REAL ESTATE JOINT VENTURES

THE CANADIAN INVESTOR'S GUIDE TO RAISING MONEY AND GETTING DEALS DONE

Don R. Campbell and Russell Westcott

John Wiley & Sons Canada, Ltd.

Library and Archives Canada Cataloguing in Publication
Campbell, Don R.
   Real estate joint ventures : the Canadian investor's guide to raising money and getting deals done / Don R. Campbell, Russell Westcott.

Includes index.
ISBN 978-0-470-73752-1

   1. Real estate investment—Canada.   2. Joint ventures—Canada.
I. Westcott, Russell   II. Title.

HD316.C319 2011   332.63'240971   C2011-906558-4

ISBN 978-0-470-67611-0 (ePub); 978-0-470-67610-3 (eMobi); 978-0-470-67609-7 (ePDF)

Production Credits
Cover and interior design: Ian Koo
Typesetter: Thomson Digital
Printer: Friesens Printing Ltd.

John Wiley & Sons Canada, Ltd.
6045 Freemont Blvd.
Mississauga, Ontario
L5R 4J3

Printed in Canada

1 2 3 4 5 FP 15 14 13 12 11

CONTENTS

MEET THE AUTHORS

Don R. Campbell is the President of the Real Estate Investment Network (REIN™), whose membership exceeds 3,000 successful Canadian real estate investors with a combined portfolio that tops $3.3 billion in residential real estate.

The author of the Canadian best-seller *Real Estate Investing in Canada 2.0*, a book that all real estate investors should have as an action tool and reference, Don is an active real estate investor who teaches proven real estate investment strategies at live workshops held across the country. A popular real estate commentator in private and public media, he has become Canadian media's go-to real estate analyst. Don has also co-authored several other real estate investment books, where he shares his market and investment research alongside years of his own hands-on experience.

In addition to helping countless investors achieve their dreams, Don and fellow REIN members have raised more than $675,000 for charities such as Habitat for Humanity. To tap into Don's experience and learn more about his workshops, visit www.reincanada.com.

Russell Westcott is the Vice-President of the Real Estate Investment Network (REIN), Canada's leading real estate education program. A sophisticated real estate investor, researcher and educator, Russell's presentations feature a welcome combination of knowledge, experience, passion and wit.

A real estate expert who speaks from personal experience, Russell manages a growing portfolio that's made him an expert on many trends in real estate investment. He is widely recognized for creative buying strategies that range from forming joint-venture partnerships to leverage financing that turns one property purchase into three or four.

Russell lives his life around four principles: (1) health, happiness and enjoyment of life, (2) family and relationships, (3) contribution and growth and (4) abundance and gratitude. He lives by his credo: "You can have anything in your life if you provide massive value that significantly improves people's lives."

MEET THE REAL ESTATE INVESTMENT NETWORK™

The Real Estate Investment Network (REIN) is a research and education company dedicated to providing investors with unbiased research and strategies for the Canadian real estate market. Now entering its nineteenth year of operation, REIN continues to provide research and support in all market conditions, regardless of whether an investor is buying, selling or holding property. With research strategies that are widely acknowledged to reduce risk and maximize returns by helping members ride the upward swings in the market and avoid the downturns, REIN has helped its members safely and securely purchase more than $3.3 billion of Canadian residential real estate.

REIN does not sell real estate, thus keeping its research and strategies unbiased. It teaches its 3,000-plus members to focus on real-life economic fundamentals that put the Authentic Canadian Real Estate (ACRE) system into action. REIN's members focus on long-term wealth as opposed to getting rich quick, and the REIN community meets monthly in select cities across Canada. Members who live outside of Canada, and those who cannot attend regular meetings, receive full recordings of the live events.

By helping its members network with other active investors and providing direct access to leading-edge experts, REIN is the most complete real estate investment program of its kind in North America. This focus on education takes the hype out of the marketplace and enables members to concentrate on what works right in their own backyards. Members are never asked to buy from, invest with or put money into any deal with anyone in or associated with REIN. There are no huge upfront seminar fees, as REIN believes that money is best spent investing in real estate—not on seminars.

To learn more about the benefits of being a member of Canada's most successful real estate investment network, with more than $3.3 billion purchased and almost 20 years of market experience, call 1-888-824-7346 or e-mail your address and telephone number to Don R. Campbell's office at info@reincanada.com. You can also visit www.reincanadamembership.com and click on the "What Is REIN?" button.

REIN offers a program dedicated to showing Canadians how to create long-term sustainable wealth with real estate investment. We look forward to helping you achieve your own Personal Belize.

Introduction ●

My first book, *Real Estate Investing in Canada*, introduced thousands of Canadians to the Authentic Canadian Real Estate (ACRE) system that is used across Canada by investors looking to invest, not speculate. To recap, I'd met Richard McTavish—he and his wife, Emma, are the central characters in the book—on a plane. He won't mind me saying that he was despondent about their financial state of affairs. As we talked, it became apparent that he was interested in real estate as a potential investment, and we agreed that as long as he was serious and willing to follow the system, I would be his coach and introduce him and Emma to other experts along the way.

That got me thinking. Since Richard's story was a lot like most of the stories hundreds of other new investors had told me, maybe I could use it to introduce and explain the ACRE system to a whole lot of people. With Richard's co-operation, we struck a deal. I would provide him with one-on-one mentoring and keep track of the process so I could write a book that would empower more Canadians to invest in real estate.

That process led to *Real Estate Investing in Canada* (which was updated a couple of years later), followed by several other books to help Canadian investors zero in on the information they need to start investing in real estate, or ramp up their investing to take their portfolios to the next level.

The Conversation Continues

This book begins where that first book left off and starts with another conversation with Richard McTavish. Richard and Emma had bought two investment properties. The second was a duplex. By living in one half of the duplex and renting out the other, they cut their family of four's housing expenses in half and took another positive step toward financial stability and long-term wealth.

But those deals were only the first two bricks in the wall of their growing portfolio. As Richard's outlook on the future improved, he was offered a new job—one that came with the chance to do a lot of driving around the town where he was already buying property. By following the economic fundamentals he had learned about when introduced to the ACRE system, Richard knew exactly where to look to find quality investment property.

Because Richard now found that talking about real estate investment was as easy as talking about his two kids, the people he worked with often asked him questions about the real estate market. They were intrigued by his knowledge of economic fundamentals and how that information helped him and Emma identify the kind of properties they should buy. Richard explained how the couple's real estate purchases factored in a host of variables that ranged from location to price to his knowledge of how the residential rental market would be impacted by local developments, including the opening of a new health-care centre and improved transit lines to service a growing industrial development. Before long, Richard's boss came on board as the first joint-venture (JV) money partner in Richard and Emma's growing portfolio.

The couple now owns five revenue-generating properties in their target area; two on their own (including the duplex they live in), one with Richard's boss, a duplex that involves two other partners, and another single-family home. Because they live in half of one duplex, their portfolio includes nine revenue-generating suites. Three properties generate positive cash flow, but one is flat and another took a dip toward the negative when the economy turned in late 2008.

WHAT'S NEXT?

People who are serious about creating long-term wealth with real estate investment are typically intrigued by what the couple has done, but have a lot of pointed questions about how real estate investment works with JV money. Some are openly skeptical and ask, "It is really possible to invest in Canadian real estate using other people's money?" Others only focus on the properties that have problems.

I know they're dubious because that's the very question a whole lot of people ask me—and often. It's also a question a lot of people are too afraid to ask. But I know they're thinking about it because they come up to me with a host of related questions about where successful joint-venture investors find one another to make a good match of skill sets. Others want to know how revenue sharing works and how fairness is maintained. Some even try to wow me with "horror stories" because they don't think that I understand the fiscal and emotional risks associated with investing with joint-venture partners.

After more than 20 years investing in real estate, I recognize that angst for what it is: a fear-based response to a serious lack of good information!

This book is my response to that lack of information. I want people who are committed to bringing money partners into their deals to expect good answers when they ask "What's next?" In fact, I want to tackle that question head on.

So, Is It Possible to Invest in Canadian Real Estate Using Other People's Money?

The answer to this question is a resounding "yes." Yes, you can invest in Canadian real estate using other people's money. The more detailed answer to the question is just as straightforward, and has two parts. First, I know that you can invest in real estate using other people's money—and I know that sophisticated real estate investors recognize these financial partnerships as a good way to make money for themselves and their investors. And second, research shows Canadians are currently sitting on a trillion dollars in cash as they wait for the right opportunity to invest. In other words, you can invest in Canadian real estate using other people's money—and your fellow Canadians have all the money you are looking for.

My first real estate investment book began with the phrase, "Oh, no, not another real estate book!" Seven years and four best-sellers later, my first hunch about real estate investment in Canada holds true. There are a lot of real estate investment books on the market, but still there aren't nearly enough that focus on the *Canadian* real estate market. Canadians are hungry for credible information about how they can generate long-term wealth in the real estate investment business. They are also leery of the massive amount of information that is readily available, since much of it is based on U.S. data that appears more concerned with selling a product than with helping them become successful real estate investors.

This book fills a particular void because it talks in detail about something no other Canadian book covers, the joint-venture deal. And take note. I am using "joint venture" as a catch-all phrase for real estate investment deals that involve other people's money. Some JV deals will be classic partnership arrangements whereby you and your money partner will each own certain shares of a real estate asset. Other deals may involve a straight financial arrangement. (As in, I will lend you $100,000 and you will use it to buy investment real estate from which you will then pay me a premium rate of interest for as long as our deal continues.) For the purposes of this book, we sometimes call both of these deals "JVs." Don't get hung up on the terminology. Our primary goal is to help you learn how to find the money you need to grow the portfolio you want!

Like every one of the other books I've authored or co-authored, this one is based on my own experience and on the experiences of the hundreds of successful investors I've met during my years at the helm of REIN. Like *Real Estate Investing in Canada*, it follows the story of Canadian investors who use JV money for their deals.

WHAT'S THE CATCH?

Sticking to a philosophy I share with co-author Russell Westcott, there is no catch to this book. This is not a get-rich-quick scheme. It is a strategy that uses systems, relationships and follow-through to help you and your co-venturers reap the financial benefits of a relationship that's built on real estate investments.

Even if you are very, very good at attracting other people's money, this book will show you there is no substitute for hard work and due diligence. Whether you want to own one property or 100 multi-family units, real estate investing is serious business. Serious investors understand the risk, especially when it involves other people's money, and they are determined to strike real estate deals that benefit both parties. They want proven and sustainable action plans, not shortcuts. They do not seek to live on the edge where the deal is everything. This isn't about winning and losing; it's about sleeping well at night knowing your investments are "safe and sound."

I can assure you that Russell Westcott and I are committed to joint-venture/capital-raising strategies that work. We know that successful investors who use capital put up by other people will investigate, adopt and continuously fine-tune tried-and-true strategies that help them invest safely and securely. To that end, this book is full of such proven strategies. But let's get one thing straight: if you are serious about growing your portfolio with other people's money, you must be prepared to work extra hard to make decisions based on market fundamentals, not emotions or hype. In a nutshell, you will need to understand that real estate investment success with other people's money is about "doing it right"—all the time, every time.

This Is About Your Future

If this all sounds too daunting, fear not! Even if you are new to real estate investing, real estate investing with money partners can be simple, fun and financially rewarding. This book will teach you how to use other people's money to make your real estate investment dreams come true, one property at a time. It accomplishes that goal by walking you through the fundamentals of investing with joint-venture cash. Think of it as a one-stop-shopping approach to JV investing.

How do I know this will work for you? Because Russell and I have been building our real estate portfolios with other people's money ever since we got into the business. That's right; we know what it's like to:

- make that first JV pitch
- have systems that turn you into a magnet for other people's money because investors see the win-win nature of the business opportunity (and tell their friends about it!)
- build on the success of others by using proven systems for every aspect of your business (from putting together your investment team, to finding solid properties and solid JV investors)
- live and work with the responsibility of building long-term wealth with JV partners
- enable success by avoiding the common pitfalls that cost non-sophisticated investors their money and reputations

In sum, our advice is tempered with real-world experience. We teach what we know. And we will share with you the templates for calls to action: how to attract JV dollars/investment cash through clear and dynamic investment opportunity presentations that include detailed marketing reports and marketing materials.

Who Will Take Something Away from This Book?

Experienced investors who want to grow their portfolios will benefit from reading this book. But Russell and I believe it is also a useful starting point for novice real estate investors. The simple truth about real estate investing is that a lot of first-time investors buy their first property with loans or gifts from people they know and care about. They borrow money from family or friends because they can. They accept money from this same group of benefactors because it's offered. Some might even let a friend or family member "in on" an investment opportunity to do him a favour, without realizing what JV money can do for their investment business.

We also know that those same investors burn some valuable relationship bridges when they enter co-venturer deals with family and friends without anticipating the level of due diligence these deals require. We can show you how to avoid those problems.

Experience also tells us that regardless of how they get the money for their property deals, real estate investors are grateful for the financial assistance that enables them to buy investment property, and they express it. In fact, Russell and I probably lead the list of experienced investors who will tell you that you need to say thanks to every person who makes a contribution to your business. But being thankful isn't enough, and we will show you that when it comes to using other people's money to expand your real estate holdings, the best kind of gratitude flows two ways. First, the investor appreciates what people with money can do for his investment portfolio, and second, the co-venturers appreciate what the investor has done for their investment portfolios and financial security.

This book is your JV/capital fund money reference, and you should treat it like any good home-study workbook! Based on what hundreds of sophisticated investors tell us works for them, I encourage you to read it with a pen and highlighter in hand, or have a notebook handy if you're reading an e-book version. Every time you write notes in the margins, complete a checklist or jot down ideas about people you need to contact or the things you need to do, you clarify your JV business strategy and fine-tune your action plan.

Why a Workshop Format?

To help you zero in on what really matters, the information is delivered in a series of 10 workshops to an audience of eight real estate investors, including Richard and Emma. Russell, REIN's joint-venture expert, leads the workshops, each of which ends with an action step to take. Each workshop is followed by a workshop tutorial that drills into the main topics and analyzes specific aspects of deals with money partners. Some of these tutorials focus on the McTavish portfolio and the way Richard and Emma approached the action steps. Other tutorials include all or some of the other workshop participants.

As an extra bonus, each of the tutorials ends with at least one Veteran Investor Insight that tells the personal success story of a real estate investor who's grown his or her portfolio with someone else's money. Written by some of the savviest JV investors Russell and I have met through our work with REIN, their stories illustrate the key messages of these workshops. Read these submissions carefully because their lessons are free—and priceless. Yes, you can learn from your own mistakes. But why would you make those mistakes if you could learn to do *better*?

Our goal with this approach is simple. We believe that investors learn a lot from each other. An uninformed outsider may look at the McTavish portfolio and think it has success written all over it. Wannabe investors who are prone to analysis paralysis may review the numbers and flee. In reality, by the time Richard and I sat down to catch up on life and business, he and Emma were "investing on the edge"—and feeling the stress associated with that position. That proximity to the edge aside, they also had much to be proud of, and I recognized, once again, that their story could help others.

That's when I invited them to build on what we'd started with *Real Estate Investing in Canada*. If they would participate in Russell's workshops and then meet me for a little one-on-one tutorial, I would help them learn how foresight and due diligence can help real-world investors avoid (or fix) problems with real estate investment deals that involve other people's money.

Let's get started. And remember, Russell and I look forward to hearing your success stories about using other people's money to grow your real estate investment portfolio.

Don R. Campbell

Workshop: The Potential of Joint-Venture Money | 1

The truth will set you free, but first it will make you miserable.
—James A. Garfield

Workshop Overview

Presenter: Russell Westcott

Welcome to our joint-venture (JV) workshop, part one. This is an exclusive workshop for the eight of you who have chosen to attend. Please note that I am using "JV" as a kind of catch-all phrase—but we'll be talking about a lot more than "joint ventures" per se. Our real topic is raising money for real estate investment, and each of you is here because you are interested in investing in real estate with money partners or improving the way you invest with money partners.

A lot of investors show up at a workshop like this prepared to jump into JV investing with both feet. They've committed to attending all 10 workshops in the series, but they are so enthusiastic about what they'll be able to do with other people's money that they figure they'll be investing with co-venturers before the first workshop ends. From the background information you provided to Don Campbell and me, I would say that's a good description of Robert and Tom. I know that you two have a growing portfolio using your own money and you want some specific guidance about how to use JV money to buy more property.

Carol and Dan, you're starting from a similar position in that you already own one revenue property and want to own more. I understand that you're both less than 10 years away from retirement and you see real estate investment as a way to secure a more interesting retirement future. Congratulations! I think you're going to find these workshops very valuable.

Others come to this kind of workshop because they know that partner cash is the only way they'll ever close their first real estate investment deal. Nolan, that's you. You're a bit more tentative, but you are clearly here to gain insight into how you can attract money for your first deal. Welcome. Believe it or not, your questions are going to help all of us remember why it's good to review the fundamentals!

Susan, I figure you're somewhere in the middle. You are enthusiastic about real estate investing, but have some reservations about doing it with JV money.

Each of the eight individuals attending this workshop has his or her own reason for being here. That's okay. But let's be clear about what we all have in common. Ask yourself:

Do I have all of the money I need to buy all of the property I need to achieve my Personal Belize?

Now, we'll refer to your Personal Belize throughout the workshops, but in short, people I know through the Real Estate Investment Network talk about Personal Belize as the fulfillment of your dreams or aspirations. It is intensely personal. Some people define their Personal Belize in terms of what they want to own or do with their lives. Others will focus on the people they want to have around them or the people and projects they want to help.

If you haven't achieved your Personal Belize, then you're at the right workshop. Regardless of the status of your portfolio, this series of workshops will help you get to where you want to go. To illustrate the power and pitfalls of JV investing, Richard and Emma McTavish have graciously agreed to participate in our workshops and have allowed us to use their investing story as the foundation of these seminars.

MEET THE WORKSHOP PARTICIPANTS

Richard and Emma McTavish: This married couple, who were introduced in Don's earlier book *Real Estate Investing in Canada*, has held up to nine properties in their portfolio. They now own five properties, including their own home, a duplex with one side rented to tenants. Richard still works full-time outside of real estate. Emma takes care of the books for their real estate portfolio, as well as doing bookkeeping for some other small businesses.

Tom and Robert: These long-time friends decided to start buying real estate investment property together in 2007. They own two single-family homes for the buy-and-hold market and would like to grow their portfolio with money partners. Both expect to

---

continue working full-time, and they believe the workshops will help them avoid classic newbie mistakes.

Nolan: Nolan is the father of two, works full-time and makes a good wage, but sees real estate investment as a way to generate long-term wealth. At 28, he is the youngest member of the group. Since the current credit crunch makes it difficult for Nolan to buy property on his own, he views joint-venture deals as an essential part of his business plan. But he's worried. Nolan has no idea where the JV money he needs will come from.

Dan and Carol: Dan works full-time and Carol is a part-time employee. At 57 and 53, they are the oldest members of our group. Dan will retire with a pension and Carol, a former teacher, is already collecting pension money. Two years ago, they took in a boarder and that experience prompted them to think about buying revenue property. Last year, a property in their neighbourhood came up for sale and they bought it. They bank the cash generated by the boarder and put every cent from the rental toward their mortgage. They would like to line their retirement nest with cash flow from two or three more revenue properties. Like Nolan, they need JV investors and are not sure where they would find them.

Susan: A full-time real estate investor and part-time bookkeeper, Susan's business plan has always focused on deals she could swing on her own. She's the group's skeptic. She owns three properties on her own (including the one she lives in, which has a suited basement) and knows that JV money is critical to growing her portfolio, but she questions the risks. Does she know how to make money in real estate? Sure. But why would anyone invest with her?

LET'S GET STARTED

We'll begin today with a quick recap of the McTavishes' portfolio and ask the question, "What can JV money do for me?" To help you understand why answering that question is so important, we'll take some time in this workshop to look at how the McTavishes got into real estate investing and how that led to deals with their money partners.

Again, their story is unique to them, but it illustrates some fundamental truths about how sophisticated investors attract—and then manage—JV money.

I can't emphasize enough how important it is that you review this first overview of the McTavish portfolio very carefully! It focuses on one couple's story, but illuminates a host of lessons applicable to all. Remember, no one is here to re-invent the real estate investment wheel. We are here to learn from experience so we can replicate the good and avoid the bad.

So Richard, I asked you to prepare a report of where you're at in terms of your portfolio. Let's hear it.

RICHARD: Thanks. Well, as some of you may already know, Emma and I are already investing with JV money. But some of our deals are going better than others, and a few of the not-so-good-deals are causing a fair bit of stress. In some cases, it's not that the deals are bad. It's the relationships we have with our co-venturers that need work.

EMMA: When you review the following chart of our portfolio, keep in mind that this is a portfolio we grew over more than seven years. We were never in a hurry to buy properties, but we were always looking.

RICHARD: That approach is the direct result of the Authentic Canadian Real Estate (ACRE) system, which helped us understand that we are in real estate investment for the long haul. We do not believe in get-rich-quick schemes, and we know that investing is hard work. I think it's fair to say that we both knew that money partners would be essential to our real estate investment business's long-term success. But we weren't really looking for joint-venture partners when the first JV deals kind of fell into our laps.

Today, our portfolio looks like the table below, and while I don't want to get into details on every property, I can tell you that three are located in the same city as we live and two are in a community with stellar fundamentals that's forecasted for continued economic growth.

I can also tell you we sold four properties in the last few years. Two were single-family homes we owned in a 50/50 JV with one partner. They were sold in 2009. We'd held those properties for five years and their sale was part of the exit strategy we'd identified with that partner. These two properties always cash flowed. When they sold in 2009, they were valued at less than what the market would have paid in 2008. But thanks to a strong economy, both were netted $50,000 more than what we'd paid in 2005.

The other two were purchased in 2005 and sold in 2010 as a direct response to market changes and complications with our JV partners. These two single-family homes were located in a community about an hour away from where we live. At the time of sale, both were breaking even but a planned rent increase wasn't possible because the rental market had changed. Two co-venturers were involved and neither was willing to extend the exit strategy. As property management presented ongoing challenges, we decided against buying out our partners or finding new money partners to hold onto those properties. Hassles aside, both JV investors got their money back and we each banked more than $15,000 on each deal.

THE McTAVISH PORTFOLIO

5 properties—9 tenants

#1. Single-family home—2 tenants
We bought this property in late 2003. It has a fully suited basement and we were using the cash flow to pay down the mortgage. Unfortunately, it's been a break-even proposition since early 2009, when we dropped the rent to prevent a vacancy. Thanks to careful cash flow management and following a proven system, we are now starting to raise our rents again and see a positive cash flow. We expect this property will improve as the years move forward.

#2. Duplex—1 tenant
We bought this property in 2004. We live in half of the duplex and rent out the other half, making it the third of our eight suites. We bought this place in 2004 and have only had three different tenants in the last seven years. The first only lasted a year—thank goodness! That suite taught us a lot about how to choose the right tenants and how to build a positive landlord/tenant relationship.

#3. Single-family home—2 tenants
We bought this three-bedroom bungalow with a fully suited basement in 2005 with Richard's boss as our money partner. He put up the money for the down payment and we provide hands-on management, from tenant relations to maintenance and bookkeeping. It cash flows nicely and we've never had to go back to this partner for more money.

#4. Duplex—2 tenants
We bought this property in 2007. Emma's sister owns 50 per cent of one half of the duplex and a man we've known for many years is a 50/50 partner in the other half. It is not located in our home city. Cash flow went flat in 2009 but a planned rental increase put it back on track today.

#5. Single-family home—2 tenants
We bought this property in 2008. It's also suited and it's in the same community as the duplex we bought in 2007. Both of these properties cash flow nicely, which is a tribute to the research we did before we bought. Still, the JV partner who's in on the single-family home wanted out of the deal when the economy dipped and the basement suite sat empty for two months. That was very stressful, especially since we've known the guy for a long time. The duplex is interesting because we have different money partners for each side. Property management is the other headache with both of these properties.

Looking back

You can see we did not purchase any properties in 2009 and 2010. We know that some investors saw this period as a buying opportunity, since market prices had dropped. We saw those opportunities, but since this was the first recession we'd worked through as real estate investors, we decided to focus on the properties we already owned and the JV partnerships we were already managing. For us, this was a good time to make sure our properties were positioned for success. To do that, we looked at property management and took steps to make sure we were holding onto good tenants, keeping our units in top condition and paying down the mortgage.

What Do the Numbers Really Mean?

This is a good time to review what we know—or, more importantly, what we *think* we know about what Richard just told us. It is easy to get caught up in the numbers. The cash-flowing properties, including one that pays the mortgage on their family home, are impressive. But what would a sophisticated investor do with this information? He would *look behind the curtain* to see what Richard and Emma really have to teach us.

The ACRE system

First and foremost, look at how Richard and Emma got into real estate investing. This is not something they "dabbled" in. From the outset, Richard and Emma chose to follow the proven ACRE system. It is a proven real estate investment system that focuses on systems, relationships and follow-through. This strategy works because

- the **systems** are designed for duplication,
- the **relationships** are win-win, and
- the **follow-through** is all about taking appropriate action toward the long-term creation of wealth and financial stability.

EMMA: Richard learned about the ACRE system first, and I admit that I was pretty skeptical in the early days. The good thing about having a system like this is that it is something you actually follow to find success and then repeat it. Some people say I'm lucky that Richard is so smart. I tell them that he's lucky he had the ACRE system to win me over!

Long-term wealth creation

Second, Richard and Emma view real estate investment as a way to generate wealth over the long term. Investing has allowed them to help

Emma's family, and Emma, who keeps the business books, likes the fact that she can now contribute to the family income and long-term financial health by working from home. Richard is still working full time, but feels more in control of his family's financial future. Thanks to real estate, he now knows how he will help his two children pay for post-secondary education and is confident that he and Emma will not face the financial uncertainty his in-laws have experienced in their elder years, especially when Emma's mom got sick.

Be the real estate expert

The biggest problem with Richard's report is that he is so uncertain about how JV money came to him and Emma in the first place. And this is a problem. When Richard says the first co-venturer deals "fell into our laps," he falls short on two counts.

1. It's an incorrect perspective to hold.
   Richard's attitude downplays the fact that others see him as a real estate investment *expert*. There was nothing accidental about why business colleagues, family and friends approached Richard to ask about JV deals, or were so keen to learn more when he approached them.
2. It demonstrates tunnel vision.
   Richard isn't being humble; with apologies to Richard, he's being foolish. He knows there are problems with some of their JV deals. Some cash-flowing properties may even need to be sold so he and Emma can escape the associated emotional hassles. By failing to see himself as a real estate expert, Richard is probably missing opportunities to bring new JV partners on board. Given the fact that most of their properties have positive cash—and the others are still good deals—new co-venturers may actually step into the deals others have been removed from.

Get Real: Commit to Chasing Your Own Dream!

When Don, Richard and I sat down to plan these workshops, I zeroed right in on the fact that Richard wasn't always being "real" with himself. This is a common trap for real estate investors. It is also avoidable. To make my point, I'm going to review highlights of Richard's real estate investment story. As you work through this with me, keep asking, *What's behind the curtain?* and *What do I want to achieve with joint-venture money?*

To recap, the year before Don Campbell wrote his first book, *Real Estate Investing in Canada*, he met Richard McTavish on a plane. Don was flying from Real Estate Investment Network (REIN) meeting to REIN meeting to REIN meeting, and Richard was returning home early from a family holiday at a favourite beach resort. It turned out that pressure from his boss, coupled with fear over losing his job, forced Richard to cut in half a two-week vacation with his wife and two kids. His family was staying at the resort, but Richard was heading back to work.

RICHARD: And keep in mind, I was not heading back to a job I loved. My decision to cut a holiday short was all about fear and obligation. I was miserable.

In fairness to Richard, his interest in financial stability and long-term wealth production began long before he met Don. Richard had read all of the valuable self-help classics written by the likes of Napoleon Hill, George C. Clason, Les Hewitt, Robert Kiyosaki, David Chilton, Brian Tracy and others. He'd even spent more than he could afford on wealth-creation and get-rich-quick programs that were supposed to give him secret insider information on everything from the stock market to real estate. But none of those ideas and schemes ever worked for Richard. It seemed like if he made money on one idea, he lost it on another. Through it all, he remained very interested in real estate investing. But every time he committed to a program, he left the expensive seminars poorer in cash and spirit. It seemed like the "best" programs, the ones that offered the most in the shortest period of time, tended to be based on information about the U.S. real estate market. No matter what he did, Richard couldn't turn any of what he was learning into action.

Besides that, Richard was haunted by what I call "learner's guilt." And I can say that because I've been where Richard was. Before I started investing in real estate with a solid plan, I was near bankruptcy. I had a university education and a pocketful of consumer debt. Was I trying to take back financial control of my future? Sure. But I wasn't successful.

Richard was in a similar position. He wanted to learn how to generate long-term wealth, and he wanted to build his own financial security. But every time he paid for a course, he left the seminar room suspicious about what had just happened. Other people seemed to be able to make the information they were getting work, but all Richard got was a gut-wrenching feeling that he was paying for information that was designed to make the instructors money. He wasn't even sure the course leaders were doing what they were teaching!

Emma: And he wasn't the only one who was worried about how much he wasn't learning compared to how much all of this was costing us. It wasn't that I didn't believe in Richard. But I sure didn't believe in what he was doing because I never saw him finish a program and put something into action. There was no reward for the money he was spending, or the time away from his family.

No matter what he did, Richard always felt like he was one more credit card payment away from learning enough to actually start investing in property. You could say he was taking just enough "action" to feel like a complete loser!

Richard: The chance meeting with Don Campbell turned that around. I think it's fair to say that after years of sitting on the sidelines, I was ready to move from the shoulder to the track. I'd recently "got real" with myself and came face-to-face with the idea that I was barely achieving mediocrity in virtually every aspect of my life. That hurt. It also helped me see how the "parts" of my life contributed to a "hole" in my life—and in my marriage. I had a job I enjoyed, but I wasn't passionate about it. I was passionate about my family, but I also felt like I was failing them miserably. I never seemed to be in a financial position where I could help others, or get ahead. I think it's fair to say I was kind of a mess when Don and I first started talking.

Richard's biggest problem is that he was at serious risk of defining himself as a loser. What a tragedy. The real problem is that he was chasing other people's dreams. Richard was not at all happy with where his life was at. But he was also dangerously uncertain about the life he wanted to lead! When Don first told Richard that he invested in real estate for a living, Richard was intrigued, but guarded. Don told me that is was like he could see the sparkle in his eye and his spine stiffen at the same time!

RICHARD: Being fairly naive about what was really involved with real estate investment, I think I actually asked Don if he had any "secrets" he could share with me. Looking back on that, I'm kind of embarrassed! Even though I thought I knew that nobody gets rich quick, I was still looking for that magic bullet to success. It's like I knew where I was at and how I got there, but I had no idea of what I had to do to get to where I wanted to be.

If I had to sum up that first meeting, I would say that Richard's biggest problem was that he was not being real. He knew all of the reasons why his life was not the way he wanted it to be, and he even took full responsibility for that fact. What he could not do was be honest about the real problem. Richard had never zeroed in on what he wanted from life. Let's say you could take your life's dream and express it as a number. If you never figure out that the answer is "four," you'll never be able to compute all of the permutations that will give that answer. (Two plus two is just the start. What about all of decimals you could use to get to your final destination?)

Indeed, once you cut through the crap and get real with yourself, you learn there is only one answer to the question "What do you need JV money to achieve for you?"

Why do you need JV money?

Because you don't yet have all the money you need to buy all the property you need to achieve your Personal Belize!

COMMIT TO SYSTEMS, WIN-WIN RELATIONSHIPS AND FOLLOW-THROUGH

If we go back to Richard's state of mind before he met Don Campbell, we can see his problem this way: he wasn't really being honest about where he was or where he wanted to go. He thought he'd done some careful reflection, but he was still prone to thinking that other people were making money without working hard. He thought that people with enough money to shape their own futures, including successful real estate investors, were simply "in the right place at the right time." These folks were lucky—and he wanted to know how to get lucky, too.

When Don offered to mentor Richard and Emma through their first real estate purchases, Richard jumped at the chance. He also agreed to follow the ACRE system and agreed to let his and Emma's journey be the foundation of Don's book *Real Estate Investing in Canada*.

Don's motivation was pretty simple. He knew the system worked, and if Richard was serious about wanting to be a successful real estate investor, he had to follow that system and its commitment to systems, win-win relationships and follow-through from start to finish. No more chasing pots of gold at the ends of rainbows and no more shortcuts to dead ends. Better still, this one-on-one mentoring process would provide Don with the crux of a book that could teach countless other Canadians about real estate investing.

RICHARD: It was tough, but worth it. But by the end of three years, Emma and I had bought our first two properties. I was still working full time, but a noticeable change in my work habits and attitude brought me to the attention of a supplier who offered me a new job. I was ready for some new responsibilities and liked the fact that the new job paid a little more. Because I was starting to think like a sophisticated real estate investor, I soon realized the job also gave me more flexibility to manage my own time—so there's way less chance I will ever have to cut a family vacation short to go back to work.

Better still, the new job gave Richard a chance to meet clients outside of the office. With copies of the Property Goldmine Score Card (see Appendix A) always sitting on the front seat of his car in a special leather binder Emma gave him for Christmas, Richard enjoys driving around town because it gives him the chance to see different neighbourhoods and more property. He picks up community newspapers, takes note of For Sale signs, and stops at corner stores to get directions and ask about different communities.

He's also put a whole lot of systems in place to make sure he can take action when he needs to. That includes going through that binder before he gets out of his car after he gets home from work. Richard sometimes circles or highlights key points he wants to revisit, or jots down notes in the margins. He then gets out of his car, recycles any needless paper on his way through the garage and stops by his office to put potential leads into his office In Box before he goes into the kitchen. Work is important. But so is family.

I call this the Reality Check part of real estate investing. Complete your own reality check here.

REALITY CHECK!

What am I doing to improve the outcomes of my real estate investing?

I am serious about real estate investing because I
- read credible material on real estate investing.
- have fostered a mentoring relationship with a successful investor.
- have joined a network of sophisticated investors.
- set aside time each day/week to focus on taking investment action.
- am building my own real estate investment team (realtor, property manager, lawyer, accountant).

MAKING THE LEAP TO JV DEALS

With Don's coaching, Richard got to the point where he was investing with other people's money. When his new boss noticed that Richard was always up-to-date on real estate investing and economic development in their city, he started asking Richard a few questions. He learned that Richard paid attention to special economic announcements, like the opening of new commercial enterprises and retail power centres, and the extension of transportation lines to carry commuters to and from work. The boss was impressed when Richard told him that commuters in walking distance of a good transportation system would pay 20 per cent higher rent, and he was intrigued by how much Richard knew about the way certain neighbourhoods were changing and what that meant in terms of real estate prices and rents. When they talked specifics about Richard's growing real estate portfolio, his boss had even more reason to be impressed. He liked

Richard's focus on cash flow and long-term property appreciation. A former renter himself, the boss also appreciated the way Richard sought win-win relationships with his tenants.

Before long, his boss came right out and asked if Richard and Emma were looking for another investment partner. If Richard would provide the investment expertise, the boss would put up the investment capital.

Do you see what was happening? Richard was starting to define himself as a *real estate expert*. When we look back on that period, we see that Richard is pretty humble about what was happening. Humility is okay, but honesty is better. Whether he knew it or not, Richard was setting the real estate investment table—and getting ready to welcome paying guests!

REALITY CHECK!

What I am doing to present myself as a real estate expert?

I keep current on the real estate markets where I invest. I can
- talk knowledgeably about the key economic fundamentals that drive real estate markets up and down (i.e., GDP growth, employment and immigration statistics).
- explain the ripple effect and how it impacts communities located near larger centres where market rents are rising rapidly.
- describe how brand new transportation changes can impact real estate values by improving access to housing and jobs.
- contact experienced and quality-driven realtors and property managers for their perspectives on what's happening in a particular market.
- anticipate some market shifts by figuring out how political and economic news impact a local housing market.
- identify potential money partners by the kinds of questions they ask me.

Okay, we're getting close to winding up for the day. Any questions? Nolan, you look confused.

NOLAN: Because I am! It seems like everyone here is nodding their heads and scratching down notes. But I'm lost. I don't know what the "ripple effect" is, and I don't know why I need to understand immigration.

RICHARD: Sorry for laughing, Nolan. But I've been where you are! I used to look at real estate investing and think there must be some secret shortcut to success. Don helped me see there are no secrets at all—but there is a lot to learn. What you really need to find is a system. When you work with a system like ACRE system, the lessons are broken down. You learn how to tell if a town will boom or bust; you learn how to identify the best properties in the best areas; and you learn how to make offers that will be accepted and how to close deals without encountering unwelcome surprises.

It looks complicated, but the real beauty of successful real estate investing is that you can learn how to do it right.

EMMA: You can also learn "who" to do it with. When Richard and I started out, we learned that we did not have to figure things out for ourselves. Don was our first mentor, but that connection led to many others. When I need direction with an issue, be it a tenant problem or a question about our tax planning, I know to call someone who is an experienced real estate investor (in my case, a fellow REIN member). I could figure out some of these things on my own—but why would I do that?

RICHARD: Before we started investing in real estate, I had a lot of excuses for why I wasn't good at making money. Learning how to take action helped turn that around. It wasn't enough to be honest about what I was doing. I needed to be honest about what I wasn't doing and about what I didn't know how to do. It was kind of painful to realize I was the problem, but making myself take responsibility for positive change was essential.

EMMA: And the changes are not all about Richard. Passive income allowed me to leave a part-time job and spend more time with my family, including my ailing mother. I keep the books for our real estate business and that keeps Richard and me on the same page when it comes to our investment decisions. We've also involved the kids, and that's been great. Sam is now 15 and Alison is 12. They've helped us do everything from clean properties to paint fences, mow grass and hand out letters in neighbourhoods where homeowners may be thinking about selling. Sam even helped us find a for-sale-by-owner deal because he knew we were interested in a particular street and he saw the sign while riding by on his bike.

The Take-Home Lesson: Acknowledge the Power of JV Money and the Need for a Proven Investment System

What are Richard and Emma telling us? I think that one of their key messages is that honesty is hard work and it begins with a look in the mirror. If you acknowledge that JV money is essential to your business plan and you want to be good at attracting JV money to your real estate deals, then you've got to be prepared to follow a proven system and do the work that a proven system entails.

Robert and Tom, you may need to pay particular attention here. You already own two single-family homes and you both know what JV money can do for your deals. But you need to be clear about why you want JV money. You want JV money because it is essential to your business plan. You need JV money to buy the property you require to attain your Personal Belize.

Dan and Carol, Nolan and Susan, I know that you are starting where Richard and Emma began. You are all looking for better returns on your investment cash. Dan and Carol and Nolan aren't sure where their money partners are and Susan has some reservations about how deals work with JV money. My advice to all of you is that you take the time to learn the nitty-gritty details of the ACRE system and pick up a copy of *Real Estate Investing in Canada 2.0* and *97 Tips for Canadian Real Estate Investors*, both written by Don Campbell. You do not need to re-invent the real estate investment business. But you can save time and money with proven insights, strategies and success stories.

Workshop #2 is going to focus on the systems you can put in place to make JV money a priority. Remember: you don't need to reinvent the real estate investment wheel, but you do need to learn how to make it turn in the right direction. To help you understand why JV money is so important to your ability to create future wealth, this workshop's action step is all about the Personal Belize.

WORKSHOP ACTION STEP: WHAT DO YOU WANT JV MONEY TO ACHIEVE FOR YOU?

You want to acquire JV money because that money is essential to growing your portfolio, building long-term financial security and attaining your Personal Belize.

Whether you're buying your first property or your fiftieth, successful real estate investors take time to figure out what they really want out of life. At REIN, we say these people are working toward their Personal Belize.

This means that they've taken some time to figure out what they really want out of life. And they don't just think about it. They get a big piece of craft paper and a bunch of magazines and start making a collage of words and pictures that gives them a visual reminder of why they want to invest in real estate and what they plan to do with their long-term wealth.

If you haven't done this yet, do it now. And be honest. If what you really want is a special edition Harley motorbike for your fortieth birthday, find a picture of that bike and hang your collage in a place you can see every day. Maybe you want a family vacation to Europe before your oldest kid graduates, or enough passive income from real estate investment to let your spouse quit the job that currently pays for the "extras." Maybe you want a more secure retirement and the chance to spoil your grandkids with trips to Disneyworld, or to help your own kids with university tuition.

This is your Personal Belize—so dream big!

JV ACTION PLAN STEP #1

I want to invest in real estate with JV money.
What am I prepared to do about it?

Thinking is great. Doing is better. To get the results you want, you must commit to action and excellence.

—Don Campbell

Ask yourself: How well do I know my own portfolio?

You can't know where you're going unless you know where you've been and where you're at right now.

1. How many properties (i.e., "doors") do I own?
2. What have I done recently to increase per-unit cash flow?
3. When was the last time I reviewed
   a. local market rent?
   b. my maintenance plan?
   c. the effectiveness of my property management strategies?
   d. my exit strategies?
5. What do I do to cultivate my image as a sophisticated investor? Have I
   a. updated my business card?
   b. looked into web-marketing?
   c. made sure my websites are visible with search engine optimization?
   d. updated the material I present to lenders and partners? (ACRE aficionados, for example, develop a Sophisticated Investor Binder to help them present their business and their deals to prospective lenders.)
5. What could I do to assess how my systems are working and what I could do better?
   a. I forget to do things that I say I will do.
      i.   What can I do to improve my record-keeping system?
      ii. What can I do to improve my message follow-up?
   b. My tax planning is in disarray.
      i.   Why are records missing or difficult to find?
      ii. Does my bookkeeper need more direction?
      iii. What can I do to improve my relationship with my bookkeeper or accountant?
   c. I am encountering problems with tenants.
      i.   What can I do or ask my property manager to do to improve tenant selection?

ii. Who is tracking tenant concerns, and are these being dealt with?
iii. What is my property manager doing to keep my units occupied?
iv. What three things could I do to build a better relationship with my property manager?

JV ACTION PLAN STEP #2

I want to attain my Personal Belize. What am I prepared to do about it?

The indispensable first step to getting the things you want out of life is this: decide what you want.
—Ben Stein

Keep your eye on the prize.

A lot of people ask if they have to physically make the collage. The answer is yes. Visualizing success helps you attain it.

John Lennon once said he could "write myself a swimming pool." Frank Lloyd Wright said "events always happen when you truly believe in them; and the belief in that event makes it happen." Similarly, professional athletes learn to visualize success. They write down goals, they watch training videos, they practise *thinking* about success. They mentally work through the process of what they need to do to put the puck in the net, take the fastest step from the starting block or render perfect form off the diving board.

Your Personal Belize poster will help you visualize what you want in life, and that vision will help you invest in your own success. It will help you visualize what you will do when you secure your first mortgage, sign the papers on your first property, sign your first Joint-Venture Agreement or send your money partner their first cash-flow cheque.

The vision will change as your business develops, but that picture will always remind you of why you are willing to do what it takes to earn long-term wealth.

What does my Personal Belize look like?

_____

_____

_____

_____

_____

_____

_____

_____

TUTORIAL: WHAT IS YOUR PERSONAL BELIZE?

1

WORKSHOP RECAP:

Acknowledge the power of JV money and the need for a proven investment system.

Be honest about why you need JV money.

Ask yourself: What are you prepared to do to attain your Personal Belize?

Presenter: Don Campbell

The take-home lesson of the first workshop asked you to be honest about what you do and do not know about real estate investing. I understand that you all plan to adopt the ACRE system, and we will use that as a foundation in future workshops and tutorials. In addition to guiding specific investment decisions, this system will help you maintain your commitment to excellence.

The workshop ended with Russell asking you to understand how JV partnerships will help you attain your Personal Belize by helping you grow your real estate investment portfolio. We are not going to review the number of properties you will each need to achieve your individual Personal Belize. But I will encourage you to review that Personal Belize at least once a year. Experience tells me that your Personal Belize may change with time and circumstances. But knowing your "end goal" is essential to mapping your journey!

We are going to review your Personal Belize collages. This collage is a fundamental component of the "systems" approach to real estate investment that Russell and I teach. As I recall what Richard and Emma's first Personal Belize looked like three years ago, I'm excited to see how it has evolved.

I want you each to tell us a little bit about the Personal Belize posters you brought with you today.

NOLAN'S PERSONAL BELIZE

Hi, everyone. My Personal Belize really focuses on my family. Here's a picture of my house. It's not the house I live in today, but it's the one that real estate investing will allow me to buy. This picture is of my real family. I know the two kids will be a bit older when we buy this place, but they're going to love it. As you can see, there is a games room and a home theatre, and that cutout of an airplane represents the times we'll leave the house for family vacations. I'd like to be flying somewhere special for a two- or three-week vacation every summer starting when the oldest is in junior high. That's nine years from now, and I figure we should get six great vacations in before she goes to university—which her mom and I will pay for, of course!

Robert's Personal Belize

Tom and I worked on our Personal Belize collages separately. And that was interesting. Even though we are real estate investment partners, our collages don't have a lot in common. First, I'm not married and I like to spend my free time at my cabin. As you can see, my Personal Belize is all about that cabin and the people I'll spend time with there. This photo is of my family. I'm really close to my brother and his wife and their three kids. Right now, that cabin isn't winterized and doesn't even have electricity. These pictures of fancy appliances are my dream appliances. My family likes to spend time together cooking, and this kitchen would be perfect for that. And see this cappuccino machine? It's more than three grand, and yes, it's part of my Personal Belize. I would just love to treat my visitors to a fabulous cup of cappuccino. If it's cold outside, we'll gather in the kitchen or around the fireplace, and if it's nice outside, we'll be on this deck.

Tom's Personal Belize

My Personal Belize is all about "free time," too. And don't get me wrong. I love Tom's cabin, but when it comes to vacations, I'm all about sandy beaches, cold drinks and maid service! My Personal Belize focuses on getting away during January and February each year. My kids will both be done university in the next couple of years, and after that, I'd like my wife and I to be able to travel to someplace new every year. But it's not like I'm abandoning my kids. This corner of my Personalize Belize is all about them. My wife, Shelley, and I aren't much for giving our kids things. But we would like to gift them money when they buy their first homes, and Shelley has plans to outfit their nurseries once our grandbabies are on the way. We didn't have much when the kids were born, and she'd like each of them to have a fancy crib and rocking chair. Our kids also grew up playing the piano, and it's a personal dream of mine to buy them each a piano once they move into their first homes.

Susan's Personal Belize

I bought my first investment property eight years ago just after I got divorced. It's the home I live in now and it has a suited basement. Since then, I've added two more single-family homes, both near the neighbourhood where I live with my daughter. I know what investing has allowed me to do as a single mom—but this is the first time I've ever thought about investing as working toward a Personal Belize. My vision is all about spending more time with the people I love. My Personal Belize includes taking my parents on a trip to Hawaii and making sure my daughter finishes college or university without any debt. Our family home needs a little work, too, and that's why my Personal Belize includes this great kitchen! I know that each of us worked on our collages alone, but I am going to steal an idea from Robert and add a fancy cappuccino maker to my dream kitchen!

Dan and Carol's Personal Belize

DAN: The Personal Belize concept was completely new to Carol and me—and that's why our collage has so much empty space! We've talked about retirement for years, but always in terms of what we might be able to do. This is the first time we talked about what we really *want* to do. The idea that we had never really planned for that period of our lives was a little unsettling.

CAROL: Unsettling at first, but very helpful once we got going! Our house is paid off, our tenant/boarder pays $500 a month that goes straight into our savings and our combined pensions and RRSPs do give us some liquidity. In fairness, those RRSPs haven't met our growth expectations, but we're starting to see how we can use that cash to buy real estate investment property that will yield higher returns.

DAN: When we combine what we "have" with what we want from real estate investments that leverage other people's money, our Personal Belize started taking shape. We've got two grandchildren and one more on the way. Phase One of our Personal Belize involves buying a recreation property within two hours of where we all live. My goal is to retire at 65. I'm now 57 and I want that recreation property in the next five years.

CAROL: I'm only working part-time and I'll quit work the day Dan's done. In the meantime, I'm going to devote one day a week to real estate investment education. As part of that, I'm also going to make a date with Dan to do some more work on our Personal Belize. Listening to all of you talk about what real estate will do for your lives has been very inspiring and it's prompted me to jot down a few questions I need to discuss with Dan. I want to talk to him about whether we plan to leave a financial legacy for our three kids and our grandkids. I share Dan's desire to have a recreation property where we can spend time with our family, but I'd also like to travel with Dan.

RICHARD AND EMMA'S PERSONAL BELIZE

EMMA: Richard and I took a night last weekend and worked on our collage together. This was fun because it's not something we've done for a few years, and it was interesting to see how our Personal Belize has changed—and stayed the same. In the early days, we dreamed of being able to help my parents and put away money for the kids' education. Now we're doing that and planning for our future. Once we started talking, we realized that we both love our summer vacations in B.C. so much that'd we'd like to retire there. This isn't even something we'd discussed before, so finding out we had the same vision of the future was awesome.

In a perfect world, we'll have a waterfront home and our grandchildren will spend most of their summers with us. That's why our collage includes a power boat and all that fishing gear. That's for Richard and our grandkids. And the garden? That's all mine. My Personal Belize definitely has a garden that stays green all year-round.

RICHARD: One of the best parts of working on our collage was that it helped Emma and I talk about the future. I mean, we "talk about the future" all the time, but we are so focused on Tuesday's hockey practice, Thursday's meeting with our lender and Saturday's trip to the grocery store that I don't think we ever really look at the bigger picture.

What I like about our Personal Belize is that it shows our family together. We're going to hang this on the door that leads from the kitchen to our garage, and this way, we'll see it every day. It's a great reminder of what we're doing for our family's future.

That was incredible! And I am glad you all took this exercise so seriously. As for Susan's apology for "stealing" an idea from Robert's collage, no apology is necessary. There is nothing wrong with looking at someone else's dream and wanting parts of it for your own. In fact, that is why it's important to have a Personal Belize you can talk about and share with other people.

I appreciated the sentiments shared by Dan and Carol, too. Some people have trouble "dreaming big" because they've never been asked to do it, or have never given themselves *permission* to do it, so I'm glad you two found this exercise helpful. A lot of people in your situation find it liberating to listen to others talk about their dreams. The process of working on a Personal Belize collage actually helps them drill down to the details about what they want for themselves.

SUSAN: That's an interesting point. Maybe that's why I'm struggling with the whole concept of bringing other people's money into my real estate deals. On the one hand, I know that I am a successful investor and I am generating long-term wealth. On the other hand, I also know that I could be closing bigger deals if I brought partners on board—and that I would be helping them in the process. Maybe I've just never given myself permission to want more!

Susan, it's like you are knocking on the door of the next workshop. While I said we wouldn't review the number of properties each of you will need to attain your Personal Belize, I want you all to start thinking about how the current state of your portfolio impacts your Personal Belize. That will help you be honest about where you are at and where you want to go. Remember the quote at the start of the first workshop? *The truth will set you free, but first it will make you miserable.* It's making the same point. Before you can move on to what's possible in the future, you have got to be honest about what is real right now.

Bonus Handout: Insights from a Veteran Investor

This isn't rocket science. Anyone can learn to invest in real estate with joint-venture partners.

—Wade Graham

Background

Wade Graham's foray into real estate investment owes much to happenstance and his own curiosity. "To be honest, I became an accidental landlord when a new work contract took me to Banff. I didn't want to sell my place in Calgary, so I found a tenant to take care of it while I was away, and that experience got me thinking. Over time, I realized that even though I did a lot of things wrong along the way, I was still making money. That insight propelled me to start looking at whether there was a 'right way' to invest in real estate. I ended up reading *Real Estate Investing in Canada* and some other books about how to generate wealth with real estate—and that set me off on a whole new path."

A computer information systems specialist by profession, Wade didn't close his first real estate investment deal until 2006, five years after his first experience as a landlord. That first deal happened because Wade impressed an acquaintance with his knowledge of how real estate investment generates long-term wealth. After a couple of meetings, the two struck a deal, with Wade as the real estate expert in a 60/40 deal cut in the money partner's favour. "We both realized that I had done this successfully before and that I knew enough to put another deal together. As Russell likes to say, 'we both saw the win-win.'"

Fast forward another five years and Wade's Higher Ground Real Estate Investments Inc. and his JV partners own just under 30 revenue property doors with assets that tally $5 million. Now living in Canmore, B.C., Wade has three properties in northeast Edmonton. The rest are in Calgary. There, he targets properties with mainfloor and basement suites and double-detached garages located in neighbourhoods in the northwest quadrant of the city. "My typical tenants are young professionals who will likely buy the next home they occupy." All of Wade's properties are professionally managed, which allows him to focus on his great talents: finding properties and attracting money partners.

Wade's advice to investors who are looking for JV money cuts to the chase: "Be clear about what you want from real estate investment, take the time to learn how to do it right and focus your energy on the joint-venture partners who make sense for your business. These people aren't really investing in a revenue property; they're investing in you and your core values. If they don't like, trust and respect you before a deal is on the table, you are wasting your time because there won't be a single dime of money that comes your way."

Here are some tips Wade has to share.

STUDY THE BUSINESS, THEN ACT

I see value in learning to do things the right way. A lot of people want to know the "secrets" to real estate investing, but I don't think there are any secrets—just hard work. When I see people getting into real estate investment because they think they can make a quick buck, I shake my head. I have structured my business to focus on sustainable cash flow for my company and my investors, and I really do believe that sophisticated real estate investment is a learned skill. That's why I joined REIN before I bought my first JV property. While I had proven that I *could* do it, I saw value in taking steps to make sure I was doing it right.

In sum: Those who take the time to learn the mechanics of investing will be rewarded. But they won't be rewarded just because of what they know; they will be rewarded because of what they *do*.

NARROW YOUR JV PROFILE

I haven't yet had to exit any JV deals prematurely, and I think that says a lot about the due diligence I apply to making sure that I am working with the right money partners. I don't work with people who want to invest their last $10,000 or with people who are risk averse. I take the time to get to know potential partners, and if I suspect they will be going through a significant life drama, then I don't work with them. I also spend a lot of time making sure my investors understand the deal. When I first started looking for money partners, I was considering everyone I knew. I understood very clearly what my property and tenant profiles looked like, and I thought that was enough to convince people to partner with me. I didn't have a lot of success until I got clear on what my JV partners looked like and what their motivations were. To do that, I looked at who was investing with me and what they had in common—and the results were clear.

Before I did this exercise, I thought I was working with "everyone." Now I knew I was working with a specific niche group. It turned out that because of where I live, my JV partners tended to be mountain guides. They were all individuals who'd been living in Canmore for several years. Most were self-employed, and they typically had families. As most tended to travel a lot, what they didn't have was time to devote to investments. Some of them had cash, and all of them had significant home equity. They were also all looking for investments that could generate future wealth. To them, it was either about long-term security, or putting their kids through university.

This JV profile would throw a lot of people off, I know. It's not the typical doctor or dentist profile that most seek out. But it provides clarity to me. It's like telling yourself to look for yellow cars. All of a sudden, you see yellow cars all over the place! I was now able to table a message that spoke directly to this niche and their motivations.

MAKE THE DEAL WORK FOR YOU

When I closed my first deals with JV partners, I probably undervalued my contribution as a real estate expert. But if I was starting out from the same place again, I wouldn't necessarily do things differently, because those first deals were a reflection of where I was at that time. They were my cost of education and experience.

My point is that it's taken me a few years to get to where I can put together JV deals that earn me the higher percentage of a 60/40 deal. But on those first deals, I did feel it was win-win even if I was getting the 40 per cent.

My current approach is a little different in that my portfolio is approaching the point where my exit strategy will allow me to meet my goals. When the next sellers' market comes up, my partners and I will be able to harvest what we've sown. That said, real estate investment always makes sense, since when I'm ready to sell, someone else will be ready to buy and hold. I love this business because it always offers investment opportunities.

WORKSHOP: SYSTEMS MAKE JV SUCCESS A PRIORITY — 2

Achieve success in any area of life by identifying the optimum strategies and repeating them until they become habits.
— Charles J. Givens

WORKSHOP OVERVIEW

Presenter: Russell Westcott

Welcome back! I know that you are still working on the highs associated with completing your Personal Belize collages. I also know that some of you were a little disappointed when you walked through that door and saw the title of this workshop: "Systems Make JV Success a Priority." You might ask, isn't this just a repeat of the fundamentals of sophisticated real estate investing? You bet. And to be successful with JV money in your deals, you need to follow a real estate investment system that works because

- the **systems** can be replicated,
- the **relationships** it nurtures are win-win, and
- the **follow-through** is all about taking appropriate action toward the long-term creation of wealth and financial stability.

We are revisiting these ideas here because I want you to see the connection between them, your Personal Belize and your goal to attract joint-venture money to your real estate deals.

RICHARD: That's an interesting point, Russell. Ever since we hung our Personal Belize collage in a high-traffic area of our home, my attitude about what that collage means has definitely changed. It's more than a dream; it represents my commitment to sophisticated real estate investing. The Personal Belize exercise is all about taking responsibility for the life I want to lead. I envision it because I want it. I will do what it takes to earn it because I can learn how to do that.

All of this helps me remember why Emma and I do what we do—and that focus keeps us loyal to an investment system that's based on market fundamentals.

Good point, Richard. And that's exactly why we asked you all to complete a detailed Personal Belize collage. Sophisticated real estate investors know where they are going and why. That's how they know what they need to do every step of the way. Everything they do supports their system because their system supports their Personal Belize.

SYSTEMS: THE FOUNDATION OF YOUR REAL ESTATE INVESTMENT STRATEGY

We're not going to repeat the basics here. What I want to stress is that real estate investing does not require any "discovery" of new information. Everything you need to be successful, from buying quality properties to attracting the right tenants to templates for quality JV agreements, has already been established. If you do not know what to do—find someone who does. That's what a quality system is all about, and the Authentic Canadian Real Estate (ACRE) system is a great place to start.

In sum, take a look at the next list. These are the specific things a quality real estate investment system will help you do.

REAL ESTATE INVESTMENT SYSTEM

Use a quality system to

- understand the fundamentals of real estate as a long-term strategy to create wealth.
- learn about the Cash Flow Zone and how you can determine if a property can make you money.
- identify cities, towns, communities and neighbourhoods with the best investment potential. (These properties work for long-term buy-and-hold. They have positive cash flow and will appreciate in value, often at rates that are above-average for a region.)
- analyze a specific property to see if it fits your system.
- negotiate positive terms with vendors, including mutually agreeable closing terms and dates.
- optimize your ability to get lenders to say yes to your deals.
- undertake and complete renovations that add lasting value to your rental properties.

- attract and keep quality tenants in your units.
- build positive working relationships with property managers who keep your suites rented and well-maintained.
- fine-tune your exit strategies in line with economic shifts.
- systems will help smooth out the ups and downs of being in business

Susan: That's awesome. What a great reminder of why I do all of the things I do to make sure an investment property works—and continues to work—in my portfolio.

Robert: I agree. Tom and I just closed on a side-by-side duplex that needs renovations. It's not the kind of property we'd bought before, but the whole deal went really well. I don't even think we realized how every one of the decisions we made, including our decision to put in all-black appliances, was based on our investment system. Every time we ran into something unexpected, we just took a step back and used our system to figure out what we should do.

Your comments are exactly why I wanted to review investment systems before we jump into how to attract joint-venture capital to your deals. Once you start investing with other people's money, the need for solid fundamentals is even more important!

THE IMPORTANCE OF RELATIONSHIPS: SURROUND YOURSELF WITH QUALITY PEOPLE

Let's take another look at that list. Everyone in this room recognizes that those items are all about *systems*. They are also about *relationships*. The relationship side of the real estate investing *system* takes some people by surprise. If you plan to invest with other people's money, relationships are even more important.

One of the things I noticed about the Personal Belize exercise is that Tom and Robert decided to work separately on their Personal Belize collages, while Richard and Emma worked together. This happened organically, but I want to look at what was behind that decision. Tom, what do you think was going on?

Tom: It's pretty obvious to me. Richard and Emma are a couple. They share a family and common goals for that family. Robert and I have been friends for a long time, but we invest together because we can help each other create long-term wealth.

Richard: I think I know where you're going with this, Russell. Whether Tom and Robert know it or not, they are already investing as joint-venture partners. They may enjoy working together, but the relationship works because they each bring different attributes to the deal. Before we got started today, Robert was telling us about his background in home renovation and construction and Tom was saying his background is all business. He delivers mail by day, but he's a number-cruncher slash deal-maker at heart.

That's exactly my point. Tom and Richard came into this workshop because they want to attract joint-venture money to their deals. What they didn't seem to realize is that they are already in a JV-type of relationship. They obviously share a keen enthusiasm for real estate investing and are committed to the idea of working together. But you also understand that you each want different things in life. I suspect you are going to learn that there are some things you need to take care of in terms of your business partnership, but we'll work on that later. For now, I just wanted to point out how some partnerships are so natural we might not even anticipate how they come to be.

The second part of my point is directed at all of you. The money partners you bring on board will also bring different dreams to the table. And every one of them will deserve the same respect as Tom and Robert give each other.

REALITY CHECK!

Relationships make the deal go "round"

The people who invest with you are working with you toward a mutual goal: wealth creation. But that doesn't mean they need to think like you, or that they should want the same things in life as you want.

We'll talk later about how real estate investors manage the different expectations of their money partners. Here, I want to focus on relationships as a fundamental component of your real estate investment system. As with a deal you close and manage on your own, real estate investing with JV partners demands the efforts of a team of quality people. For those of you who are already investing and aspire to be recognized as sophisticated real estate investors, this list may look a little redundant. Read it anyway. If you are committed to investing with proven systems, you should recognize the value of using lists like this to review what you're doing. That simple act of linking names to a list like this sometimes triggers a strategic response.

THE REAL ESTATE INVESTMENT TEAM

Property sources/realtors

Mortgage brokers/bankers

Property managers

Home inspectors

Property appraisers

Lawyers

Bookkeepers/accountants

Renovators/contractors

Other investors

Life partners and joint-venture partners

THE TAKE-HOME LESSON: THE TEAM APPROACH IS THE ONLY APPROACH

Why do you need a real estate investment team? Because you need other people to get your deals done—and those deals are essential to your Personal Belize. Long before you bring a joint-venture partner into a deal, you need real estate agents who will bring you the deals you're looking for and not waste your time showing you properties that do not fit your system. You need lenders and brokers who know, understand and respect your long-term investment plans. For example, if you plan to buy 10 or more properties, that's something your lender and broker need to know because that long-term plan should shape your first borrowing decisions. (You may be able to avoid one conventional lender's lending "cap" by strategically working with a less-conventional lender, maybe even a money partner, on your first deals.)

You also need accountants and lawyers who have real estate experience. They will understand the importance of meeting deal deadlines and will help you steer clear of tax and legal issues.

Knowledgeable home inspectors and quality renovators will also be critical to your team. You need to trust these people to be honest with you about what's wrong with a property and how you can fix it without compromising your place in the Cash Flow Zone.

Quality property managers will also be essential. Even if you decide to handle this function on your own (a common practice with new investors), you need go-to people to get information about why a property may not be not renting and what you can do about it.

CASH FLOW ZONE

(Gross Annual Rent / Purchase Price) $\times$ 100 = Cash Flow Zone %

If this formula tallies 10 per cent or more, there is a very good chance the property will yield positive cash flow. For sophisticated investors, however, the key numbers lie in the zone between 8 and 10 per cent. Sophisticated investors will look at properties in this zone very carefully, since they may be able to find ways to make a property work at 8 per cent.

RICHARD: Whoa! When I first saw this list, I was thinking this exercise was just a simple review. But your comments got me thinking. I don't have a good relationship with the property managers who look after the two properties that aren't in our home city. Because property management was a major hassle with two of the properties we recently sold, this is really eating away at me. I know we're not going to walk away from these properties, but this is causing a great deal of stress and I've been dealing with it by pretending I don't have a problem!

ROBERT: It's funny you should say that. Tom and I know the lawyer we're working with has no experience with JV real estate deals. He's done a good job with our first deals because they're really straight-forward. But the last time we met, he made a couple of comments about how Tom and I need to find a lawyer who can vet JV deals. We're going to have to deal with this sooner than later, especially if we want JV partners. I look at this list and think, "What are we waiting for?" Given that Tom and I seem to have missed the boat in terms of making sure our own business relationship is set up properly so as to protect us both, I don't think a lack of legal know-how with regard to complicated JV deals is something we want to deal with in the middle of closing a deal that involves other people's money.

SOPHISTICATED JV INVESTOR INSIGHT

Get experience on your team

Sophisticated real estate investors do not have to be experts at all aspects of real estate investing, but *do* need to know what they're lacking—and where to get it. A good real estate lawyer for your JV deals should have several years of real estate experience and should be actively investing in real estate. When you are dealing with other people's money, you must ensure that the legal agreement that binds you and your partner together takes care of both of your interests. This is no time to learn a lesson! Identify what your strengths are and focus on these specialties, then delegate the rest of the duties to people who are the experts.

FOLLOW-THROUGH MEANS TAKING ACTION

That last sophisticated JV investor insight makes the point that this section is all about: taking action. Real estate investment is about taking action. If you can talk about it, but can't seem to actually buy a property, complete a deal with a JV partner or get the right lawyer on your team, you need to figure out what's holding you back.

Some would-be investors never buy real estate because they are wary of the commitment. Others can't seem to close a deal with a money partner. These people are willing to *talk* about what they are prepared to do, but they aren't willing to actually do it.

The key is to trust your system. If you are committed to a proven real estate investing system and follow it, you will close deals. Richard has some experience here, so let's hear what he has to say.

RICHARD: I sure do. If you want to invest in real estate, or want to invest in real estate with a money partner, then you have to find a way to do that. For Emma and me, it was about finding the ACRE system and letting it show us which properties to buy. We used the Goldmine Score Card to help us target communities with the best investing potential. We used the REIN Property Analyzer form (see Appendix B) to figure out if a particular property made sense. We followed proven due diligence checklists to make sure we weren't missing anything. Of course, you never buy all of the properties you look at. But by the time we worked through those forms a few times, we knew why we were using them. These systems gave us information we could trust. Investing wasn't scary anymore. It made sense!

DON'T LET ANALYSIS PARALYSIS HOLD YOU BACK

Analysis paralysis occurs when an almost-investor is so busy collecting the facts that they never get around to buying property, or never get around to buying property with a JV partner. These individuals will look for "one more reason" to not make an offer, close a deal or approve a co-venturer. They are often very knowledgeable about real estate markets and investing. In fact, some of them can talk at great length about "what might have been" if only they'd used their vast knowledge of the industry and got into real estate investment a few years earlier. These individuals are not looking for the right time to invest. They're looking for reasons why it's the wrong time to invest. They are paralyzed by "what ifs."

Nolan, you look like you have something to say. Do you want to share?

NOLAN: I sure do. You're describing me to a "T." I know that I can't invest in real estate without a money partner. I've tried! I've talked to lenders and mortgage brokers, and I have a plan that involves JV deals. What I really need to do now is to trust my system. Until Richard spoke, I hadn't thought about the fact that my first deal might not even go through. I've always seen that as failure and figured my money partners would see it that way, too.

Now I realize that I'm coming at this from the wrong perspective. I am a real estate expert. I follow proven investing systems to generate long-term wealth. I respect all of the people who help me run my business—and every time I work through a deal that doesn't close, I still win because my systems will be intact—and strengthened by experience.

Trust your system

I like where you're headed, Nolan. Experience is a good teacher, and that's why investors like Don and I are so committed to systems that are built on experience.

We also believe that real estate investing should be fun and financially rewarding. I can see you all squirming, but I'm serious. You should find a way to celebrate every deal that closes. But real estate investing is not something you do to add excitement to your life, nor is it about getting rich quick. By the time you sign the papers to close a deal on a piece of real estate, you should feel nothing but confidence in a deal well done. You should also feel good about taking one more step to long-term financial security.

But what do you do if a deal goes bad? The sophisticated investor knows she won't buy every property on which she makes an offer. All that really means is that the deal did not work on her terms. She learns from it and moves on. Similarly, a sophisticated investor sells a poorly performing property with the same lack of emotion she bought it with. That's easier to do when you invest with a system like the ACRE system.

One of the things the ACRE system does is provide you with valuable filters like the Cash Flow Zone. A real estate investor's two biggest assets are cash flow and time. You want properties that cash flow, but you cannot analyze every property on the market. That's a tall order given the sheer number of properties that could be on the market in your targeted area. The Cash Flow Zone filter saves you time and money by keeping you from wasting valuable time on properties that won't deliver a positive return.

As Don says, an experienced investor may be able to make a property work if it scores 8 per cent. But if you're not an experienced investor, why waste your time? Every deal is not the only deal, and the time you spend trying to make a deal work would be better spent finding a property that's already in the Cash Flow Zone.

Workshop Action Step: Review Your Real Estate Investment Team

Why do you want JV money? You want JV money because that money is essential to growing your portfolio, building long-term financial security and attaining your Personal Belize.

Why do you need to review your real estate investment team? Because the whole is bigger than the sum of its parts, but a weak link puts the whole chain at risk.

Sophisticated real estate investors are always building their network of actual and potential team members. This is not about disloyalty. If your property manager is a valued member of your team but needs to upgrade her knowledge of tenant communication, you can make that happen. If your accountant would like your bookkeeper to use a different software package, you can facilitate the switch and provide appropriate training.

This is not rocket science. It's good business.

JV ACTION PLAN STEP #3

I aim to build the best real estate investment team I can. What am I prepared to do about it?

TEAM = Together Everyone Achieves More
—Unknown

I value relationships.

What am I doing to make sure my real estate investment relationships are on track?

---

1. I will make a list of everyone involved in my business: lawyer, realtor, mortgage broker, property manager, home inspector, accountant and partners.
2. I will identify three things I like about each of those relationships and three things I don't like. I will brainstorm possible actions and a timeline.

Example:

Positive: My accountant is knowledgeable, accessible and answers my questions in a timely way.

Negative: My accountant's bill is higher than I think it should be. My accountant's staff bullies my bookkeeper about deadlines. My accountant's tax advice sometimes comes a little late.

Action Plan: I will take my accountant out for lunch to talk about the "big picture" issues with this part of my business. I will ask why my bill is so high and seek input about how it can be lower. I'll take those ideas back to my bookkeeper and see what we can do to improve our ability to meet deadlines. I will ask for advice about strategic tax planning. Maybe this is something we should be doing in the summer or fall versus December.

Workshop recap:
Trust the system. Look behind the curtain when issues arise.

Presenter: Don Campbell
I've been going over the notes of the second workshop, and I'm really impressed. How did that issue with your property manager work out, Richard?

Richard: Awesome. One of the units in a suited single-family home we bought with a JV partner sat empty for two months this past fall. I never felt like I was getting the whole story about what was going on. The unit had been rented to the same people for two years, and the property manager told me that she needed a month to do some maintenance upgrades before she put it on the market. It turned out that those upgrades included new paint and the property manager was doing all of the work herself. When the project took longer than planned, she didn't put it on the market and we lost another month's rent. Our reserve fund prevented us from having to go back to our partner for money, but he sure noticed the fact there was no cash flow cheque and he started talking about getting out of the deal early.

That must have been frustrating. What you do about it?

Richard: To be honest, I took responsibility for what happened; after all it is my property. This property manager is pretty serious about her job. This kind of work actually falls into her budget, but she made the mistake of trying to do the work herself because it was cheaper. It wasn't long before she knew she'd made a mistake, but she didn't know she could come to me for help.

As we hadn't really talked about the situation, all of our recent interactions were kind of tense. It's like she was waiting for me to ask, and I was waiting for her to tell!

The main floor of that home will be in the same situation in the next six months when the existing tenants move out. We haven't raised the rent on that suite for 18 months, which will improve cash flow, but it should be painted before it goes back on the market.

This time, we'll hire painters and the property manager is already getting estimates.

Then it's all good. You didn't just fix a problem, you learned a lesson. Let's look at your review of your real estate investment team. Remember, your goal is not find fault, but to fix problems or prevent them from ever being problems.

Look Behind the Curtain

If there's a take-home lesson from this tutorial, it's got to be this: look behind the curtain. It can be easy for us to say that about an issue that involves someone we don't know, like a new vendor, for example.

But every one of our relationships merits this kind of treatment. If a relationship is not working, find out why and look at what you can do to make it better. Similarly, it's not enough to adopt formal check-lists and forms. If you choose to adopt the proven systems delivered by the ACRE system, learn to *use* that information to its fullest. Use your relationships to look for information that's available, but not necessarily obvious.

For example, knowing a seller's motivation can help you get a better deal. It can also help you fine-tune the negotiations. But always make sure you are working on the same deal by getting the details in writing. If you think the appliances are part of the deal, put it in the offer. If they are taking a light fixture with sentimental value, but agreed to replace it with another fixture, write it down.

RICHARD: What you're saying is exactly where I went wrong with the property manager we talked about above. We fired two other property mangers before we found this one and when we encountered that problem with a longer-than-expected vacancy, I just didn't know what to do. Which is silly! It's our money and it's my *responsibility* to find out what's really happening when a property is not performing as expected.

Looking back, I see that this problem with the vacancy affecting cash flow arose just as Emma's sister was telling us that she wanted out of her deal with one-half of a duplex early. In the end, both of these problems were solved by relying on our system. With the single-family property, we pulled out the Joint-Venture

Agreement and looked at our options with our partner. In the end, he and Emma's sister stuck with the agreed-to strategy and opted against us buying them out. With the property manager, the issue was the need for better communication. In both cases, my first responses were all about fear. All I had to do was look behind the curtain!

BACK TO THE FUNDAMENTALS

One of the best things I'm hearing from you, Richard, is that you are willing to take responsibility for what's not working with these relationships. That is critical. Even though an investor can never control every aspect of a deal or a relationship, the buck always stops at their feet. Here are a few other points you want to keep in mind as you are building and strengthening relationships.

Keep it legal!

Investors who want to be in business for a long time will protect their reputations because it makes business sense. They take care to steer clear of anything that's illegal or dishonest. They don't sign documents that aren't truthful because they know that mortgage fraud can send them to jail and devastate their portfolios. They look for information that can help them make a deal, but they don't use a seller's motivation against him. They know that a motivated vendor may have other properties to sell, or know of others who would like to sell in the area where they're looking to buy. In terms of JV money, they also know that motivated vendors may be interested in working out a second-mortgage deal.

Let's review the information below. It's a concise summary of areas where sophisticated investors might anticipate trouble.

EXERCISE CAUTION

Real estate investment involves financial risk. Real estate investment with joint-venture partners involves financial risk to all parties. Never think that other people's money decreases your responsibility to put together a good deal. If anything, JV money

---

makes due diligence even more critical. As part of your system, do the following:

1. Be wary of anyone who tries to teach *and* sell you real estate.
2. Never sign a document that is not true. Anyone who tells you to do this to secure a mortgage is already dealing in a legal grey area. Walk away from the deal. (This includes telling lenders you plan to live in a property you are buying for investment.)
3. Never listen to anyone who says you can't get a second legal opinion. This is a huge red flag. In fact, in JV deals, you will be telling your partners that they need to seek independent legal advice. (And you will never take no for an answer.)
4. Stay away from deals where you are told you don't have to declare every aspect of your real estate transaction. You do not want to withhold information from a banker, lawyer or buyer.

Cover the JV angle

When you commit to an investment system, you commit to practising good habits. That's information your money partners need to have. They do not have to know how to run your business, but helping them understand your good habits can put money in your deals.

Educate your JV partners

If someone you know is interested in what you do as a real estate investor and wants to learn more about using real estate investing systems to reduce the risks, get them a copy of the latest edition of *Real Estate Investing in Canada 2.0*. Send it to them with a cover letter that tells them how you use the book to create wealth. While a small minority of these individuals may want to start investing in real estate on their own, others will be open to JV arrangements.

If these people have questions about how you find or qualify properties, suggest they read Chapter 8, "Not Any Port in the Storm: How to Find the Best Properties in the Best Areas," and Chapter 9, "The Property Analyzer Form: Where the Rubber Meets the Road." You can also recommend Chapter 4, "The Four Most Important Words in Real Estate," as this will reassure prospective investors that your approach to real estate investment is based on solid systems.

Remember: when all you have is a nail, every tool at your disposal will look like a hammer. The same principle applies to investing in real estate with JV partners. Here, every person you meet has the potential to help you grow your business. Some may want to invest in your business. Others may know of other money you can attract. Sophisticated investors use this information wisely. They know that their relationships with other people can impact their business and they take their role as a relationship-builder very seriously. The better their bridges, the fewer they will have to burn—-and the more they will be able to build.

EDUCATE YOURSELF

Teaching other people how your business works is important. But you also have to nurture your own understanding of real estate investing with JV partners. To learn more about how proven systems reduce risk, read *97 Tips for Canadian Real Estate Investors* by Don Campbell and *81 Financial Management and Tax Tips for Canadian Real Estate Investors* by Don Campbell, Navaz Murji and George Dube. Both also offer special insight into what makes a good JV deal.

What do I do really well? I build the right team.
—Mark Loeffler

BACKGROUND

A realtor and veteran real estate investor who says joint-venture partners are essential to his business, Mark Loeffler of Toronto owns a portfolio of more than 30 properties. Mark, who recently launched a limited partnership to raise $10 million to buy investment rental property, says there's a direct connection between his business success and the professional strength of his investment team. His team doesn't just know what Mark wants—they deliver what Mark needs.

A consummate networker and a major proponent of "informed investing" through education, Mark admits he should have done more homework before he got into real estate investing. "I made some mistakes because I was learning as I went. In hindsight, I could have avoided those problems with a little more education. And that education is out there for those who look."

Here, in his own words, is what Mark has to say about the role of **systems** and the need to stay on top of your **real estate investment team**.

NETWORK. NETWORK. NETWORK.

A lot of new investors don't understand that networking is a critical component of a real estate investment system. Networking is a "system" because it's something you do over and over, and it directly impacts your ability to meet your investment objectives. It is especially important for investors who want to work with JV partners.

I typically spend four days a week talking with people who are interested in real estate investment. I'm a member of REIN and belong to several smaller networking groups that meet regularly. When I was starting out, I also participated in Cashflow game nights. [Cashflow™ is an educational board game that teaches the basic concepts of investing.] These days, my networking system includes the time I spend teaching my own courses to investors who want to learn about the rent-to-own market. Some of the people are serious about investing and really do want to learn how it works, but they do not want to do the work. They sometimes approach me to talk about JV partnerships, and they like my track record and the fact that I already have an investment team in place.

In the early days, it was hard to get in front of people—but investors should not let that hold them back. When you're starting out, you need to be making presentations to five to 10 people a month. I'd been in sales before, so the rejections didn't bother me. I focused on the feedback I was getting and the fact that every "no" brought me one person closer to a "yes." That kept me moving forward.

Today, a lot of my presentations are to individuals on a list of people who have told me they are interested in working with me. I still try to meet new people and develop new relationships, but I've been at it long enough to know who I need to talk to when a certain deal comes up.

I think I "put myself out there" more than some investors who are looking for JV money, but that approach has really paid off for me, and I do think that new investors need to look for ways to talk to people about real estate investing. I know that a lot of investors rely on family and friends and other people they know for their JV deals, and if that makes sense for you, then I say, "go for it." My own approach took a different path. My JV deals are all with people I didn't know before, but that doesn't mean I will work with anybody. In fact, even though I still believe that I need to network to meet new potential investors, every one of my JV deals to date has been made with the same core group of partners. Networking is really important to growing my business, but I'm really careful about who I bring on board.

LEARN. LEARN. LEARN.

I started buying investment properties before I went to any seminars or really looked into how the business works. I now wish I'd learned first and invested second.

For example, my first property was about 25 minutes away from my home and that seemed reasonable. But I was managing the property myself, and I really underestimated what that involved. Every trip there cost me at least one hour of my time and that was before I dealt with any tenant or property issue. Looking back, that property only would have made sense if I had hired a professional property manager, which is what I eventually did. Today, I only self-manage one of my properties. It's about two minutes from my home and I used to live there, so it's a property I know really well. My other properties, which are mostly in Ontario (although I do have one in Edmonton and one in Fort McMurray), are all managed professionally. I've actually got four property management companies on my team—and it's great.

If I'd sought information from experienced investors, I also would have learned to avoid the JV partner who's given you his "last" $50,000. Instead, I brought the guy into a deal, and I can tell you that he called me every day. It was really frustrating, and I now know that he is not the kind of person I want to invest with.

A lack of experience and knowledge also led me to invest in expensive single-family homes (worth $1.2 to $1.3 million) that were built for the spec market. [Short for "speculative market," homes built for the spec market are built before they have a buyer. The market can offer great returns, but the risk is definitely higher.] In retrospect, I had no experience in that market and neither did my partner, so it was a mistake for either of us to think we could just jump into that niche.

Some of my current deals are property flips, and these exemplify how partners can complement each other's strengths. In this case, I find the deals and my partner does the renovation work. It's a great relationship, and I'm glad to have him on my team.

Other successful investors have since taught me to look beyond property value for my long-term deals. Because I focus on cash flow and mortgage pay down, my investments are all about profits and payments. JV investors like that—and it kept us out of trouble when the last recession hit. Our properties still cash flowed, and because we didn't have to sell any, reduced property values weren't an issue.

Team. Team. Team.

My investment team is my biggest asset. That's something I've learned over time, but it's an area I could have improved on faster if only I'd sought more education first. I think that my team is my biggest asset. I couldn't close deals and make them work without these people. For example, my mortgage broker is incredible. He makes what I do easy.

I'm also grateful to have such a good relationship with a JV partner who can do deals where we buy, renovate and resell; or we buy, renovate, add value and rent. Property managers are another big component of my success.

Some people just don't get the value of the team. I tell them that the team is what gives them credibility, especially when they're first starting out and making those first deals. Sure, you can move from realtor to realtor, or jump from broker to broker, but who will you go to when you have a problem? Your team should evolve over time, but you don't want to be burning bridges when you're starting out.

Workshop: Learn the Principles of JV Wealth Attraction   3

Genius is one per cent inspiration and ninety-nine per cent perspiration. Accordingly a genius is often merely a talented person who has done all of his or her homework.

—Thomas Edison

Workshop Overview

Presenter: Russell Westcott

I'm sure you've all heard about people who are "lucky" because they attract money to their real estate deals. I'm here to dispel that myth. Attracting other people's money to your JV deals has nothing to do with luck. It is a learned skill, and like all learned skills, it is something that gets better with practice. Workshop #4 is going to teach you how to identify potential JV investors, and Workshop #5 is going to get into the nitty-gritty of how you market your business—and specific deals—to money partners. That's exciting stuff. But before you can tackle those strategies, you need to know why they work.

Why Is it Possible to Attract Money to JV Deals?

The simplest answer to this question is embedded in the principles of wealth attraction. Investors who put those principles into action understand that they are *choosing* to do things that attract wealth. Building on the key points of Workshops #1 and #2, these individuals are taking responsibility for achieving their business goals. They are doing what it takes to be successful.

Before we delve into these principles in more detail, I want to tell you a little bit about a guy I knew. He was smart, held a university degree and was attracting a lot of positive attention from the higher-ups in the company where he held a full-time management-level position. From the outside in, life looked pretty good. From the inside out, it was a mess. He'd borrowed money for a lot of things that added remarkably little value to his life, and when he finally put that university accounting education to work on his personal books, the pages were bleeding red. He wasn't just worried about his future. He was scared. And I know that, because I'm talking about myself prior to getting involved with real estate investment.

How did I turn my situation around? I did it by taking personal responsibility for where I was at—and for where I wanted to be. I share this story now because I think it's a great illustration of the difference between building a Personal Belize and daydreaming about what you *wish* your life could be like.

When I sat down and wrote a seven-year life plan a couple of years out of university, I had a full-time job, a lifestyle built on credit and enough financial awareness to recognize that I was on a slow-but-steady path to personal bankruptcy.

Was my situation extreme compared to what you are all at right now? Absolutely. But looking back, I realize the goal of my life plan was my Personal Belize. If none of you has those issues, congratulations! You are already leaps and bounds ahead of where I started. Which brings me to my first rule of thumb for people who want to attract other people's money to their deals: keep it real. Be honest about your motivation. If your goal is to make money for yourself and your part-ners, put that upfront. Money is not the most important thing in the world, but it matters. It matters a lot—and sophisticated real estate investors do not shy away from that fact.

This is *your* life; act like it matters

My point here is that if you want to be a magnet for other people's money, I can teach you how to do it. But you have to take re-sponsibility for why you want that money. When I had my own epiphany, my motivation was fired by my decision to turn around my financial future. I was a little embarrassed about where I was at, but I knew that I was the only one who could put my life back on track. Between keeping that full-time job and pursuing my new interest in real estate investing, I figure I worked 60 hours a week during the first few years I was buying real estate. Now as one of the executives of REIN and a guy who owns a significant number of properties with 19 co-venturers, I can honestly say I never want to work that hard again. But let's be honest. I started in a bit of a hole. I could have kept digging that hole, but I chose to build a ladder to financial freedom.

RICHARD: That's a cool story, Russell. And it makes me feel a little bit better about where Emma and I started from. When we started working with Don Campbell, our Personal Belize was all about financial security, spending more time with family and being able to help Emma's mother. Because we took the time to think about what real estate investing could help us do in the future, we understood what we needed to do at that moment.

And what you all need to do now is answer a simple question.

Who has all the money they need to buy all the property they require to achieve their Personal Belize?

That's the question Don Campbell asked Richard soon after Don started mentoring him through his early days of real estate investing. Don knew that many novice investors think there is some kind of trick to attracting JV money to real estate investment deals. Since the task looks so daunting, they figure that money magnetism must be a skill you're born with. Not true! The ability to attract money to real estate investment deals is a learned skill that is honed with practice and perfected over time.

That doesn't mean it's easy. Attracting money to your deals is where the going gets tough. It's also where the tough get down to business. If you already have all the money you need to achieve your Personal Belize, great. If you don't, keep listening.

We will keep reminding you about why you need to spend some time thinking about and planning your Personal Belize. Believe it or not, this step is fundamental to the success of your efforts to attract JV money.

REALITY CHECK!

Review that Personal Belize

It takes time and effort to become a money magnet. Every time you wonder if the time and effort is worthwhile, review your Personal Belize. Unless you already have all the money you need to bring that Personal Belize to life, you need to bring other people's money into your deals.

Commit to the Three JV Pillars: Systems, Relationships and Follow-Through

Before we look at the principles of wealth attraction, let's review the fundamentals. That makes sense because your action step is going to involve looking at those principles and seeing how you can apply them to the fundamentals. To review, success in real estate is based on three key pillars: systems, relationships and follow-through. If you plan to attract JV money to build your portfolio, those three pillars are even more important. Let's take a look at why that's true.

1. Systems

Systems, like those discussed in Workshop #2, take the guesswork out of the day-to-day operation of running a real estate investment business. Score cards and checklists help you find and assess potential properties. They also speed up the process whereby you discard properties that do not fit your system and help you identify JV money worth pursuing (or not, as the case may be).

Bookkeeping systems ensure you know where every receipt is filed. Why rely on the memory of a hard-working investor who is juggling multiple properties when you can put in place filing systems that never let you down?

The same holds true for every other aspect of your business. Systems help you find and keep quality tenants. They help you track which suite's bathroom needs a new washer in the faucet and which one needs new fluorescent bulbs. They let you monitor an investment's financial performance and guide decisions about what you need to do to keep your business on track. All of this information, and knowing where to find it and what it means, will be critical to making sure your JV partners understand how real estate investing works. It will also build JV-partner confidence in your management decisions because it shows what you're doing to keep a shared investment on track.

2. Relationships

To the sophisticated investor, positive relationships are like the people side of systems. You fine-tune systems that promote business success and you nurture the relationships that grow your business. You also wean yourself off relationships that cost your business in terms of time, frustration and money.

When you are investing with other people's money, these relationships are even more important. Believe it or not, even the newest real estate investor comes into the business already knowing most of the people he will need to raise money for his real estate deals. The next workshop will teach you how to identify those people. For now, all you really need to do is prepare to shift the way you think about the people you know.

3. Follow-Through

Follow-through implies doing what it takes to make sure every one of your real estate deals goes through and is successfully managed. You can't make your Personal Belize come true without taking action, and if you need other people's money to grow your portfolio, then you also need to do what it takes to find that money.

Think about it: You can't buy a property without securing a mortgage and signing the legal documents. You can't find quality tenants without securing a quality property, and you can't attract other people's money to your deals without following up on conversations with people who are interested in expanding their personal long-term wealth. Without follow-through, that money will find a new home!

This does not mean you relentlessly pursue every property that meets what your system demands, or every JV dollar that might make your next deal happen. Due diligence still matters. You must close the deals you can and move on from the deals you can't. You must open discussions about JV deals, but only commit to those that fit your systems and your long-term goals. Once you are clear about your systems, relationships and follow-through, you are ready to become a money magnet. Let's look at how that all works by studying the principles of wealth attraction.

SUSAN: Before we do that, I just want to say, wow! When you opened this session with your personal story, you might as well have been talking about me, Russell. I know I am the skeptic in the group because I have some serious reservations about using other people's money in my deals. But I'm starting to see things very differently. If I'm being honest about my Personal Belize, I should also be honest about the fact that I do need other people's money to grow my portfolio. Yesterday, that would have scared me. Today, I'm thinking, why not? I am good at what I do. My real estate investment business is founded on the principles of systems, relationships and follow-through. If I don't bring people into my deals, I'm not the only one losing. That never occurred to me before.

EMMA: Susan, one of our first JV deals involved Richard's boss, and I worried that the nature of that relationship would add a new dimension of stress to the deal. In hindsight, I recognize this is exactly the kind of deal we needed to pursue.

TOM: I like Russell's story, too. I think it's fair to say that Robert and I were thinking that we were facing issues no one faced before. Learning that other real estate investors have successfully met the same challenges is liberating. We don't have to re-invent the JV wheel, we just have to learn how to ride it forward.

THE TAKE-HOME LESSON: THE PRINCIPLES OF JV WEALTH ATTRACTION

Building on those three pillars, it's time to learn how to help JV money make it to the table of your next deal. For that, you need to understand the eight principles of wealth attraction and know how to use them to take action.

PRINCIPLES OF JV WEALTH ATTRACTION

Attraction versus Pursuit

Abundance

Expectancy

Imagination

Giving

Decisiveness

Expertise

Resiliency

The Principle of Attraction versus Pursuit

There is a reason the Principle of Attraction versus Pursuit tops this list! We've probably all experienced what it's like to have someone try to sell us something we don't want. Sophisticated investors who use other people's money to get their deals done *never* want to be confused with a pushy salesman! We aim to attract good money to good deals because that's how we generate long-term wealth.

Take JV action

The pursuit of JV money for real estate deals begins with people who've expressed an interest in the topic. The next workshop is going to teach you how to identify potential JV partners. For now, we want to focus on a simple truth related to the Principle of Attraction versus Pursuit.

Remember when we told you that you probably already know all of the people you need to know to find JV money? This is where that idea takes flight. Real estate investors should be proud of what they do, and they should be willing to talk about their investments. But keep it smart. While you should always be prepared to talk about what you do for a living (or do to enhance your workaday earnings), do talk about something else if the person is not interested.

Our basic rule of thumb is this: tell, don't sell. You want to attract people who are interested in more details. But you do not want to scare away family, friends and acquaintances by making them think you can only talk about real estate and why they should invest with you. By sticking to the tell-not-sell approach, you leave the door open for future discussions with people who might not yet be ready to talk about JV deals. This principle also applies to your marketing program, and we're going to talk about that in a later workshop that details what we like to call solid oak marketing strategies.

The Principle of Abundance

Is your glass half full or half empty? The Principle of Abundance is all about attitude and how your approach to life colours (or discolours) your relationships with other people—and their money. Sophisticated investors seek win-win situations. They don't approach business decisions based on the idea that they "win" only when someone else "loses." They also don't hold much stock in "shortages." If they need something, be it quality properties, tenants, investment team members or JV money, they find it.

Take JV action

Look for ways to complete the deals you want to complete. When a prospective investor tells me he doesn't want to do a deal, I thank him and move on. That takes a little practice, but my point here is that I know it's not a personal rejection, it's a business decision. It may not be a business decision I agree with, but that is not for me to judge because it's not my money. Besides, every time I hear a no, I am one person closer to hearing a yes.

That's the Principle of Abundance in action. Instead of getting sidelined by a negative response, I realize that I'm not talking to the right person and I move on.

Tom: Want to hear something funny? When Robert and I first talked about working together on real estate investing, I didn't just turn the idea down, I was kind of ticked that he even asked me. As you all know, Robert and I have full-time jobs in addition to our work as investors. I brought up his idea with my other business partner, and it was that individual who made me realize what was going on. I was acting as if Robert's pitch was personal, and it wasn't about our personal relationship at all! He was offering me an opportunity, and I nearly missed it!

That kind of situation isn't uncommon. I have a good friend who I talk to about everything from our personal lives to our business endeavours. He never asked about investing in real estate with me, so it's a line of conversation I never pursued. He knew what I did, and we often talked about my money partners.

One day, six years after I started investing, I was telling him about some deals I was involved with, and their geographic location caught his attention. He had some ties to the community, knew what was driving its economic strength and realized the people moving there needed places to live. Before I knew it, he was *asking* me to call him the next time I needed a money partner to buy an investment property in that town. Now we're friends—and business partners.

THE PRINCIPLE OF EXPECTANCY

This next principle feeds into what we were just talking about. I assume by now that you all understand that you need other people's money to build your Personal Belize. But do you all *expect* to raise the capital you need to complete a deal with other people's money? Sophisticated investors have that expectation because they've planned for it.

Take JV action

Expectancy is based on confidence. Be confident. After Richard's boss expressed an interest in investing with him, Richard put together a deal that he expected his boss would like. After Tom expressed an interest in working with Robert, the two of them sat down and talked about the kind of deals they should pursue. In both instances, they expected to find deals that could benefit both parties and then made those deals happen.

If we stay true to the Principle of Abundance, we realize that if one deal doesn't work out, we will find another deal. It is never all or nothing.

THE PRINCIPLE OF IMAGINATION

Sophisticated investors use their knowledge of systems, relationships and follow-through to see solutions where others cannot. Because they have the imagination to see their way through to a completed deal, they solve problems by creating opportunities.

Take JV action

Help prospective JV partners imagine how their own visions of the future can be a good fit with the way you operate your real estate investing business. In the spirit of abundance and expectation, remember that everyone you talk to is a potential money partner. You don't have to sell, but do tell!

When you talk to potential investors, be honest and uncomplicated. If they talk about their retirement plans or the education of their children, tell them how real estate investments can help them achieve their long-term financial goals. If they are concerned about cash flow, let them know how you use the Cash Flow Zone filter we talked about in the last workshop. If they want to focus on potential problems with tenants or maintenance, counter their fears with facts about how you follow proven systems to find quality tenants and plan for maintenance and upkeep. Be prepared to show them the REIN Property Analyzer form and talk about how you use solid financial data to make sound management decisions.

REALITY CHECK!

Information changes people

You can't unknow information—and neither can your potential investors. If they're curious about your systems, show them how they work. Use a REIN Property Analyzer form (see Appendix B) to walk them through the process of figuring out if a real estate deal works in your investment system. Give them the tools they need to ask better questions and then answer them head on.

THE PRINCIPLE OF GIVING

People who attract wealth are some of the world's greatest philanthropists. Experience has taught them that the more they give, the more they receive. Sometimes they leverage cash. Other times they leverage ideas or skills.

Take JV action

A lot of novice investors wonder how giving can possibly be a principle of wealth attraction, especially if they're just starting out. The simple answer is that giving is about a lot more than money. Do you have skills you can "give" to help complete a real estate deal? Are you the investor who "knows" other people with money to invest? Can you do the renovations yourself? Do you have marketing skills to offer? Do you have special ties to a prospective pool of tenants or rent-to-own investors?

When it comes to giving, think outside the box. Use the principles of wealth management to come up with innovative ways to make deals work based on your commitment to finding the right properties and the right partners.

NOLAN: Thank you! I've been talking to some experienced real estate investors, and they're telling me the same thing. But I think I get it now. I've been so hung up on needing a money partner that I sometimes don't focus enough on what I bring to the table.

My current job is in oil and gas, but I before this, I worked for a new home builder whose company also does home renovations. The other day, I called up my former boss and we went for coffee. It turns out his son, who's the same age as me, is interested in real estate investment. Like me, he wants to do at least some of the hands-on work involved with making an undervalued property fetch top rental dollars. But whereas I'm a kind of job site gofer, he really knows his stuff. He's a journeyman carpenter and has great connections with the other trades. I already know that we work well together, so we're now talking about how we could make a JV deal work. He has access to some great capital and likes the idea of teaming up with an investor who wants to manage the buy-and-hold part of the deal. He also likes the idea that our joint venture could feed his company work. It seems so obvious now, but I hadn't realized how many connections I already had to people in the trades. A lot of these people own their own homes and can access some serious capital.

CAROL: Dan and I have also been surprised to learn how much we bring to the investment table. The big surprise for us was learning that our son wants to invest with us. He trusts our business acumen and likes the idea that he could invest with us and not have to do any of the work.

THE PRINCIPLE OF DECISIVENESS

This increased awareness of what you bring to a potential JV deal is a factor in your ability to display decisiveness. Decisiveness is about putting to work what you know. Experienced real estate investors make decisions based on their due diligence, and the fruit of that due diligence is solid information. This is especially important when working with JV money. Novice investors who are attracted to your deals will expect you to be a decision maker, not a procrastinator.

Take JV action

Real estate investors who work with other people's money know that they will need to support their decisions with due diligence. If a potential JV partnership depends on finding the right deal, find it. If you have already attracted JV money to a particular deal, take responsibility for keeping that deal on track. If due diligence shows that you need to walk away from a deal, do it.

Always be prepared to explain your actions, and then move on. Facts in. Emotions out. Show that you can make good decisions because you have good information.

THE PRINCIPLE OF EXPERTISE

People are attracted to expertise because knowledge gives them comfort and confidence. If your real estate portfolio has a particular focus, market that focus to attract JV money. Do you

- invest with RRSP money?
- help people who've experienced financial trouble buy a home?
- renovate and sell properties in neighbourhoods undergoing gentrification?
- use the strategy of rent-to-own investing?
- have a geographic expertise that allows you to know everything about a region and brand yourself the expert (i.e., Mr. Hamilton— Erwin Szeto)?
- buy multi-family units in walking distance of commuter trains or large employers?
- buy and hold residential properties for cash flow and long-term wealth accumulation through market appreciation?

If you self-manage the rental properties you buy, do you do an especially good job of screening tenants or identifying communities with higher-than-average rates of real estate appreciation?

Once you identify your area of expertise, showcase it.

Take JV action

Become a real estate investing expert and follow a system like the Authentic Canadian Real Estate (ACRE) system taught by REIN and detailed in *Real Estate Investing in Canada 2.0.* If you don't have an expertise yet, think about areas you would like to develop. If you only buy properties with positive cash flow, let your investors know why you do that and what it could mean to them. If you want to focus on student housing, learn everything you can about that market.

THE PRINCIPLE OF RESILIENCY

The Principle of Resiliency helps you get out of bed those mornings when you know you've got problems to solve. It is the ability to adapt to changing circumstances, even when the circumstances are discouraging. When a potential investor turns down a particular deal, I ask them what it would take for them to say yes. I listen carefully to the answer, and then take that information and use it to put together my next deal. Over time, that approach has fine-tuned my strategies for attracting JV money to my deals. Again, I never take a negative response personally. Resiliency is about moving forward and not getting discouraged if you get knocked down from time to time.

Take JV action

Resiliency is not about taking a particular course of action; it's about finding lasting solutions that work for you in a given situation. It's about moving forward with lessons based on your experience, including mistakes. It's about learning from others, but not blindly following another person's strategy. It about turning excuses into conquests.

• If you can find great properties but not JV partners, link up with someone else who can.

- Find out what's holding prospective partners back and then look for deals that address those concerns.
- If you don't have time to deal with tenants, hire a property manager to secure and maintain the tenants you want.

REALITY CHECK!

Seek solutions

If you are surrounded by people who say they want to invest, but don't understand the principles of wealth attraction and the need for action, take your business plans somewhere else. Your Personal Belize depends on it!

WORKSHOP ACTION STEP: RESOLVE TO DO THE EXTRA 10 PER CENT

Real estate investing is simple but it demands real work, which means it is not an "easy" way to change lives and create long-term wealth. Unless you already have all of the money you need to attain your Personal Belize, you will need money partners to build your real estate portfolio and bring that Personal Belize to life.

Novice investors who are serious about successful real estate investing should remember that the rewards come to those who do the extra 10 per cent. This is especially important when you are working with other people's money, since the extra 10 per cent is all about taking care of business for this deal and the next. While you can and should empower your team, you must never forget that the business buck stops with you. Quality systems, relationships and follow-through work because you make them work. When things go bad, you fix them. You take responsibility for your decisions and exhibit the win-win attitude that puts into play all eight principles of wealth attraction.

Even the most naive JV partner should realize that things sometimes go wrong. To keep that partner onside, make your response to those problems what counts. Sophisticated investors plan for success by making sure they know what to do no matter what happens. They go the extra 10 per cent.

JV ACTION PLAN STEP #4

I will become a money magnet

Here is a motto to say to yourselves regularly: "To be a magnet for other people's money, I will take responsibility for my results, both good and bad."

Sophisticated real estate investors who use JV partners to buy property must eliminate the excuses from their lives. Focus on the deals you can make, not those that may be speculative or uphill battles. If your current partners don't want to invest more of their money, find people who do. If someone turns a deal down, find out what's missing from the presentation or where they might be confused. Do they need more information about a deal? Do they want more security? Are timelines the issue? Use their answers to polish your JV strategy.

Review the following eight principles of wealth attraction and identify two excuses per principle that you currently use to keep yourself from attracting money partners. Once articulated, the excuses can be banished.

Attraction versus Pursuit

Abundance

Expectancy

Imagination

Giving

Decisiveness

Expertise

Resiliency

TUTORIAL: PRACTICE THE PRINCIPLES

3

WORKSHOP RECAP:
Practise the principles of JV wealth attraction.
Resolve to do the extra 10 per cent.
Become a money magnet.

Presenter: Don Campbell
It's good to see you again, Richard and Emma, and I'm dying to see your action step. This past session was pretty specific in terms of what Russell wanted you to do. How did you make out?

EMMA: We approached it the way you taught us, Don. Seriously and with a pen and paper in hand. We literally took the assignment and started brainstorming about issues related to each principle of wealth attraction.

RICHARD: It was tough to start with, and then we remembered how Russell opened the workshop by reviewing the three pillars of real estate investment: systems, relationships and follow-through. Once we applied each of the pillars to the question, things got much clearer.

EMMA: Russell's instructions to find "two excuses per principle" was also a really helpful approach. This forced us to look past what we're already doing right to see if we could be doing it better. The whole exercise helped us realize that it's easy to be complacent, but complacency works against our true goal, which is constant improvement.

RICHARD: It's like we now understand the phrase, "I will become a money magnet," as code for systems, relationships and follow-through. As you can see from our action step, we banished our excuses using two key phrases from the workshop: "The extra 10 per cent" and "I will become a money magnet." We see those phrases as calls to action. We talked about what each one meant in the context of each principle and excuse, and then each of us tackled one of those phrases.

I'm intrigued. Let's look at what you've got.

Excuses the McTavishes Use to Keep Themselves from Attracting Money Partners

Attraction versus Pursuit

1. We choose not to talk about our real estate investments with friends and family.
2. We frequently recommend specific books or workshops to people who are interested in learning more about real estate investment, but we rarely follow up those recommendations to see whether we could do more to help.

The extra 10 per cent

RICHARD: The buck stops here. We are practising our sophisticated investor responses to questions we are frequently asked. This is a new system we've developed, and it directly influences relationships and follow-through.

I will become a money magnet

EMMA: We know that some of the people we refer to other sources do the follow-up. Others don't, but that doesn't mean they're not interested in real estate investment. Richard is writing a letter we will now send to individuals who show an interest in what we do, but aren't yet ready for an Expression of Interest Letter, which has more detail. (Examples of the Follow-Up and Expression of Interest Letters are in Appendix C and E respectively.)

This follow-up letter provides a brief overview of our real estate investment business, including JV deals, lists the resources we gave them verbally and tells them that we benefited from the mentorship of sophisticated real estate investors and would like to play a similar role for them if they're interested. Our main goal is to set up a face-to-face meeting or generate enough interest that we are invited to send the contact more detail about what we do.

Abundance

1. We catch ourselves making excuses for not looking for more properties.
2. When Richard talks about a potential deal, Emma gets defensive about what this will mean to her time.

The extra 10 per cent

RICHARD: It's okay to not buy more properties, but it's not okay to make excuses about why we're not ready to look! We know too much about the fundamentals of the real estate market to be giving other people the impression that the market is tapped out. We're not just *not* doing the extra 10 per cent—we're undermining our business with the wrong attitude.

I will become a money magnet

EMMA: I get overwhelmed with the thought of buying more property because I know I'm on the hook for bookkeeping and property management. Even though we're not actively managing our properties, there's still work involved. Some of the issues are really just bad habits. I don't always keep our filing system up-to-date and that causes a flurry of stress if I'm asked to check something like a receipt or warranty information on an appliance, or to pull up the name and contact information of an electrician or plumber that we've just started working with. I also spend too much time reviewing property management decisions. I'm going to take two mornings next week to clean up my office and get those files in order. On a third morning, I'm going to develop a new e-mail system of tracking property management. Instead of expecting them to clear every decision with me, I'll ask them to handle repair and maintenance issues under $100 per month. I will still need receipts and reports, but I will start collecting these by e-mail every Wednesday morning.

I want our property managers to flag issues so Richard and I can keep our property maintenance program up-to-date. But I've got to make sure my time is spent on investment activities that matter.

Expectancy

1. The economic downturn of 2008 and the emotional fallout from selling two properties we weren't planning to sell in 2010 left us with some other bad habits. Because we know that money is not as readily available as it was a few years back, we create reasons for not talking about what we need to grow our portfolio.
2. We've confused new market realities with rejection.

The extra 10 per cent

RICHARD: Our properties are making money and accumulating appreciated wealth. Our partners are happy. We've made money every step of the way in this business and because we are not embarrassed about making money, we're going share that outlook with more people. It's all about "tell versus sell."

I will become a money magnet

EMMA: Richard has a few friends who've asked questions about our real estate investments, and we've kind of brushed them off because we didn't think they could "afford" to invest. That's not our call to make! Our JV deals to date have all been pretty straightforward with us running the deal and the partner putting up the cash. We're going to find out more about what our friends are interested in doing and then see if we can find deals that work for both of us. We are *expecting* success.

Imagination

1. Thinking inside the box is limiting our potential!
2. We "think small" because it seems easier.

The extra 10 per cent

EMMA: Time is a big issue for us, and it's our number one excuse for not taking action. We're going to set aside 90 minutes every Saturday morning to talk about our portfolio and some specific actions we can take to make the business run more smoothly. I've been wanting to make some bookkeeping changes for awhile, and I feel that Richard's been holding me back even though he's not the one managing the books. By the same token, I've been hovering over the property managers. We're going to look for ways to improve how our team members do their jobs.

I will become a money magnet

RICHARD: We're going to go back to the write, scratch, question technique we learned when we got started. As soon as we hear ourselves making an excuse for not getting something done, we're going to write it down. If we can't figure out a positive spin question that scratches out the excuse, we'll bring it to our Saturday morning meetings and come up with something together.

For example, Emma is okay with handling the bulk of the office work related to our investment properties, but says she doesn't have time to call up everyone I've talked to who might be interested in investing with us. We scratched out that excuse, composed a positive spin question and took action. Now, I bring Emma the postal or e-mail addresses of the people I need to follow up with. Emma sends the follow-up letter we wrote together when we were brainstorming ideas under the Principle of Attraction versus Pursuit.

Giving

1. We don't know what to do when people we don't know very well ask us questions about real estate investing.
2. We don't have time to work with would-be investors who can't bring money to the table.

The extra 10 per cent

EMMA: After hearing from Mark Loeffler, we're starting to realize that we are leaving a whole lot of money on the table by ignoring individuals who don't fit our current JV deals. Richard knows a few experienced tradespeople who want to spend their evenings and weekends renovating investment properties, but they don't know where to start. Emma's younger siblings and their friends want to buy their own homes but can't qualify for traditional mortgages even though they have secure jobs.

I will become a money magnet

RICHARD: We're going to expand our working definition of who qualifies to be in our JV deals. We've got a good track record and the kind of knowledge and expertise that can help other people change their financial futures. This is a good way for us to give back to other people.

Decisiveness

1. We recently passed on a good deal because we couldn't set up a time to complete the extra due diligence required after the property inspection report was delivered.
2. We know we've got a problem with how we oversee property management, but we don't do anything to change it.

The extra 10 per cent

RICHARD: We've got good contractors we can call for advice on how we can make a renovation deal work. We're going to meet with these people in the coming weeks and ask about the timelines they would need to come and look at a property and get back to us with an estimate that will help us fine-tune an offer. The very fact that we've been acting like this would be seen as "bother" shows we need to do some serious relationship-building in this area.

I will become a money magnet

EMMA: We know that real estate investment is about finding, buying and renting out or selling quality residential properties. We're going to be more serious about working with our team to pursue good deals.

Expertise

1. When people ask us about our real estate investments in social situations, we often downplay what we do, saying things like, "it's not that hard" or "anyone can do it."
2. When people say derogatory things about real estate investment or the real estate market, we shy away from the conversation.

The extra 10 per cent

EMMA: We're proud of what we do, and we're good at what we do. We're going to role play some of these situations we've been in and practise better responses.

I will become a money magnet

RICHARD: We are real estate investment experts. We know that sophisticated investors are successful because they know what they're doing. We resolve to counter negative comments with positive ones. For example, if someone says, "it's crazy how real estate prices have dropped since 2008," we will counter with, "people are still making money in real estate investment. They're not speculators, they're business people." Or when we hear, "Bob and Shirley lost everything on that multi-family complex they bought," we can answer, "The fundamentals of real estate investing hold true in down and up markets. Our own portfolio is holding its own and appreciating nicely. We've weathered a few storms of our own and have still made money. In fact, we're in this for the long term and we like what we see."

Resiliency

1. Is the pursuit of long-term wealth really worth the effort we're making?
2. There's so much doom-and-gloom economic news. Why are we saving for a rainy day when the neighbours are using their line of credit to fund winter vacations?

The extra 10 per cent

EMMA: There is nothing wrong with enjoying the fruits of our labour, but we're proud of how real estate investment is helping us take care of our financial future. We are absolutely prepared to do the extra 10 per cent now, but our discussion about resiliency was a good reminder that we need to enjoy the journey, too. We're going to take a look at our portfolio and set some financial and family goals. One of our properties is nearly mortgage free. We'll look for ways to complete that process and then celebrate with a family vacation.

I will become a money magnet

RICHARD: We are really proud of what we've been able to do thanks to real estate investment. Thanks to a good grounding in market fundamentals, our financial risks have been mitigated by knowledge. But this is not a hobby, it's a business. The Principle of Resiliency helps us adapt to market changes. Because we don't expect things to stay the same, we are quick to recover when markets change.

TO SUM UP

DON: That's incredible. I really like how you approached this assignment. Other investors, novice and sophisticated, should read through your notes and hear how you address each issue because your thought process is so clear. I am especially pleased to see the way you are using what you already know! Success in real estate investment really does boil down to systems, relationships and follow-through. When things aren't going well, or when you want to make things go better, these three pillars should always be your starting point.

Follow-up information

I like what the McTavishes are doing to nurture relationships with potential money partners. Once you have a few solid JV deals under your belt, you will probably be able to follow-up requests for more information with an Expression of Interest Letter (see Appendix E) that outlines more about what you're really looking for: money. That's a very direct approach. But if you don't have a detailed package ready to send, or aren't yet sure that this prospect merits the time and energy to pull one together, don't use that as an excuse to do nothing! Never neglect an opportunity to cultivate your list of potential money partners.

A word about resiliency

I need to say a little bit more about resiliency because this is a huge stumbling block for a lot of real estate investors, especially since late 2008. Russell and I also tell investors they need to read the latest economic news. You need to know what's happening with everything from housing starts to corporate expansions and retractions. Where are jobs being created and lost? What's up with interest rates? What are local real estate boards saying about residential supply and demand? Richard, I see you're nodding and shaking your head.

RICHARD: I sure am. Emma and I subscribe to our local daily newspaper, read a national news magazine and check out the business news from two on-line sources. But sometimes it feels like it's too much news. It's hard to make sense of what's happening, especially since Canada is still climbing out of the last recession.

That's my point exactly. Resilience demands a deliberate effort to look behind the doom-and-gloom and ignore the overly optimistic headlines of the day to identify real trends about market fundamentals. Bad news is especially troublesome for investors who don't understand that headlines and those 15-second broadcast news "teasers" are written for emotional impact. They get people to buy the newspaper or tune into a certain broadcast. People who actually read the whole story or listen to the particular news item are often disappointed when it doesn't support the sky-is-falling prediction of the headline or teaser.

I guess my main point is that you really need to take some steps to make sure you are getting your information from credible sources that offer information that real estate investors can rely on. This is why so many sophisticated investors belong to an investment network. They want solid information and the opportunity to hear what other investors and market analysts have to say about that information. That feedback helps them hone their ability to look behind the curtain. These investors know that they need to be especially wary of market information that comes from people who have real estate to sell.

The bottom line is that resilience is never about putting your head in the sand. But discerning the "real news" demands a special kind due diligence. It is your job to find out what's really going on, and that means learning to steel yourself against negative news.

EMMA: Always ask "what's behind the curtain?" Right?

That's right, Emma. Given all of your hard work on this assignment, I think you and Richard are going to be really excited about what Russell's got planned for Workshop #4 because it really builds on what you've started here.

Bonus Handout: Insights from a Veteran Investor

Put the principle of attraction to work by turning every conversation into real estate.

—Cindy Wennerstrom

Background

Cindy Wennerstrom bought her first investment property when she was 24 years old. Then attending university in Toronto and working toward her MBA degree, the Sudbury native rented out the house while living in its upstairs apartment. The experience whetted her appetite for business, education—and investing.

Since that first property, she has purchased nine others and managed more than 10 renovation projects, all while working full time for a multinational corporation. Cindy left full-time employment on July 1, 2010, and launched Oro Properties, specializing in investment real estate located in Toronto's southeast end.

Currently managing a portfolio that includes six duplexes and one triplex, she has 14 rental doors and lives in a home with a basement suite (fully tenanted, of course). Cindy believes her hands-on approach to the business is good preparation for when she transitions her growing portfolio to more multi-unit properties. "I will know exactly what needs to be done with my properties and for my tenants. Many of my tenants tend to stay a long time, and we develop strong relationships. I wouldn't want that to change."

Still living and investing in Toronto, Cindy credits her steady success to an investing strategy that emphasizes cash flow and appreciation, two fundamentals stressed by her REIN mentors. She's also committed to providing value to her JV partners. "If I lost somebody's money, I would be devastated. I know that my investors have worked hard for their money, and I am never going to default on the commitments I make to them. I take my work very seriously—and my partners reap the rewards."

An advocate of the principles of wealth attraction, Cindy says her JV deals hinge on three lessons with direct ties to those principles. Here's her story:

Turn Every Conversation
to Real Estate

Three of my properties were bought with a JV, and I take very seriously Russell's advice to turn every conversation to real estate! That approach is how I got my first investor. I was standing in line at a conference in Halifax and chatting with people about how I'd just faxed in an offer on an investment property in Toronto. I was nervous, excited and very enthusiastic. It turns out the man who was standing behind me was eavesdropping. He became my first joint-venture partner, and we owned that first property together for several years.

That experience, and my subsequent work with JV partners, taught me that a lot of people think about investing in real estate, but don't know how to get into the business or don't want to do the heavy lifting. Every time I talk about my business, I'm giving people like that an opportunity to get involved in real estate investment.

I've also learned to be creative when it comes to finding ways for my partners to get involved in real estate investment on their own terms. I have one partner who's strictly a money partner, and he comes and goes from my deals when I need private financing. On one deal, I needed $70,000 to finance the renovation. He had the money, but didn't care about the details, and that worked fine for me. I had a 70/30 deal with another partner who couldn't fund 100 per cent of the money to purchase and renovate, and the triplex involves three separate partners. I did another deal with a woman who wanted to live in the property once we'd bought it and fixed it up, and that guided how we divided the ownership percentage as we were able to put a smaller down payment on the home.

The one thing that never changes is that I always make sure the partner understands how that particular deal works and why it works the way it does. The fact that you should never shortchange your worth as an expert in any deal is a valuable lesson taught by Russell and Don.

In 2009, I started leveraging my experience via a new consulting practice. I work with new investors to help them find viable cash-flowing properties and complete renovations that will maximize cash flow and property resale value. I also help veteran investors who want to increase their cash flows or resale values. Over time, it is common to let properties get "worn" or "tired." A Cindy-style facelift helps boost rent and property values substantially (upward of 30 to 40 per cent) in a matter of mere weeks! Lastly, I have found a real niche in attracting amazing tenants. I find great satisfaction in helping fellow investors market their homes for rent and finding them the best possible tenants for complete peace of mind knowing that their homes are being wonderfully cared for. With hundreds (soon to be thousands) of tenants on my property watch lists, my services are invaluable to landlords who wish to be more hands-off.

Never (Ever) Second-Guess Your Value

Experience has taught me that I know what I'm doing and that my knowledge is worth something to a deal. When the recession hit and I got my statements from my mutual funds, I realized my investment portfolio had dropped over $60,000. At the same time, my real estate portfolio was still cash flowing and appreciation was up 3 to 6 per cent. Not bad!

Conveying information about what I bring to the deal can be difficult, but it's also essential. Let's say I'm working with a new partner on a classic 50/50 deal. To help them understand what I bring to the table as a real estate expert, I am prepared to write down all of the things I do for my 50 per cent of the deal. Sure, my partners have to drop into the bank and lawyers' offices to sign papers, but my to-do list will be five pages long. Don't sell yourself short!

I also like the REIN philosophy that teaches me to treat my real estate investments like a business. As I see it, each of my properties is a separate business entity. I buy properties with cash flow and appreciation and thus I know I'm never going to default. This commitment guides the properties I buy. My properties generate a minimum of $650 per month *after* all expenses (including 10 per cent management and 9.2 per cent slush fund allowances), and most hover between $1,000 and $1,100, depending on whether or not they've been re-financed, post-renovation, for a higher value—and that's "net-net." I know that other investors work within different margins, but this is what works for me. I know I can put together deals that meet these parameters and that lets me sleep at night.

Plan for the Divorce

I take a very business-minded approach to real estate investment. If you think of each property as its own business entity, then what you're really doing is running several businesses, each valued at approximately $500,000.

Because I focus on cash flow and appreciation, I know that my profits depend on buying the right properties. But I also know that JV partnerships aren't solely about real estate, they are also about relationships. Be clear about that!

I look for people I want to work with because I know that I may have to deal with this person on a day-to-day basis. That can be difficult, but it's manageable if I like that person. My golden rule: if you don't like the person you're dealing with, do not take their money. Never, ever ignore your intuition or gut feeling.

I've also learned why it's so important to make sure your partner understands how the partnership works and why the deal is structured the way it is. I've worked with JV partners who bring renovation expertise to the table. I may do the design work, marketing and all the tenant-finding and tenant-selection work, but they'll help with the physical completion. Obviously, those deals will be structured to reflect our contributions. If a partner is strictly a money partner, and has no real estate experience, then they remain basically silent and trust that they are investing in me and my company. It's similar to a mutual fund, but with way better returns!

The greatest discovery of my generation is that human beings can alter their lives by altering their attitudes of mind.

—William James

WORKSHOP OVERVIEW

Presenter: Russell Westcott

Who has all the money they need to buy all the property they require to achieve their Personal Belize?

There's that question again! I put it there to remind you of why we are all here. If you do not have all the money you need to buy all the property you need to achieve your Personal Belize, you need to attract money to your deals. The last workshop introduced us to the principles of wealth attraction. In sum, when it comes to attracting other people's money to their deals, sophisticated real estate investors do the following:

1. Tell, not sell (attraction versus pursuit).
2. Believe they live in an abundant universe (when one person says no, another says yes).
3. Expect success—and do what it takes to make success happen.
4. Imagine possibilities.
5. Give to others.
6. Make decisions (and move on).
7. Know they are real estate experts.
8. Adapt to changing circumstances by investing according to market fundamentals.

Once you commit to those principles of wealth attraction, you will start to understand the central truth about investing with joint-venture partners. Namely, you already know most of the people you need to raise money for your next real estate deal. That is the Principle of Abundance, as applied to investors. Think about it. There is no such thing as a shortage of investors when you commit to the Principle of Abundance.

RICHARD: That's a key aspect of understanding what joint ventures are all about. Emma and I don't have all the money we need to buy the property required to achieve our own Personal Belize, but that's not the same thing as knowing or meeting the right people. We've got a lot to learn about accessing more JV partners, but we know it's a challenge that can be overcome.

REIN Joint-Venture Circle of Influence

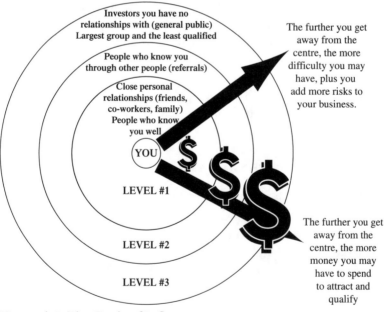

Figure 4.1: The Circle of Influence

That's right, Richard. And the first step to finding JV partners begins with your own Circle of Influence and learning to be what sophisticated JV investors call a "money magnet."

BE A MONEY MAGNET

To attract JV partners to your real estate deals, you need access to people who are interested in putting their money to work, but perhaps aren't educated about real estate. Sophisticated real estate investors love the Circle of Influence because it unveils a fundamental truth about real estate investing: even the greenest investor already knows a lot of people, and many of these people represent a JV opportunity. Once you understand how your Inner Circle works, you are a giant step closer to acting like the money magnet you already are!

NOLAN: This is all making a great deal of sense, and I'm starting to see why you and Don Campbell said I should be at these workshops. Before now, I thought the money I need to attract would be coming from people I don't know. I was keen to build a network of potential money partners, but confused about where to begin. If I think about how a magnet works, I realize that what I really need to do is attract money from people who are already close to me. That might change as I become a bigger magnet, but the Circle of Influence is beginning to alter my understanding of where I need to put my focus right now.

ROBERT: As Russell was talking, Tom and I were each jotting names into the various circles. We just switched copies, and I'm totally shocked. We have a few of the same names in each of our Inner Circles, but most are different. Because we're working together, our Circle of Influence is actually going to be massive.

TOM: Imagine what our Level 2 list is going to look like once we really delve into this.

This is great. What Tom and Robert are doing is exactly what I'm going to ask each of you to do right now. To come face-to-face with the potential your own Inner Circle holds, I want you each to get out a piece of paper and draw a circle of your own. You "linear" thinkers might want to draw up a chart with three vertical lists, the first and longest being for those who are in your Inner Circle.

Now think about what you "know" about each individual on your list. Ask yourself

- who has or will have children in university or college?
- who is planning to retire?
- who is a single parent concerned about long-term financial security?
- who wants to buy their own home but is having trouble putting the deal together?
- who's looking to put some of their savings to work so one spouse can switch to part-time employment or stay at home full-time with children?
- who has a circle of friends who want to rent quality housing near post-secondary institutions, health-care facilities or transit systems?

Brainstorming about the people you know will help you on two fronts. First, it helps you fine-tune the list of potential joint-venture investors you can approach, and second, it provides valuable insight into the kind of investment you may want to pursue, now or later. This helps you identify JV possibilities when certain kinds of deals come your way.

SUSAN: Remember when I said how the principles of wealth attraction were helping me understand that I could help others with my real estate expertise? This makes that Principle of Giving even clearer. What

I know about the people in my Inner Circle makes me think every one of them should be investing in real estate because of the long-term implications for their financial security. I know I can't expect everyone of them to come on board with my deals, but I am increasingly sure that I should be opening the door for that to happen.

DAN: Carol and I had a similar revelation when we talked about applying the principles of wealth attraction to our search for JV partners. Our closest friends are at a similar stage in life and we know that they have money and are frustrated by conventional investments. In fact, we talk about our investment woes all of the time. Imagine what the conversation will be about the next time we have our friends and neighbours over for coffee!

That's great, Susan and Dan. What I am hearing you say is that real estate investment can be win-win for all of the partners in a real estate deal. That's a smart way to approach the investment business. What you're really saying to potential investors is that you will take care of their money. People like that.

Now take a closer look at the names on Level 1, the people in your Inner Circle. How did you meet these individuals? If they started out at Level 2 or 3, what brought them into Level 1 and made them people with whom you have a close personal relationship? Now think back to the principles of JV wealth attraction. Look at how you used the principles of expectancy, imagination, giving, decisiveness, expertise and resiliency to draw prospective investors closer to your Inner Circle.

The most important thing you need to realize here is that the people in your Level 1 Inner Circle are like gold. While novice investors may find it easier to try and attract virtual strangers to their deals, sophisticated JV investors know that strategy is seldom worth their time. I see a few frowns, so let's look at why that's true.

FROM CIRCLE OF INFLUENCE TO JV PARTNER

Not everyone in your Circle of Influence will be interested in real estate investment, and some of those who are interested might not be people you want to invest with. That is okay. The due diligence of real estate investing includes taking a close look at prospective partners. You do not want to do business with everyone, but it makes sense to begin your quest for JV partners by taking a closer look at those within your Circle of Influence.

Level 1

Let's start with the people on Level 1. When it comes to sharing news of your real estate investments and searching for money partners, the individuals on Level 1 have several key advantages, especially for novice JV investors. These individuals are

- inexpensive to reach
- responsive to your ideas
- a lower risk because you already know them and you both value your relationship. (They can say no and still have you over for supper. They can say yes, and you will have more reason to believe they'll follow through.)

These are all very good reasons to target your Level 1 people first. Employing the Principle of Attraction versus Pursuit, you focus your time and energy on talking with people who reciprocate your interest in real estate investment. You can talk to all the people on your Level 1 list about what you are doing, but never compromise those relationships by making people feel like that's the *only* thing you can talk about.

I've got a great example from my own experience. I often talk to my friends about what I do as a real estate investor and what I know about the market. As I said before, one of my friends always listened intently, but told me he just didn't think real estate investment was for him. That was cool. So about six years goes by, and then he calls to say that the next time I was buying investment property, he'd be interested. I ended up calling him the next time I was putting together a deal, and he jumped in.

I was never worried that it took six years for our friendship to lead to a business relationship. Because of the win-win nature of my business strategy, I was grateful he came to me when he was ready to invest.

RICHARD: Our first JV deal with my boss is kind of similar to Russell's story in that my boss approached me about investing. We already had a great working relationship founded on mutual respect, and the whole thing felt pretty natural.

And why not? It is natural to work with people we like, and it's natural to want to help people we like. Real estate investing delivers on both fronts. In all honesty, your relationship with Level 1 people also provides useful information you can use to *pre-screen* them as investors. Not every member of your Inner Circle will make a good co-venturer, but it's a great place to start thinking about the kind of person you want to invest with. Because they know you and what you do, Level 1 investors are also a good place to generate leads about quality lenders, available property, prospective tenants and more investors.

I see some of you scratching your heads. It's normal to start this process and feel like you don't know anyone you can put on your Level 1 list! If that's where you're at, then brainstorm a list of the places where you know and interact with people. Now write specific names by those places. Here's a list to get you started:

- your place of business
- business events
- events that involve co-workers/consultants
- family events
- events hosted by friends
- meetings with a local investment club
- business association meetings, like the chamber of commerce
- Toastmasters
- other professional or personal development meetings
- political fundraisers
- church
- volunteer assignments
- wine tastings
- car shows
- sporting events

REALITY CHECK!

Go for the dough

As a real estate investor, you're looking for *money* and that doesn't necessarily mean you'll find a JV investor. Some investors may want a return on their loan versus the chance to own a percentage of the property you're investing in. These are money partners versus co-venturers and some sophisticated investors prefer these partners to co-owner relationships. As long as the person with the cash is someone you want to work with, it's okay to be creative when setting up the deal.

Level 2

These investors are people you know through other people, and they represent your secondary focus. In terms of their potential as investors, your Level 2 people aren't just people you know because you've met people they know. Think of them as prospective investors who have been *referred* to you by people from your own Level 1.

Most importantly, Level 2 people know what you do and are interested in your investing business or your knowledge of real estate investing. They could be people you meet hosting investment events, like a Cashflow party, where people play the Cashflow™ board game to learn about long-term wealth creation and real estate investment. Others may have already decided they want to invest in real estate and may be checking you out as a potential partner.

The next workshop will look at some cost-effective ways to attract Level 2 investors to your business and what's involved with moving them into your Inner Circle.

Like Level 1 people, Level 2 contacts are typically eager to meet you, already responsive to your ideas, and because you have Level 1 people in common, they are likely to value honesty in your relationship. They owe you nothing, but may not want to compromise their own Level 1 relationships. This makes them less risky than a Level 3 contact.

Level 3

Level 3 investors are people with whom you do not have a previous connection. They do not know you, you do not know them, and you may not have any Level 1 or 2 relationships in common. These individuals may respond to classified or Internet advertisements or the flashy I BUY INVESTMENT PROPERTY signs you've posted on billboards or vehicles. Those cold calls are welcome, but do heed the voices of JV experience and be honest about the three main problems with Level 3 leads.

1. Level 3 leads are the lowest-quality leads and will require the most demanding follow-up.
2. These individuals are more likely to back out of deals and often have trouble making decisions.
3. They do not know you, but they may think it's your job to make them money, fast.

REALITY CHECK!

Attracting JV capital from Level 3 takes you into securities regulations. Make sure you know your provincial regulations and stay in compliance.

WORKSHOP ACTION STEP: APPROACH YOUR INNER CIRCLE CONTACTS AS JV INVESTMENT GOLD

Your Circle of Influence is essential to your JV investment strategy, and the vast majority of the time and money you spend cultivating money partners for your deals should focus on the people who occupy the Inner Circle, or Level 1, of your Circle of Influence.

Implicit in that fact is a simple message: steer clear of those who encourage you to pursue JV partners you do not know. They are complicating your strategy and risking your deals.

It can be difficult to do business with people you know and like. Do not let that be your excuse for not cultivating this market. Approach this as a real estate expert, and your due diligence will ensure you do not work with people who are not a good fit with you and your deals.

In sum, attracting people to potential deals is not the same as working with them. Investors who value their relationships with people inside and outside of real estate deals will tell you it's always better to work with people you know. If your due diligence reveals that a potential money partner is not a good fit with your business strategy, you can opt against working with a particular contact and still maintain your Level 1 relationship. (See Workshop #9: Closing the Deal—How to Avoid Partner Pitfalls.) Again, it's all about seeking the win-win.

JV ACTION PLAN STEP #5

I will build bridges with my Level 1 contacts.

The reality of successful real estate investing with JV partners is that one deal leads to another. Existing partners may invest in more than one deal, or refer you to others who have money to invest in your deals. But be mindful. Savvy JV partners will also go looking for different partners if they think they can strike a better deal or develop a better partnership.

Your goal is to build bridges, not burn them. If a JV partnership works, nurture it. Seek to be the "next deal" and the "better relationship."

Resolve to complete and study your Circle of Influence. Take three people in your Inner Circle and brainstorm what you *know* about them. Design a deal that would work for each one. These do not have to be the kind of real estate deals you want to pursue. The exercise is meant to stretch your imagination and keep you open to the possibilities.

Potential Investor #1:

The Deal:

_____

_____

_____

_____

Potential Investor #2:

The Deal:

_____

_____

_____

_____

Potential Investor #3:

The Deal:

_____

_____

_____

_____

TUTORIAL: RECOGNIZING JV INVESTMENT GOLD

4

WORKSHOP RECAP:
Inner Circle contacts are investment gold.
Build bridges with your Level 1 contacts.

Presenter: Don Campbell

Russell tells me the last workshop led to a few epiphanies all around the table. Nolan now knows where to start looking for JV money. Susan, Dan and Carol now understand why it would be a good thing—with win-win opportunities—to bring members of their Inner Circles into real estate deals. Tom and Robert are reeling from the exciting discovery that their investment business can benefit from combining their Inner Circles to create a kind of massive investment pool. Of course, they're not expecting unanimous buy-in, but just knowing they have so many people to talk to is downright exhilarating.

What about you two? Did you go into that session believing that you already know all of the people you need to know to buy the properties you need to buy to make your Personal Belize come true?

RICHARD: I think that real estate investing helped Emma and I realize that our priorities were family and long-term financial security for our family. In that sense, we already valued our Inner Circle. We know why those people are there and why we want a close relationship with them. But did we expect a workshop on how to find JV investors would point us in a such an obvious direction? Definitely not!

EMMA: The workshop did clarify why our portfolio has evolved the way it has, and we feel kind of silly about not recognizing what was happening. For several years, we've hosted an annual summer barbecue where all of our JV investors get together so we can show our appreciation for this particular angle of our relationship with them. Other than telling them how much we appreciate the opportunity to work with them, we never "talk business" at that event. We do talk about how lucky we are to have these people in our lives, and we do tell them that we will approach them if we come across a JV deal that we think would work for them. The last workshop helped us realize what's really going on. Our business relationships with these individuals feel so natural because they evolved from positive personal relationships. We were setting up deals with our Level 1 contacts without really realizing why that made sense. How lucky is that?

Hey! Remember what I said about so-called luck. There is nothing lucky about the situation you've just described to me. It may be lucky that you are learning more about how the Inner Circle works, but the fact that you were already tapping this resource says more about your due diligence than it does luck. Once again, it all comes down to recognizing opportunity and taking action. You can live your life looking backward and regretting what you "should have" or "could have" done, or live it looking forward and capitalizing on the variety of advantages you can bring to a real estate investment deal.

Let's look at how you did with your action step.

POTENTIAL INVESTOR #1

RICHARD: This woman is a close friend of Emma's family, and we all call her Auntie. She's widowed, is financially secure thanks to her late husband's insurance plan and the sale of the family business, and is retired with a healthy pension plan from 30 years in the civil service. She's got a real eye and ear for business, values home ownership and has helped her own grandkids buy their first homes.

The Deal

RICHARD: Auntie always asks about our portfolio, but we've never pursued the conversation beyond that. We kind of thought she didn't "need" the money. In reality, she'd be a great money partner. She's financially secure, so she's less concerned with cash flow. But she loves teaching her kids and grandkids about the value of money, so she would enjoy the opportunity to build her own financial legacy through real estate appreciation.

POTENTIAL INVESTOR #2

RICHARD: At the end of the last tutorial, we said we knew people, friends of Emma's siblings, in fact, who wanted to buy homes but were having trouble with the down payment. We have done *nothing* about that.

The Deal

RICHARD: This next week, we're going to meet with one of Emma's brothers and his wife to talk specifically about helping them with a lease-to-own JV deal. They'd never even heard of this, but Emma tells me they plan to come to that first meeting with information about how much money they can put into the deal and a plan to pay down the mortgage. Emma's mom told us they're talking about selling the sports car that they're still making payments on to make home ownership a fiscal priority. We know they have good jobs and can make payments, but it's nice to know that our JV agreement will protect us if something goes wrong, because until it's paid for, the property will be in our name, not theirs. Based on what this couple has told other family members, it's like they appreciate knowing that, too. They want our help, but don't want to feel like they "owe" us. As always, it's win-win.

POTENTIAL INVESTOR #3

EMMA: Richard has a friend he's known since high school. He's a journeyman carpenter and a kind of jack-of-all-trades when it comes to home renovation. We've seen some of the places he's renovated, and his work is impeccable.

The Deal

EMMA: This guy's not in a position to put up much money for a JV deal. We don't usually do fixer-uppers because the fixing-up part is just too time consuming. But we do come across properties we'd like to renovate for the buy-and-hold market, and are going to talk to this carpenter about getting involved.

This is a good start. Sometimes people brainstorm about their Level 1 contacts and come up with ideas for deals that are quite a way outside their comfort zone. Others miss the point and want to focus on ways to get Level 3 investors on board. What a waste of time that is when you're first getting into JV deals.

Your approach is way more disciplined, and I can see you making each of these deals work for you and your investors. Good job!

Notes of Caution

At the end of Tutorial #3 we looked at what it means to go the extra 10 per cent with your real estate investment deals. Keep that principle in mind as you review the points below. Sophisticated real estate investors are money magnets because they see opportunities to apply that extra 10 per cent logic to every action they take.

Keep it win-win

You've designed these deals with a win-win strategy. That's good. It demonstrates a commitment to the people in your Inner Circle. If you slack off on that approach, you risk your current relationships with these potential investors, and you risk other Inner Circle relationships should others "take sides" in a dispute.

Stick to your plan

Protecting your Level 1 relationships does not mean compromising your business goals. Russell is going to walk you through the details of a solid joint-venture agreement at a later workshop. For now, always remember that your goal as the lead in a partnership arrangement is to under-promise and over-deliver. Things will go wrong. Properties will need unscheduled maintenance. Markets will weather unexpected ups and downs. "Quality" tenants will renege on their responsibilities. Through it all, a good joint-venture agreement will keep the deal on track.

Brainstorm both ways

This exercise encouraged you to think about a potential investor and then match that individual with a particular joint-venture real estate deal. You can also work in reverse. Think about deals you would like to make and then brainstorm the kind of partner you would need to make that deal come true. Does the deal require

- a partner with money?
- a partner with time?
- a partner with expertise?
- a partner with access to credit?
- a partner who can qualify for more mortgage financing?
- a partner with access to additional partners?

Tapping into your Inner Circle proves there's investment gold in your closest relationships.

—Derek Peever

BACKGROUND

When Derek Peever first got excited about the potential to make money in real estate investment, he did what any good friend would do and invited his best friend into the mix. That was five years ago, and today, he and Carson Conn are the principals behind PeeverConn Properties, a growing real estate investment business that's headquartered in the Fraser Valley of British Columbia.

By the time they joined REIN a year later in early 2007, the duo already held several properties. They also knew that they needed the support of the successful mentors in a real estate investment network to take their business to the next level. Their relationship with REIN proved especially important to their plan to bring more joint-venture partners into their deals. In addition to taking a "Joint-Venture Secrets" course taught by Russell Westcott, Derek and Carson set out to learn from their peers. Derek figures he's missed just two REIN meetings since March of 2007.

That work, learn and invest strategy paid off. Working with 23 different JV partnerships (including several couples), PeeverConn currently owns close to 40 revenue properties and sublets another 11, most of them located in the Abbotsford, B.C., area. As part of their Super Suites program, their portfolio features a number of furnished suites, which clients rent for one month to a year.

How does a real estate investment company run by two young guns (Derek is 27 and Carson, 28) amass such an impressive stable of properties and partners in such a short time? "Carefully—learning as we went," says Derek. Here's his take on what's worked for PeeverConn Properties.

FAMILY AND FRIENDS

PeeverConn bought its first property in Agassiz, B.C., for $65,000. With two family members on board, the four partners each invested only $5,000. Because we were all figuring out how real estate investment worked, we put in equal amounts and we all did the work. Five years later, Carson and I are more likely to be the "experts" and have our partners put up all of the money.

Most of our partners are still from our Inner Circle of family, friends, our parents' friends and the people we've worked with before. That works for us, but you still have to be careful about the people you bring into your deals. The recession taught us some valuable lessons about the fact that money partners need to understand how real estate investment works. We're lucky that we were listening when Russell and Don Campbell taught us about reserve funds, and we keep healthy reserve funds for every one of our properties, which means we haven't yet had to go back to our partners for more money.

I am upfront with investors who question those reserve funds. But the one-vacant-month-and-a-major-appliance rule of thumb we used to use can create a real cash crunch, and if you own 50 per cent of the deal, you're on the hook for 50 per cent of those expenses. That could become a big problem—very fast—if you own several properties that encounter problems at the same time. Our cash reserves help us avoid that, and we explain that to our partners. With experience, I would now recommend a larger reserve amount of at least 2 to 3 per cent of the purchase price as a better rule of thumb.

BUILD ON WHAT YOU KNOW

Carson and I have learned that working with people you know is no substitute for due diligence on a partner and that partner's expectations. We've been burned a few times, and I think that's helped us become much wiser at choosing who we get into business with. For example, we brought in one partner who was going to do the renovations as part of his commitment to the deal. Unfortunately, he did not complete the work as agreed or operate with any integrity, which meant we had to come up with $40,000 to complete the required work. Moving forward, we are clearer about expectations, would not pay for any work upfront and would, in fact, have holdbacks to make sure the work is completed before a contractor or tradesman, including a JV partner, gets paid. We're also more specific about our work timelines, because a property that's not on the market is a vacancy that costs us and the partner. A property that's not completed on time is also a liability if you have committed it to clients for a certain date.

Our first deals gave some pretty healthy profits to our investors, but may have been a little too rich for what the properties could support in terms of cash flow. As the real estate experts on our deals, we've also learned to make sure that our deals don't sell us short. For example, it's sometimes better to maintain ownership of the property in return for having a debt investor put up the money for a 10 to 15 per cent return. Let's be honest: for a lot of people who have money to invest, a 12 per cent return is pretty good.

We plan to make our investors a lot of money and as a result, we too will benefit.

Property management is our number one hassle. We manage our own properties in the Fraser Valley, which makes for a lot of work—but at least it gets done right. The four properties we own in Red Deer are professionally managed, and it's an ongoing concern. In Red Deer, we own three condos in one building, and we bought them for the same reason we bought the properties in B.C.: Red Deer is economically strong and we got a smokin' deal on the properties.

Unfortunately, the one Red Deer property lacks curb appeal, and because we're not there to make sure it's well managed, maintenance, vacancy and repair issues cost us money. These are issues we will deal with, but it's frustrating to know that quality property management and hard work on the ground could solve the whole problem.

In all honesty, our Red Deer experience has taught us to pay close attention to the properties we buy. We know what our target market for renters looks like, and that makes curb appeal a higher priority than it might be for some investors. For us, enhanced curb appeal means higher rents, and that has a direct link to tenants who pay on time and are generally a pleasure to deal with.

Super Suites: Developing a Niche Market

Our business has changed over time, and I'd say our main strategies are now re-positioning multi-family and commercial properties/condo conversions by upgrading them for higher market returns, platinum standard super suites (through our Super Suites properties business), long-term holds and the odd lease to own, in that order. The Super

Suites strategy evolved into our primary market after we learned that a niche demand for this kind of accommodation was not being met in the Fraser Valley.

Like any niche market, you've got to pay close attention to what the market is telling you. When we bought our first suites, we couldn't bring them onto the market fast enough. Then we overshot demand, and that was a problem, too. We currently have 24 of these suites in Abbotsford and three in Surrey, and this side of the business is going well.

But this market is complicated. Our suites are all stylishly furnished for an upmarket renter. With high-end furniture, plush linens and superior customer service, they demand a great deal of attention. My stepmom handles the suites in Surrey, but I manage the Abbotsford properties. Sometimes I'm out there at one in the morning so that people who are in flying in from overseas will check into a suite that's fully functioning. We keep the suites stocked with basic supplies (all soaps, detergents, toiletries and paper towels, etc.), offer regular cleaning services and supply high-speed wireless Internet, digital cable and in-suite laundry. It can be labour intensive because we can have eight suites empty one week and be fully occupied the next.

Some of our investors are getting a 30 per cent return on their money for these Super Suites. In hindsight, Carson and I believe we may have given away too much as we encountered some cash flow challenges while in the process of building the Super Suites brand and clientele. One of the biggest challenges is making sure that potential short-term renters know what we offer. To reach the human resources departments of local corporations, we typically take our brochures directly to the people who have to book accommodation for out-of-town colleagues and consultants. Several of our units are rented to players with the Abbotsford Heat, the local American Hockey League team.

We've also learned to look for clientele who might need what we offer—but not know we even exist. These include people who are relocating to or from our target area. They sometimes need temporary accommodation prior to or after the move. Insurance companies also like what we offer, but we have to take our marketing messages to them directly so that adjusters know we can offer short-term accommodation to home owners who have to vacate their properties due to insurance issues.

Management intensity aside, I really like this side of the real estate investment business. We're typically dealing with great people and the rental cheques are sent, in advance, by the companies who employ them. Over time, I think we'll find that these capital assets also appreciate in value.

It's work, sure. But whereas our partners make money and then hold that money in real estate, real estate is our business. And since those JV partners are essential to our business, we've learned to do what it takes to bring them aboard—and put their money to work for them and us.

WORKSHOP: HOW TO GENERATE JV LEADS WITH SUPERIOR MARKETING

The aim of marketing is to make selling superfluous. The aim of marketing is to know and understand the customer so well that the product or service fits him and sells itself.

—Peter Drucker

WORKSHOP OVERVIEW
Presenter: Russell Westcott

The last workshop zeroed on in on what we call the Circle of Influence. My goal was to make you understand the following two points:

1. You do not yet have all the money you need to create your Personal Belize.
2. You *do* know the people who have the money you need.

A lot of new investors are astonished by all of the JV investment doors that knowledge opens up! It makes you see your friends and relatives in a whole new light—not because they have money but because you can help them make more.

Sophisticated real estate investors know that Level 1 investors are their primary source of the JV money they need to complete their next deal. Level 1 individuals are the least expensive to reach with marketing messages. They are also the most responsive, and they represent the lowest risk. But that does not mean that a deal will sell itself.

This workshop targets two key ideas. First, success depends on adherence to two marketing rules; and second, you can use those rules to generate leads that will help you find joint-venture money for your deals.

REALITY CHECK!

Marketing matters

You may know why a particular Level 1 contact should invest with you, but does *he* know why? This is where a focused marketing plan comes into play. To generate JV leads, you must let others know what your business is all about.

Solid Oak Marketing Rules

Don Campbell and I like to tell investors that they need to focus their marketing strategy on two Solid Oak Marketing Rules. They are:

1. Stand out from the crowd.
2. Always tell people what's in it for them.

Savvy investors realize that both of these statements embody everything we know and believe to be true about the principles of wealth attraction. Both statements encompass a commitment to attraction, abundance, expectancy, imagination, giving, decisiveness, expertise and resiliency. This point is important because it leads us toward a bigger truth about taking personal responsibility for adopting superior marketing strategies. When we are trying to stand out from the crowd and tell people about the win-win nature of our JV deals, the principles of wealth attraction will help us stay the course and fine-tune the details. Let's take a look at how this works.

Standing out from the crowd is critical, but complicated.

Your willingness to be recognized as a real estate investor demonstrates that you are proud of what you do. It showcases your expertise, decisiveness and resiliency.

Just make sure you stand out from the crowd in the right way. Even if you invest part time, your quest for JV money will depend on showing that you have what it takes to be a sophisticated real estate investor who earns the confidence of JV partners by delivering what you promise.

To stand out in the right way, focus on presenting yourself as a professional. If the people in your Inner Circle (Level 1) hold any negative stereotypes about real estate investors or real estate investing, make it your job to put those stereotypes to rest. Project a positive image in the way you dress and carry yourself. Treat this like the business that it is and remember that every successful business spends money, time and resources on attracting new prospects. This is not an extra, it is an essential. Make sure that your most basic marketing tools, like business cards, advertisements and signage, project a professional demeanor. Always resist the temptation to share the details of a particular real estate business frustration with members of your Inner Circle. These are not the people with whom you should vent about tenants, leaky pipes or the problems you may encounter with JV partners. You are a problem solver, not a complainer.

REALITY CHECK!

Share what you know

Sophisticated real estate investors welcome opportunities to talk about why their business is a lot less risky than others might assume. If a member of your Inner Circle seems reluctant to invest in real estate because they don't understand its win-win possibilities, offer to help them learn how the business works. Instead of overwhelming them with details about prospective deals, send them a "follow-up letter" like the one in Appendix C.

Congruency

One of the most important aspects of standing out from the crowd in a positive way involves what sophisticated JV investors call "congruency." Congruency is all about harmony, compatibility and working with people who work well together. To be the person others will invest with, you need to be aware of the image you project and take responsibility for making sure that image is always positive.

If you show up late and disheveled for every family gathering, what does that say about the way you run your business? If you are given to rants about the problems you face with tenants, lenders, renovators or existing and potential JV partners, ask yourself what that says about your ability to build positive working relationships with the people you need to make your business dreams come true? To be the person others will invest with, be the person you would want to invest with.

The business cards you hand out, the letters you write and the real estate proposals you distribute to interested Level 1 contacts should all project the following messages:

- I am a successful real estate investor.
- I am proud of what I do.
- I know what I am doing.
- I am building long-term wealth for my family and me.
- I can help other people create long-term wealth, too.

Let them know what's in it for them

When you project these positive messages to your Inner Circle, you impress people with your business smarts and open a line of communication about your real estate investments. In effect, you are letting people know what's in it for you—and by default, what might be in it for them. It's all about "tell, not sell."

Tom and Robert, you look confused. What's up?

ROBERT: This is an area we struggle with a lot. We have professional business cards and stationery and have put some real thought into how we handle every e-mail message we send out.

TOM: But we sometimes leave events where we've been asked questions about our real estate business, and find ourselves whining to each other about what we didn't do or say. We now realize these personal interactions put us in a pool of potential investors. How can we market our deals without seeming pushy?

The answer to your question is to be honest about what you do. Think about all of the negative messages that keep investors out of the real estate investment market and anticipate how you can counter those messages with solid information about your business. If you're excited about a new property, talk about it. Let people know why you like it—but stick to the investment details. For example, if you anticipate certain questions, prepare yourselves to talk about them. Maybe you need to share details about what makes a particular property's location and features so great for quality renters. When negative messages about tenants cloud the conversation, talk about how you find and keep good tenants. Maybe you've just reviewed a renovation plan that will allow you to boost rent and improve long-term cash flow. That's the kind of business information that's likely to catch the attention of potential money partners. "Hmm. Robert and Tom seem to have a plan to make money. Maybe I could get in on it?" That's the kind of questions your Level 1 contacts will start asking themselves, and then will ask you.

Now that you two know that you want to work with JV partners, you need to be a bit more assertive when you're talking to people you've identified as potential partners. Ask them if they've ever thought about real estate investment. Let them know you are putting together deals with co-venturers and encourage them to call you if they want to know more.

CAROL: Dan and I have started to talk about our plans to invest in real estate with JV partners. We had a few friends and neighbours over last week and when some of the guys started complaining about their stock market returns, I got out pictures of our rental property and showed them information on other revenue properties we'd been looking at. Dan also shared his research on the local rental market and that opened the door for a conversation about how we were planning to leverage our experience as real estate investors to help other people invest in buy-and-hold real estate.

Excellent! And once you get your first money partners, you will need to start talking to other people about what makes those partnerships work. You obviously do not want to be dropping names and numbers that could present a problem in your Inner Circle, but you should be willing and able to talk about what JV deals let you do for you and your partners. Maybe you use cash flow to pay down a line of credit on a property, and your JV partner banks hers so she can save for a holiday.

If you think about it, what better way is there to stand out from the crowd than by using your own success stories to show that you take your business seriously. Let's review the ways you can do that.

THE TAKE-HOME LESSON: PUT THE SOLID OAK MARKETING RULES TO WORK

Like systems and the principles of JV wealth attraction, the Solid Oak Marketing rules are all about *action*. Sophisticated investors are students of their own strategies and they seek constant improvement. What do you do to stand out from the crowd? How do you let prospective investors know how your deals can help them build long-term financial security.

1. Stand out from the crowd.

Solid Oak Marketing Rule #1, stand out from the crowd, is linked to the principle of wealth attraction that encourages you to tell, not sell. Keeping that in mind, always be willing to talk about your vision for your real estate business and how that translates into real-world specifics.

In the tutorial for Workshop #6, we're going to take a detailed look at a formal Expression of Interest Letter and a Letter of Intent. Here, our focus is on helping you turn day-to-day interaction with your Level 1 contacts into potential JV deals. If you're not sure how to make that work, approach the topic like a business assignment. Decide what you will say when people from your Inner Circle ask you what real estate investing enables you to do. Level 1 contacts are the people with whom you can be very honest. Since you already have a relationship with these people, sharing what you do and why you are successful at it is one more way to cultivate that relationship. Tell them that real estate investing allows you to

- improve cash flow, perhaps to renovate your home without borrowing money, or to finance regular family holidays.
- build long-term financial security and finance a comfortable post-retirement lifestyle.
- put your children or grandchildren through post-secondary school.
- help your parents or in-laws pay for a good retirement home.
- be financially supportive of a charitable organization that's especially important to you.

When your vision includes or needs JV partners, share that information, too. Talk about the way you and your partners share risk and profit. If you bring something extra to the table, like real estate market knowledge, lender contacts, insider knowledge about what a certain tenant pool wants in rental housing or renovation expertise, plan how you will talk about those things when people ask you about your real estate investments. People in your Inner Circle may already see you as a real estate investment expert. But they won't necessarily know what that means, so make sure you know how to educate them when they show an interest.

Real estate investors who don't know where to begin this conversation with Level 1 contacts should take some time to think about their business. Write down your goals and how you meet them. Fine-tune the way you might talk about this information with a member of your Inner Circle. If you leave a conversation wishing you'd said more, or less, think about what you can do to improve your presentation the next time the subject comes up. Studying your own business is a great way to prepare for future opportunities to market your business.

RICHARD: This gets easier with practice. My boss was our first JV partner, and when he first started asking me very specific questions about our portfolio and the way we managed our investment properties, I totally missed the clues until Emma pointed out what was happening.

SUSAN: I love talking about my investment portfolio, but I can think of several recent conversations where I also missed the clues. Some of the names I just jotted down aren't even on the Inner Circle list I developed after the last workshop.

You've both just given excellent examples of why the Circle of Influence is such a powerful tool. Experience has taught me that our Inner Circles are always much larger than we first think. Real estate investors who commit to "standing out from the crowd" also notice more migration from their Level 2 to Level 1 contact pools. Good news really does travel fast!

2. Always tell people what's in it for them.

The second Solid Oak Marketing rule focuses on the win-win side of real estate investing. Always assume the individual you're speaking with does not yet know how investing in real estate with *you* can benefit *both of you*. If you've got successful JV deals you can talk about, go for it. If you know why a particular kind of deal may work well for the person you're talking to, let them know why.

Quality presentations

Quality presentations depend on quality information, so practise your presentation by thinking about the details of what you do. For example, tell people who ask about your business that you buy

- properties with positive cash flow.
- single-family homes for the rental market in the top 10 towns (rankings based upon the economic fundamentals as outlined by qualified experts).
- fixer-uppers to renovate and re-sell.
- properties you manage on a rent-to-own basis for families who need help buying a home.
- student rental properties in easy commuting distance of universities and colleges.
- multi-family properties near transit stations.

Erase excuses with action

If you find it difficult to talk about your real estate business, ask yourself why that is. Some novice investors think it's rude to talk business with friends. Others worry that members of their Inner Circle might think you value their money more than your relationship. That attitude needs to change. If you can help a long-time friend build financial wealth, why would you withhold that information from them? If they're not interested in a JV deal, that's okay, too. The principle of abundance tells you others will be interested, and those who aren't yet interested know where to find you if they change their minds.

By talking honestly about what you do, you also extend your Inner Circle to people outside of that circle, since informed members of your own Level 1 now have quality information about real estate investing that they can tell people outside your Level 1 group. This means your friends are now marketing your business to prospective clients.

Sophisticated JV investors fine-tune their strategies to generate leads by reviewing the information in this chart. Study it closely. Who could you send a personal letter to? Whose help could you enlist to legally generate leads among people who aren't in your Inner Circle?

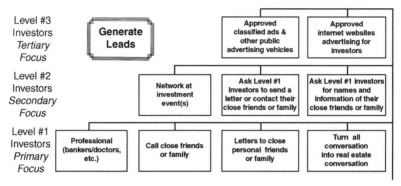

Figure 5.1: Generate Leads Chart

How to Generate Level 1 Leads

The most important point to remember about marketing your real estate investing business is that it is a *business*. Once you commit to that idea, it will be easy to adopt specific strategies that will help you project a positive business image and talk about your vision. But knowing that we should value our Level 1 contacts like the golden marketing opportunities they are does not help us convert a Level 1 contact from personal contact to business lead.

To generate business leads from your Inner Circle, you must take action. As American success guru Napoleon Hill says, "Your ship cannot come in unless you first send it out." If you've been a real estate investor for awhile, the people in your Inner Circle likely know what you do. If you're just starting out, you need to find a quality way to let them know how you can use their money to benefit you both. Your best bets are

1. direct communication.
2. an interest letter.

Direct communication

One of the best ways to open a direct line of communication about investing is to talk to the people in your Inner Circle face to face. You can also send them an e-mail, or pick up the phone and give them a call. Again, focus on the principles of wealth attraction and include a call to action so you can discuss the information in more detail. Nothing ventured, nothing gained.

Your opening line. How does a novice investor turn all conversations to real estate? With practice.

- Rehearse your response to questions like: "What do you do?" Or, "What are you up to these days?" Questions like that cue your opening line, your first pitch.
- Practise a 20-second "elevator speech" about what you do. If that was all the time you had to make an enthusiastic statement about your business, what would you say?
- Plan what to do if someone expresses interest in your business and business vision.

This last point is critical. First, you may not be in a place that facilitates a professional discussion about what you do. Second, you want to show the individual that you value your personal relationship enough that you want to arrange a more suitable time and place for a business discussion. Here are some ideas about how you can ease the transition

- Ask, "Do you want to talk about this later?" Offer to send them a letter or e-mail with the names of some of your favourite real estate investment books. Set a date and time when you can call to set up a longer meeting. Make sure they know you are interested in talking to them and interested in setting up a meeting that respects both of your timetables. Let them know that you have some information you would like to send them, and get their address or e-mail. An educated JV partner is a quality JV partner. That's why many sophisticated real estate investors send prospective JV partners a copy of *Real Estate Investing in Canada 2.0* or *51 Success Stories from Canadian Real Estate Investors.* Both focus on the Canadian investment market. The first details proven investment systems. The second provides a very personal look at how real estate investing, often with JV partners, changed the lives of fellow Canadians.
- Offer to send them information about a deal you worked on, including property and financial details. (Do not include your money partner's name.) Let them know you think they will find it interesting and that you would gladly meet to review the details. If they know one of your JV partners, and it's okay to share that information, let them know you're already working with him or her.

This helps them see that you have nothing to hide and like it when people who know your real estate investing business talk about it.
- Offer to send them the details of a deal you're looking at. Building on your conversation, tell them to pay particular attention to the information you highlight. If they are especially interested in cash flow, timelines or certain markets, make sure you highlight supportive information in the data you send over.

Your Expression of Interest Letter
The people in your Inner Circle probably know a lot about you, but never assume they know anything about your real estate investment business or the win-win situations it creates for your JV partners.

Send an Expression of Interest Letter (like the samples that workshop participants wrote for the following tutorial) to people who've expressed an interest in knowing more about what you do. Every letter must provide top-level details about some of your real estate deals, or the ones you want to emulate. If you belong to a network of real estate investors, tell your contact why you think that matters. For example, you may want to explain that these meetings provide great leads on everything from acquiring quality properties to obtaining legal and accounting advice. If this is where you get your best market data, let them know that, too.

Also provide these Inner Circle contacts with details about the other things you do to make sure you stay on top of market changes. Where appropriate, provide references (fellow investors, your lender, your lawyer) and include a call to action, such as a face-to-face meeting.

GENERATING LEADS FROM LEVEL 2 AND LEVEL 3 INVESTORS
All of this focus on Level 1 leads does not negate the fact that quality leads can also be generated from Level 2 and Level 3 contacts. When it comes to generating leads, the people in your Inner Circle should be your key focus. But they should not be your only focus, since secondary and tertiary contacts can prove fruitful, too.

Networking
Based on my experience, Level 2 leads are best generated by networking at real estate investment events or unpaid referrals from Level 1. If you belong to a network of real estate investors, attend the meetings

and get to know people. You can also host investment events, like a Cashflow™ board game party or wine-and-cheese-type event that includes a presentation about what you do. Some investors host this kind of event at one of the properties they are getting ready to place on the market. Just don't advertise these to strangers.

Take another look at the Generate Leads chart on page 105. It will remind you that networking is always about reaching out. You can ask Level 1 investors to send letters or contact their close personal friends and family, or to give you the names and contact information of close friends or family they think you should approach. These letters should be brief introductions about who you are, what you do and how you help your Level 1 investors create long-term wealth.

Again, always include a call to action. "For more information about how you could use my expertise to secure your financial future, please feel free to call or e-mail me directly. I look forward to meeting you."

Advertising

If you want to attract interest in your business from people at Level 3, advertising is your best bet. Classified ads and other public advertising vehicles are one way to generate leads from people you do not know. You can also use Internet websites and social media, like LinkedIn and Facebook, to advertise for and connect with investors. Like any marketing information you release, Level 3 marketing messages must be very professional. And, once again, make sure your public advertising complies with your provincial securities commission rules. Do *not* break these rules.

REALITY CHECK!

What they see is what you get

When it comes to generating leads, make quality, not quantity, your goal. Investors who use a "get-rich-quick" theme to attract Level 3 leads may generate a whole lot of interest from the wrong kind of investor.

Traditional and web-based advertising are not sophisticated JV investment strategies and should not be the crux of your business development program. But they can supplement other strategies. For instance, you could encourage Level 1 investors to refer Level 2 and 3 individuals to your websites (including blogs). Always follow the Solid Oak Marketing rules by making sure that your ads stand out from the crowd and tell people what's in it for them. One savvy investor I know takes relevant questions from Level 3 contacts and turns them into material for his blogs and tweets. This gives him a way to get important information to Level 1 and 2 contacts without spending a lot of time cultivating a lead that has very little chance of producing fruit.

Workshop Action Step: Seek Out Sophisticated JV Investor Insight

Newcomers to real estate network meetings are often surprised by what they see and hear. They expect a crowd of enthusiastic individual real estate investors who are keen to learn how they can take their business to the next level. They expect "experts" to be present to do the teaching, but they rarely expect to be in a room full of experts.

Look for a grassroots network of real estate investors who give each other an opportunity to share their personal success stories about what it felt like to buy their first (or tenth or thirtieth) property. Maybe you can start a monthly breakfast club with individuals who are willing to share experience and marketing tools, like letters of introduction and packages of information about market research or investment opportunities. Seek win-win relationships.

Think about joining groups that share real estate investment information through courses or newsletters. Real estate investment is a competitive enterprise. But successful investors who follow the principles of wealth attraction are often willing to share information about what makes them successful. They are proud of their expertise, and they know that helping others will help their businesses, too.

Develop your elevator speech

Once you commit to the Solid Oak Marketing Rules (stand out from the crowd and always tell people what's in it for them), you need to think about specific ways to communicate about real estate investment with your Level 1 contacts. Your goal here is to come up with a 20-second elevator speech. The concept is based on a typical elevator ride. If 20 seconds is all the time you had to talk to a Level 1 contact about what you do and why it matters to them, what would you say?

Make sure that your first response to questions about what you do always includes the fact that you are a professional real estate investor. This is the easiest way to make sure that your presentation is following the cardinal rule of prospect development: turn all conversations into real estate conversations.

Your elevator speech must also

- address the values of the people you are talking to. You want to make people feel comfortable about asking you questions.
- gain the listener's interest. Share information that is relevant to the person you're talking to.
- leave the door open for longer discussions and show that you respect that this may not be the time and place to go into greater detail.

PRACTICE MAKES PERFECT

Elevator speeches get better with practice. Decide what you want to say and then spend some time delivering your speech. For example:

I am a professional real estate investor who provides well-managed, profitable real estate investments that have predictable cash flows, and mitigate risks for the individual investors that have limited time or expertise to invest on their own.

JV ACTION PLAN STEP #6

I will zero in on the Yes Zone.

Every time you talk to a potential JV partner, you are making a presentation. To improve their odds of success, sophisticated investors perfect their pitch through constant practice. They do not aim to bring every prospect on board, but they want to make sure that every prospect remains interested—and impressed. Here is a checklist you can use to keep these interactions on track.

RUSSELL'S RESPONSE: HOW I DEAL WITH OBJECTIONS (BEFORE THEY BECOME REJECTIONS)

1. I do my homework.

I know my market. I know my product. I know why my JV deals are a good investment for my co-venturers.

2. I listen actively.

I pay attention to what people tell me. Are they rejecting my presentation—or looking for more details?

3. I filter prospects.

I would rather be treated like a prospect than a suspect, and my presentations afford the same level of respect to the people I talk to about real estate investment.

4. I am positive.

I seek solutions versus problems, and I know that solid information quashes objections.

5. I am prepared for anything.

I never let a question take me by surprise. If that happens, I learn from the experience (so that particular surprise won't happen again!).

6. I like to answer questions with a question.

I expect some prospects to "test" me with their questions. To find out what's really going on, I turn their questions around. For example:

Question: "Do you really make money at real estate investment?"

My response: "Do you really think my growing portfolio is an illusion?"

Question: "What if your partner wants out of the deal early?"

My response: "Are you telling me that you would back out of a legal deal?"

7. I aim for substance.

I try to understand the root of the question or concern. What is the individual really asking?

8. **I know it's okay to not know everything!**
   Where appropriate, I ask for time to get back to the potential JV partner. I'd rather be right than have to backtrack.
9. **I let myself get excited.**
   I like what I do—and it shows. I don't need to give away every detail of a new deal, but if I'm laying the groundwork for a new co-venture, or have just completed a great deal, I will tell people why I'm particularly happy.
10. **I am confident.**
    Confidence is catchy. Don't leave home without it!
11. **I am prepared to walk away.**
    I can answer every objection—and still not close a deal or advance a potential partnership. That's okay. As long as I've accomplished the first ten things on this checklist, I know that I'm moving in the right direction.

JV ACTION PLAN STEP #7

I will market my business better.

To launch your quest for JV money—or more JV money—get serious about how you market your real estate enterprise as a first-class business. Get business cards and letterhead. Professionally package requests for information. Prepare yourself to talk about the details of real estate deals and get serious about the people your real estate investment business could help toward long-term financial security.

Novice investors may view Level 3 as a "safe" place to troll for prospective co-venturers. They find it easier to talk to people they don't know all that well, and they like not having to worry about the way that a business deal might compromise a personal relationship. However, it is full of risk.

At best, that approach is short-sighted. At worst, it's a big mistake. Level 3 individuals do not know you—and you do not know them. "Qualifying" them as partners is complicated.

It can be done, but it will take time and money to secure your interests. It is far easier to work with Level 1 or 2 investors. These people already know you as a person. Use your marketing tools and investment knowledge to introduce them to the possibilities inherent in your role as a professional real estate investor.

Keep it professional

Level 1, 2 and 3 contacts will only generate leads if your communication is positive and professional. Interest letters must be personalized, well written, use the "tell, not sell" approach and be two or three pages, maximum. Your primary goal is a call to action. You want to create interest in setting up a meeting so you can talk about real estate investing.

1. Review your marketing materials.
2. Identify three ways you can draw people into your Level 1 Circle of Influence.

WORKSHOP RECAP:

Build your own real estate investment network.
Develop your elevator speech.
Zero in on the Yes Zone.

Presenter: Don Campbell

This assignment was a tough one. I know that you two are already doing a pretty good job on your marketing messages and materials, and the next workshop and tutorial are going to zero in on some of the written material you can develop to market your business. This tutorial focuses on what you've already developed, like business cards and the information you share during verbal interactions with members of your Inner Circle. My primary goal is to help you see this marketing review as a golden opportunity to make some positive changes.

EMMA: That's exactly what we did. We reviewed all of our marketing material, and we liked what we saw. Our message is professionally presented and congruent; we know the type of investor we want to attract, and our marketing materials help spell that out. We are looking for money partners who can access cash for our deals and seek long-term financial wealth. We are also upfront about the fact that we are the real estate experts and want partners who recognize our expertise versus those who want to take a hands-on role.

RICHARD: We did come across some problems with our website. Russell warned us about website jargon that could attract Level 3 investors who might think we are offering them a way to make a fast buck. We've had a few cold calls from Internet surfers who seemed confused about what real estate investing was about. We now understand that our website may have given the wrong impression about what we do. We were using boldfaced tag lines like: **Put your money to work right now!** and **Have condo, make cash!** We knew what that meant to us and our business, but some of those callers sure didn't.

EMMA: The big lesson there was that we were giving people who didn't know us a reason to waste our time. That site was designed to help investors and potential investors learn about our business. It's also a way for our investors to pass our information along to their Level 1 contacts. We tell people to let us know if there's someone they think we should talk to about investing. It makes those "cold calls" a little easier if we know they've already been to our site.

It looks like that review of your marketing materials gave you a head start on the second part of the workshop's tutorial: identify three ways you can draw people into your Level 1 Circle of Influence. Where did that lead you?

RICHARD: To more good ideas that we can put into action. Here's how we tackled that assignment.

IDENTIFY THREE WAYS YOU CAN DRAW PEOPLE INTO YOUR LEVEL 1 CIRCLE OF INFLUENCE

1. Improve our web site.

RICHARD: We've made this a family project. Both of us and our two kids are *each* committed to two hours of research. We are looking for examples of great real estate marketing websites. We've set a date to two weeks from now to hash over our findings. Emma will order in pizza from our favourite place, and we'll make this a working family supper meeting. I will borrow a giant easel from the office so we can also show the kids how professionals brainstorm solutions to business problems.

Our goals are
• to showcase real estate investment as a way to build long-term financial security.
• to give some examples of what investors can do with the wealth they generate.
• to promote the win-win nature of our investments.

---

2. Recruit Level 1 support from Level 2 contacts.

EMMA: Our dentist recently expressed an interest in investing in real estate with us, and he's happy with where that relationship is headed. We are ready to close on our first deal and once that's done, we are going to send him a letter asking him to send his dentist friends a letter of introduction to our business. He's also told us that he's willing to let us use his name when we send out letters to our doctors and some of our relatives who have great connections in our local business community.

Our goals are
- to focus on several principles of wealth attraction.
- to showcase our area of expertise, our experience and our commitment to helping others achieve their investment goals.
- to include a clear call to action so readers know we anticipate their calls or e-mails—and will take quick action to help them out.

Once we developed this set of goals, we used it to refresh our elevator speech. When people ask us what we do for a living, our response now sounds like this:

"Richard and I are successful real estate investors who know how to buy and manage revenue-generating properties. We work with a growing list of money partners who like the fact that we manage our joint investments for cash flow and long-term wealth creation."

3. Convert our Level 2 contacts to Level 1.

RICHARD: We are going to have an open house at one of our properties. We will invite Level 2 contacts to come and see one of the houses we are renovating for the buy-and-hold rental market. That deal was completed with a JV partner, and our property managers have already lined up a renter. We've got two weeks before the work is done and three before the renter moves in. We'll use that time to set up an open house for the Friday before the renter takes possession.

It's furniture free, but we'll move in a table so we can serve a few refreshments and add a few potted plants and vases of fresh flowers to make the kitchen, bathrooms and living area look especially nice.

Our goals are
- to bring in some Level 2 contacts who've heard about our business and may have already been asking members of our Inner Circle some questions.
- to give visitors a chance to see that our business values the connection between quality housing and quality tenants.
- to provide a one-page handout that profiles that project: initial cost of the house, cost of renovations, JV partner's commitment, projected monthly cash flow, building a repair-and-maintenance account, details of the deal exit strategy and an estimate of what the property will be worth in five years based on current projections of property value increases.

Well done! These are great ideas. The best thing you've done is take Russell up on his call to action. There is nothing wrong with an investor who decides he only wants to hold X number of cash-flowing properties for X number of years. But since that's not where you're at—your Personal Belize calls for a larger portfolio—you have to take responsibility for finding more JV partners.

These three ideas are going to keep you busy for awhile. Here's a list of other actions you could take to recruit more investors to your Inner Circle:

- identify one person from your Inner Circle who would benefit from one of your deals and ask him or her to a business lunch.
- identify one person from your Inner Circle whose business acumen you admire. Ask him or her if they will meet with you to look at what you're doing and offer advice on what you could do better.
- call up your existing money partners and let them know you are looking to buy more properties with co-venturers. Ask them to let

the people in their Inner Circles know you are available to talk. (This also encourages existing partners to think about closing more deals.)

DEALING WITH OBJECTIONS

RICHARD: We also reviewed Russell's comments about how to move people past their objections and into the Yes Zone. I even made another poster with the 11 main points, and Emma is going to review our marketing materials one more time to see if we're missing any of these items.

EMMA: We thought the list was a good reminder of key principles, and we're going to use the list to challenge ourselves as well. For example, *active listening* is very important, but we're not sure if we're really doing it right. The next time we do a formal presentation, we're going to do a kind of post-mortem to see if we're both hearing the same things. I suspect that while Richard tends to hear all of the "hard" information about financing and timelines, I hear slightly different information about why they want to invest. Since a partner's motivation is so important to how the deal works out, I think we could capitalize on this information a little better.

RICHARD: One of our current JV partners is interested in another deal. Emma thinks he is motivated by concern about paying for his children's post-secondary education. If she's right, I think that information can help us make the deal, with win-win repercussions for both parties.

Questions with questions

EMMA: As much as we like most of that list, we struggled with Russell's suggestion that we answer prospect's questions with questions. Richard and I agree that the tactic makes sense, and we actually use it with our teenagers all of the time. When they ask what time they should come home from a movie night or want money to buy something, we use this technique to turn the question around. By asking them "what time do you think you should come home?" or "how much money will that cost?" they have to take responsibility for the answer.

RICHARD: But how do we do that with potential JV partners? Don't we run a serious risk of turning them off?

I'm glad you asked about this because it's an area a lot of new investors do not understand. Russell's point is that while you don't want to be confrontational, you do need to recognize that potential partners may ask questions solely to throw you off. They may want to shake you up a bit and then use your response as their excuse for not investing. Others will ask one question when they really should be asking something completely different. They may ask what you'd do if they backed out of a joint-venture agreement early, when what they really want to know is what they can do if *you* do that.

Your answers may not make or break a deal, but they could make or break a deal with that individual. Your goal, as a savvy real estate investor, is to get past the question to the crux of the issue.

To help you understand this better, I'd like you to look at the following 12 most common objections to a JV deal. The list comes from Russell's own experience. Instead of being troubled by how often the same questions are asked, Russell wrote them down and devised a plan to deal with them. You will need to develop your own responses, but I've included some of the smartest responses Russell compiled. As you review this list, look at how Russell uses the question technique to target the bigger issue: fear (that is, ignorance of how sophisticated real estate investors run their businesses).

THE 12 MOST COMMON OBJECTIONS TO A JV DEAL—AND HOW RUSSELL DEALS WITH THEM HEAD ON

1. **Did you know that people can lose money on real estate?**
   Will the thought of this investment going down in value keep you up at night? I know that I do not want to lose money on a deal. That's why I . . .

2. **What happens if a tenant trashes our property?**
   Is this a scenario you've heard about? I haven't ever had any real problems in this area, but I do have a plan of action.

First, the investment will include a reserve fund to help us deal with unexpected financial costs. Second, if you own a rental property by yourself, you are 100 per cent responsible for any maintenance and repair costs. The good news is that if we're JVs, I would share the costs. As the real estate expert on the deal, I also know exactly how we would deal with this situation in terms of legal remedies. I also know who to call to clean things up quickly and efficiently. We sure don't want a unit sitting empty for any longer than it has to!

One of the ways I've avoided this situation is by thoroughly vetting prospective tenants. I'm really diligent about tenant screening and have a whole system in place to make sure I don't miss anything. At least five people, from employers to previous landlords, will approve a tenant before I'd let him or her move into an asset that's worth more than $200,000.

3. **What happens if you go bankrupt?**
Are you planning to go bankrupt? Me neither! But this is a great question. If we are co-owners of a property and one of us goes bankrupt, that individual's assets will be turned over to a trustee to liquidate and pay off the creditors. But no one can go after the co-owner's assets. Some JV partners want more security, so they qualify for the mortgage (with or without me) so that their name is on the property title.

Is there anything else you would like to see from me to ease this concern?

4. **What happens if you die?**
Have you met my wife? Seriously, under the terms of our JV agreement, if I die all of my assets go to her, and that means you'll be dealing with her going forward. That's why she will be at several meetings with us. If that doesn't work for you, we could also take out insurance on each other. If either one of us dies, the policy would buy out the partner's share.

5. **What happens if you abandon the investment?**
Would you walk away from a formal legal agreement? If I did that, I would abandon the investment and forego all of

the potential profits. (I'd also risk the reputation I've worked so hard to build!) A joint-venture agreement, which will be vetted by your lawyer and my lawyer (who will not be the same person), will spell out exactly what would happen in this situation.

6. **What happens if I need to sell and get my money out quickly?**
   Is there something I need to know about? This investment is going to be a five-year commitment, maybe more. If you suspect that won't work for you, we need to talk about that now. I know that things happen in life, and if you ran into a problem, we could certainly look at getting your money out earlier than planned. But I can't make any promises. Is that fair?

7. **Why do I need to qualify for a mortgage?**
   Does qualifying for a mortgage concern you? If you were to invest in real estate without me, would you have to qualify for a mortgage? Obviously. All of my properties are well managed and produce a positive cash flow. But Canadian banks do not look favourably on investors who already hold several mortgages in their name, which is why it makes sense for you to qualify for the mortgage.

   But you are not in this deal alone. I have arranged access to my private mortgage broker, and he will give you preferential treatment. Since I own 50 per cent of the property with you, it's in my interest to negotiate the best interest rate and deal possible. Since that broker wants my business, it's in his interest to do the same.

8. **Why do I have to tie up my money for five or more years?**
   How long does it take to make money in the stock market? What about accumulating wealth through bank interest or RRSPs? Real estate investment is about long-term wealth creation. My portfolio focuses on cash flow. That makes our investment work in the short term. In the long term, which is five-plus years, we should also be able to bank on property appreciation.

If five years is just too long, maybe we should talk about a different kind of deal. You would come in as a lender versus a partner, and we could set up the deal accordingly.

9. **Can you pay my line of credit interest?**
If you used a line of credit to buy stock in a company, would that company pay your interest? Probably not. Real estate investments accrue their largest expenses in the first year. Once the property is cash flowing, we have more options. Would you be willing to wait two years before we entertain paying your line of credit? One year? Could we look at cash flow after one year, then pay your line of credit out of the positive cash flow?

10. **Why aren't you putting any money into the deal?**
Did I give you the impression I wasn't putting any money in? I'm sorry, because that's really not the case. This is my business. It costs me money to develop my expertise and it costs me money to run it. What I'm not doing is contributing to the initial investment. But I am providing all of the work in advance to find a cash-flowing asset. After the initial investment, we share all of the expenses going forward on a 50/50 basis, good and bad.

Can you show me another investment where one person takes 50 per cent of the downside, does all the work and doesn't expect to get any profits until the investment makes a profit? This is an area that catches a lot of new JV investors by surprise. Honestly, it's because they don't understand what's really involved with putting together solid deals that will cash flow and appreciate.

11. **Why do you get 50 per cent (or more) of the deal?**
Can you show me an investment where one partner takes 50 per cent of the risk and, after the initial investment, puts in 50 per cent of the cash calls going forward, works at least five years for free and, at the end of the deal, only makes money if his partner makes money? I didn't think so!

12. Why do I need you to make the deal work?

What are you really prepared to do to make a real estate investment deal successful? Do I think you could do this on your own? Absolutely. I also know that it's already what I do—and I'm good at it.

BONUS DOWNLOAD

Go to www.jvsecrets.ca to register your book and download a FREE 60-minute audio recording that will help you close more money partners. Listen as a JV master overcomes all of these objections—live—and discover the exact techniques you can use to close more money partners and answer over 90 per cent of all the objections a real estate investor might face.

Success breeds success. Use your investment experience to generate leads.
—Jared Hope

BACKGROUND

Jared Hope wasn't even looking for a money partner when his first joint venturer knocked on the door of his growing real estate investment portfolio. Well on his way to realizing an ambitious business plan to buy 100 doors in his first four years of business, Jared was investing while working full time as a personal trainer to wealthy Edmontonians. In between exercises to build physical strength and endurance, Jared and his clients shared information about what was going on in their lives. Jared knew his clients were listening—but he didn't know they were also telling others what he was up to. Without even knowing it, his enthusiasm for real estate investment was building the muscles of a marketing campaign that would bring hundreds of thousands of dollars into his real estate business.

"I came into this business thinking I would do it on my own. I had some experience in business, and I didn't want the headache or hassle of dealing with partners," recalls Jared. That changed when the husband of long-time training client asked to meet him to talk business. It was 2006, and Jared, who had been investing for three years, knew his business would soon face a critical juncture. The young investor was nearing the end of his lending limit, but wanted to buy more property. A member of REIN, Jared knew what other investors were doing with other people's money, so he set up a formal meeting after the client's husband initiated contact.

With all of his properties located in Grande Prairie, Alberta, a market whose future he liked, Jared pulled together a three-page document about the Grande Prairie market using information he pulled from the REIN website. "My whole plan revolved around talking to this man about two possible strategies. The investor could come in with $75,000 on one property. It would be a five-year deal that focused on mortgage buy-down and cash flow. Version two of that deal would look at $150,000. Essentially, we'd do the first deal twice."

The conversation began much as Jared expected, but quickly veered off in a direction Jared didn't anticipate when the prospect told him he had $750,000 to invest in real estate. In hindsight, Jared realized that while he didn't know the man he was meeting, the prospect already had a solid understanding of the deals Jared was making—and knew he wanted in.

Responding to the offer on the table, Jared never presented his two-pronged scenario. Instead, he showed the prospect an executive summary of his portfolio's performance, told him more about his experience as a real estate expert and talked about why the Grande Prairie market was getting all of his investment attention. "The amount took me off guard, but I was never intimidated by what the JV partner was offering. I'd learned this business with my own money, so I knew his money was not going to be at risk in my portfolio. We bought 64 doors that year, and none of those deals involved my own money. I was the real estate expert, he was the money guy."

Today, Jared owns more than 100 doors with three JV partners. He also owns several other properties with an equal-money partner and co-owns a business, JP Management (jpmanagement.ca), which helps investors self-manage another 150-plus doors. "I am very careful about the partners I work with, but I've never had any trouble finding money when I need it. That said, the recession was tough. That's where I learned that Joint-Venture Agreements are invaluable. Regardless of who's putting in the money, real estate investment deals are two-way relationships and both parties need to know exactly what will happen if one wants out early. I faced that situation during the tough times of 2008 and 2009, and those agreements laid the groundwork for a fair solution."

Jared agrees with Russell Westcott's contention that finding the capital to invest in real estate is a lot easier than many investors anticipate, especially if they follow in the footsteps of other successful investors and focus their search on people with whom they already have good relationships.

"Taking care of other people's money is more difficult—but is also a learned skill," says Jared. Here is an overview of the lessons Jared's learned since buying his first investment property.

LOOK AT YOUR INNER CIRCLE

My experience shows that you don't necessarily have to be *looking* for money. As soon as you start investing in real estate, you are building a track record of information you can share with the people in your

Inner Circle. Most of us don't know *who* is in our Inner Circle because we've never taken the time to sit down and think about it. I know I'm not the only real estate investor who's been approached by potential partners simply because they've heard about what I do and they want to know more. To use that to your advantage, don't wait for the money to come to you. Start talking about what you do and what you want to do with real estate investment.

GET A LAWYER

I don't care who you are dealing with, a handshake or verbal understanding is never enough. You must have a formal Joint-Venture Agreement, and it needs to be written by your lawyer and vetted by your partner's lawyer. Every time I bring a new partner into the business, I explain why this step is so important. I make sure that both sides understand how the lawyers protect our interests.

This is a lesson I learned the hard way. In my case, it involved a misunderstanding over whether a deal was based on a loan or a co-owner partnership. Without a Joint-Venture Agreement, I had to do a whole lot of extra work to trace the paper trail of decisions.

That experience was a wake-up call to the fact that people's circumstances change, and when someone wants out of a deal early, it's important to have a path to follow. That's what a good system delivers. I had to buy out a deal that I wasn't prepared to buy out at that time. In contrast, when other JV partners have wanted out early, we simply followed the legal agreement; we came up with values for the properties involved and followed the process outlined in our legally binding agreement.

PARTNERS COME AND PARTNERS GO

The number one reason you need a legally binding agreement is that partners come and partners go. Every one of my partners wanted out when the recession hit in 2008–09. I ended up taking over two of those portfolios. The third came close to leaving but stayed on. It still wasn't easy. I had to go back to him for two cash calls, and under the terms of our agreement, we're equal cash partners. So if he put in $5,000 or $10,000, so did I. It was very helpful to have an agreement in place that we both trusted. We didn't have to negotiate terms, they were understood.

Learn from the Pros

There are investors who think they can do this all on their own. I ask them why they'd want to do that when they can learn so much from investors who are already doing what they want to do. By the same token, it's the "start" that stops most people. I've met potential investors who can't seem to get beyond the seminars and the books. They want to learn and they want to talk, but they don't seem to be able to do. My comment back to these people is that I've been investing since 2003, and I've been investing with partners since 2006. I run a portfolio of $20 million in real estate. I still don't know it all, so the time I spend with other successful investors is still very important to my business. I think REIN cut my learning curve significantly. You can also hire people to walk you through the process. Again, you won't be an investor unless you invest!

I do think you can use other people's JV investor stories to bring new partners on board when you haven't invested before. But as soon as you back that up with your own experience, you will be worth more to a prospective money partner. When I sit down with potential partners, I'm honest about the money and the mistakes I've made. This is how I show them that I know what I'm doing. I walk the talk.

Put Your Lessons in the Bank

When I got into real estate investing, I bought properties with strong cash flow, properties that were flush with cash month-to-month. We cut quarterly cheques from cash flow for thousands of dollars, sometimes more. When the downturn came, that all changed. Fast. When times are good, your JV partners will love getting money. But they will hate cutting cheques if times are bad. In fairness, it wasn't just our portfolio; the world had changed as well, and no one wanted those changes.

That experience changed the way I manage my business. I haven't taken money out of the portfolio since 2008. My new JV partners all know this upfront. It makes more sense to buy the right properties, manage them well and pay down the debt, since this is all about long-term wealth creation.

When I lost the income from my portfolio in the recession, I had to create a new job with JP Management, which helps landlords self-manage their properties. That was a direct response to market changes, and it grew from my own experience. As my properties are in Grande Prairie and I live in Edmonton, I went with professional property management at first. By 2005, I was tired of the hassles. Now I employ maintenance people on the ground, but handle the management myself. I'm not throwing property management under the bus because I know it works well for some investors. It wasn't working for me.

When the recession hit, a lot of investors I knew were really frustrated by issues related to property management, and I realized that because I was self-managing my properties differently, I had an expertise others might want. For a flat monthly retainer, JP Management gives owners options to deal with the day-to-day issues of tenants, maintenance and repair. If a leaky toilet is going to cost $172 to repair, you can hire us to do it at that cost, hire your own contractor, or do the work yourself. It's a hands-on support for investors who manage their own properties.

You Buy Real Estate to Retire On

I left my job in 2008 because I thought I could live off my real estate investments. I now coach investors on portfolio acquisition and management, and I tell them that while I don't live on my real estate investments, I will retire on them.

That outlook is why my business is still in the growth mode. I know it's not about how many doors you own, but by the end of 2013, I figure I will own 200 doors, most with money partners.

WORKSHOP: HOW TO CHOOSE THE RIGHT JV PARTNER

Successful people are always looking for opportunities to help others. Unsuccessful people are always asking, "What's in it for me?"
—Brian Tracy

WORKSHOP OVERVIEW

Presenter: Russell Westcott

I took a look at what some of you are doing to generate new leads on prospective JV partners—good work. I've also heard that some of you now have leads, but you are undecided about moving forward with them. Your timing is impeccable because that's what we're going to focus on today: how can you filter leads so that you're not wasting time on JV deals that won't work?

There are two particularly negative types of investor-wannabes:

1. Those who do not share your investment goals.
2. Those who don't bring what you need to the deal.

Don't get me wrong. Sophisticated real estate investors working with money partners know that their goal is to create future wealth with their partners. They also know that they cannot work with everyone who knocks on their investment door, and they know that time is the investor's greatest resource. You can lose money on a deal and make it up later. You cannot recoup wasted time. That's why it is so important to learn *who* you can work with—and who you can't.

NARROW THE JV FIELD

A lot of novice investors think they can "play the JV field." I respectfully disagree with that approach. Yes, investing with other people's money is a surefire way to build a real estate portfolio and create win-win relationships with JV partners, but this is a serious business and must be pursued with the appropriate checks and balances. Investing with JV partners carries serious risks, and you do not want to burn financial and relationship bridges. To successfully invest with JV money, we encourage you to narrow the JV field using tried-and-true business filters. Your goal is to focus your attention on partners who share your business plan and vision.

Let's say you've successfully "turned all conversations to real estate" and a few individuals have asked for more information about investing with you. Perhaps a physician who is a colleague of your family doctor has sent an e-mail to you requesting more information.

Following the system advocated by sophisticated JV investors, a system we discussed in Workshop #5, you will follow up the e-mail with more direct communication. Because this is a Level 2 contact who is approaching Level 1 status, you might send this individual a copy of *Real Estate Investing in Canada 2.0* and a letter that opens the door for a face-to-face meeting. Depending on your relationship with that individual, you could send a Follow-Up Letter like the one Richard and Emma shared at Workshop #3 (see Appendix C). That's a good letter to send to someone when you are "testing the water" to gauge their interest.

My key point here is the importance of follow-through. You want to "tell, not sell," but you can't wait for other people to open the business door for you. Since your investing system emphasizes that talking about something is not the same as doing it, you must always follow up any written correspondence with a phone call or e-mail that includes a specific call to action expressing your interest in continuing a dialogue about real estate investing.

SUSAN: This is exactly where I'm at with a dentist who is a friend and business colleague of my daughter's orthodontist. They work in the same medical business complex. I haven't invested with either of these men, but both are interested, and I feel like I'm on the verge of something really important to the long-term health of my business. I opened the door to an investment conversation by sending them a very brief letter about what I do, along with a copy of *Real Estate Investing in Canada 2.0.*

Now it's time to follow that up, but I am worried that I'm in over my head. What if I can't deliver a deal that works? What if this person isn't someone I want to work with? If I can't strike a JV deal with this dentist, does that compromise my reputation with every medical practitioner in the building? I was there just last week, and I counted 12 different practices in that office building. This has the potential to be huge, or disastrous.

I understand your fear, Susan, but believe me, this is all good news. Once you get to this point, it is important to acknowledge the three key things you are doing well. First, you are following a *systems* approach to real estate investing with JV partners. Second, you are building *relationships,* and third, you are demonstrating *follow-through.* Congratulations! You are sticking to the fundamentals of JV investing and putting yourself on the path to success.

Now we'll address Susan's concerns, which are not unfounded. Let's say her lead takes her up on her call to action and wants to discuss an investment opportunity at a face-to-face meeting. Well done. You should celebrate your initial success, but exercise caution. While Don Campbell and I are big believers in celebrating steps along the road to success, we worry when less-sophisticated investors get caught up in the emotional momentum of progress. It's great to generate leads, but the real work is just beginning. There is still a lot to do, and future progress means more of the *right* action now. For Susan, that probably means sending a more detailed letter along with a Potential for Relationship questionnaire (see Appendix D). For now, let's skip ahead and say a potential money partner says he wants to talk about making an investment deal.

FILTER POTENTIAL PARTNERS
At this stage in the process, the action you need to take is all about filters. The wonderful truth about Level 1 contacts is that once they express an interest in working with you, they are less likely to fish and cut bait. As long as you are respectful of their time, they are less apt to waste yours. Better yet, you can narrow the field of prospective JV partners by using a tested filtering process that will help you prescreen your leads and zero in on the "right" JV partner.

But there is a flip side, too. The nasty truth about Level 1 contacts is that even though your best leads come from this group, some of the people who express an interest in doing business with you will never follow through. Others may have the resources it takes to follow through, but may prove to be individuals with whom you do not want to invest. Those problems are more pronounced with Level 2 and 3 contacts, but you should know it's a potential problem at Level 1, too. Here's what you do about it.

Prescreen your leads

To increase your chances of spending time on prospective investors with the most potential, sophisticated investors prescreen every lead, regardless of whether they are generated by a Level 1, 2 or 3 contact. This typically happens before a face-to-face meeting, and the goal is clear. Since time is always an issue, you want to spend your time on the leads that are most likely to generate deals. If an investment deal is unlikely to occur with a particular partner, why pursue that aspect of your relationship? Sophisticated investors say it's like leading someone on—and who has time for that?

The prescreening process also respects your prospective partner's time and situation. By working through the prescreening process, these individuals learn more about real estate investing and their own expectations. That will benefit both parties if a face-to-face meeting goes ahead. Similarly, if that meeting doesn't happen because of what the questionnaire reveals, the investor will be able to cite specific issues. It's far better to say, "I don't think I can meet your expected rate of return," or "I need X dollars upfront before I can afford to look for property," than to leave a Level 1 or 2 individual thinking that you just don't like them!

PRESCREEN LEADS

Step #1: Investor questionnaire

↓

Step #2: Face-to-face meeting: Review questionnaire and present information package

↓

Step #3: Continue: yes or no?

Figure 6.1: Prescreen Leads

The graphic opposite highlights specific actions that sophisticated investors take to help them analyze the quality of a prospective JV partner. These actions weed out problem partners. That's right. Not everyone who expresses an interest in real estate investing with you will follow through. Others might follow through but may not be the kind of people you want to work with, or want to work with right now. Since successful JV partnerships depend on successful JV relationships, you cannot skip any part of this prescreening process.

Step #1: The questionnaire

Sophisticated investors view this tool as a prerequisite to a face-to-face meeting. Sometimes called a Potential for Relationship questionnaire, the prescreening questionnaire is exactly what the name implies—a formal list of questions that provides specific information to help you determine whether the lead is a good candidate for the kind of JV relationship you seek. It's also a good way to determine whether the prospect really understands what you do and how the two of you can work together.

An example of a Potential for Relationship questionnaire is located in Appendix D. Its questions range from what returns the potential investor seeks to investment timelines, what financial resources they bring to the table and whether those funds will be borrowed. The tool also gives the real estate investor some basic information about how "hands-on" the JV investor wants to be and whether a spouse or business partner may be involved in decisions related to the investment.

REALITY CHECK!

Templates can be changed

Proven templates save sophisticated real estate investors a great deal of time. But never think you must use a template "as is." If you don't plan to use RRSP money in your deals, you may want to leave that question out lest it confuse your potential partner. Similarly, maybe you know something about a Level 1 or 2 prospect that could help make the case for real estate

---

investment. Perhaps you should ask a question that helps them start thinking along the same lines. This could facilitate a more detailed discussion at the face-to-face meeting. For example, you could ask the following questions:

- if the prospect is a carpenter ask: what could you bring to an investment deal in terms of renovation expertise/ contacts?
- if the prospect recently inherited money ask: are you looking for ways to diversify wealth creation?
- if the prospect wants to buy a home but cannot afford to finance the mortgage on her own ask: are you open to ideas about how you could afford to buy a home for your family?

TOM: A formal questionnaire also reveals red flags in unexpected places. Robert and I have been talking to a Level 1 contact who was chomping at the bit to strike a JV deal. From what we know of the guy, it looked like we were heading toward a classic 50/50 deal with the money partner putting up the down payment. Then we learned he planned to put the $40,000 down payment we needed to complete the deal on a credit card. We asked a few questions about that plan and learned his gross debt ratio (GDR) was over 42 per cent. We knew this deal could spell big trouble for us. If our partner couldn't meet a traditional lender's evaluation on a simpler deal, we should take a second look, too.

ROBERT: It turned out he had a few credit issues and recognized that our deal could make him money. That's great. But we felt that his situation put our deal at risk; we were looking for a 50 per cent equity stake, and we didn't want his financial woes to put that at risk.

RICHARD: That's very smart. Emma and I know we are in business with partners because we can help them make money. But we are darn careful to make sure those partnerships won't cost us.

Everyone must complete a questionnaire

A lot of novice investors ask me if every potential investor should complete the prescreening questionnaire regardless of whether they're from Level 1, 2 or 3. The answer is yes. My own mother completed a questionnaire before we sat down, face to face, to discuss what we would want in a co-venturer deal. These days, my co-venturers are often referred to me by trusted members of my Inner Circle. Regardless, every new investor is vetted the same way. The process saves valuable time and ensures I can focus on individuals with the most potential to invest as JV partners.

Why would I prescreen my own mother? Because I have to! A prescreening questionnaire gives me objective information about each investor's expectations and expected contributions. You may know a Level 1 contact very well. But can you really answer for him or her? For example, you may think your mother is worried about her financial future. She may be more worried about yours and see investing with you as a way to help you grow your portfolio and secure your future wealth. The reverse may also be true. You may think she wants to show that she trusts you; but she may be worried about whether she can afford to retire. The only way to avoid trouble is to make sure that you can make decisions based on real information versus assumptions. Besides, you know what they say about people who make assumptions!

SUSAN: I'm feeling a lot better. It looks like I could send out the questionnaire along with an introductory letter that explains its purpose. But the bottom line is that I need to see the answers to that questionnaire because it's a very professional way to vet a potential partner. I think I was focusing on the personal aspects of my link to this potential partner and worrying about the face-to-face meeting and what we might both learn about each other. But this part of our relationship is all business, and I can see that having a completed questionnaire in my hand will guide that first formal business meeting. As long as I keep the boundaries clear, this man is going to respect any decisions I make for what they are: business decisions. In fact, the questionnaire makes it clear that I have certain expectations about my partners. That makes my job easier as it implies that I won't be working with everyone who completes a form.

That's exactly right. The questionnaire makes your job easier. When you read through the questions in the Potential for Relationship questionnaire, think about the different answers you might get. You should also review the list of questions you may want to add. Where appropriate, personalize the list of questions, especially if there are specific things you need to know.

RICHARD: That's a good point, Russell. One of our JV deals is with a friend and his wife. We knew that she was the one pushing for the investment, and he was really reluctant. That helped us fine-tune the questions we asked upfront, and the answers helped us avoid future problems. Our friend was still reluctant, but he knew exactly what he'd agreed to.

REALITY CHECK!

Look behind the curtain

Prescreening people you know very well can be just as difficult as prescreening relative strangers. Your goal is to always look behind the curtain. If you know (or suspect) information that's not being put on the proverbial table, ask about it!

The people completing these questions will likely know what you do and will be sincerely interested in learning more. Don't lose sight of the fact that they are willing to complete the questionnaire because they think you can help them make money. This isn't about anyone's feelings, it's about gathering the facts.

Their answers will show you where to focus your attention before you sit down with them to go over a particular deal or meet to discuss the details of the kind of deal they want you to find. Always remember to customize the questions and never trivialize the answers. Some answers may show an interest in real estate investments that do not interest you. Others may demonstrate investment naivety and reveal an individual who needs to be tutored in the ways of real estate investment.

RICHARD: Tutoring sounds complicated, but Russell's right. Sometimes people aren't ready to invest because they don't know enough. When Emma and I run into a questionnaire that leads us to believe an individual needs more information, we make that the crux of our face-to-face meeting. We let them know that we think they are "able" to invest, but not "ready." Then we talk about what we could do to help them become active investors. This isn't something you can do with every potential investor, but this kind of investment in time can really pay off when the prospect is a Level 1 candidate.

The biggest problem with trying to work with someone who doesn't understand or share your investment goals involves the risk of the "snowball effect." As your primary objective is a working business relationship that can lead to more deals with a partner or to deals with that partner's Level 1 contacts, caution is a prerequisite, since those with unrealistic expectations can compromise your next deal.

Let's say Cousin Gerry shares his view of a pending deal at the next family gathering, and you learn from others that Cousin Gerry is telling people that you've committed to making him wealthy at no risk to him. That could generate a torrent of leads from people who do not understand the basics of long-term wealth creation. Others hearing the same story might take their investment money elsewhere, fearing you don't know what you're doing.

My final word of caution is to remember that individual answers will not make or break a future JV relationship. They will, however, give you some critical information about the specific topics you will need to address in a face-to-face meeting. There, you can use solid investment information to temper unrealistic expectations.

A note about the details
Sophisticated investors pay particularly close attention to the individual's expectations about return on investment (ROI). As you review a questionnaire, ask yourself, are these expectations realistic? For example, if a lead wants an ROI of 75 per cent per year, that's trouble. Similarly, a positive ROI in 12 months may be possible on properties purchased to renovate and resell, but you can't count on appreciation in such a short time period.

Also look at what the individual expects in terms of monthly cash flow. While $300 may be possible, $1,200 may not. Similarly, pay close attention to whether the individual completing the questionnaire needs someone else's financial or moral support to complete the deal. You may need to know whether the other spouse, for example, will make a positive or negative contribution to future negotiations. If this input is going to be negative, the deal may be done before it's started. Remember: you are a real estate investor, not a marriage counselor.

Step #2: Prepare for the face-to-face meeting

The answers you get on the questionnaire will help you focus on individuals with the most potential to put their money to work in your real estate investment deals. Analyzing the questionnaire responses will also help you identify individuals you do not want to work with, or do not want to work with right now. Savvy JV investors review the answers and ask themselves three critical questions:

1. Is this someone I want to deal with?
2. Do they have assets or skills I lack?
   - do they have cash savings or assets they can convert to cash?
   - are they looking to re-invest RRSP or stock market money in real estate?
   - do they want a return on home equity?
   - if they have great renovating skills, can they put sweat equity into a deal?
   - will their strong business connections give me access to a greater pool of JV money?
3. Can I meet their expectations?
   - be specific about what you bring to the deal in terms of investment or renovation expertise, cash or property management skills.

Take your personal inventory

The last two questions are really about you and your efforts to find a JV partner with complementary skills and assets. Since success breeds success, sophisticated investors take this part of the process very seriously and complete detailed summaries of their strengths and expertise by asking themselves: What do I have to offer? They also assess the skills and expertise they are missing by asking: What am I looking for in a JV partner?

Honesty is critical. Here's what Richard and Emma McTavishes' personal inventory looked like when they first started investing with a JV partner.

Richard and Emma's response to: What do we have to offer?

- investing experience (we hold one single-family home and rent out half of a duplex).
- members of REIN.
- access to great information on market fundamentals.
- access to sophisticated mentors.
- quality bookkeeping systems that will allow us to keep our investors up to date.
- a real estate investment team that includes a real estate expert, real estate agent, broker, insurance agent, home inspector.

Richard's response to: What am I looking for in a JV partner? (What skills and experience am I missing?)

- money to buy more properties.
- quality property management.
- expertise beyond the long-term buy-and-hold market.

RICHARD: I haven't seen that list in awhile, but I remember how helpful it was when Emma and I first started investing with money partners. The first partnership was already in progress when Don Campbell asked me that question. It really helped me focus on what I needed in the partnerships that followed.

Identify your ideal JV partner

And that is exactly what we want to do now: look at what you bring to a JV deal and use that information to identify what you need in a partner.

Once Richard was clear about what he brought to the JV table, he had to take a hard look at what he needed from a JV partner. Sophisticated investors with JV experience view this exercise as a key component of their system and aim to describe their ideal candidate in detail. When you think about what your ideal candidate will look like, how they dress, where they live, whether they have a family and how much investment capital they have, you create a vision you can work toward.

For example, in terms of age and financial position, Don Campbell's investors tend to look remarkably like him and his wife Connie, minus the fact that his ideal candidates are not interested in playing a hands-on role in joint investments. How does Don describe these people? They have the money; Don has the expertise.

In contrast, my co-venturers are people who are highly invested in pension plans, own homes that have appreciated in value and are looking to connect with a real estate insider like me. Some of these individuals want a hands-off role, while others want to learn more about what I do and how I make decisions. Over time, some of the individuals who were interested in a more hands-on role have invited me into their own deals.

RICHARD: Like a lot of JV newbies, I was sensing some interest in JV deals from family members and professional contacts long before I really started thinking about what my "ideal" money partner would look like. Once Don got me thinking about what I brought to the table, I realized that my JV partners should complement my resources. In the end, my profile of an ideal investor for Emma and me looked something like this:

RICHARD AND EMMA'S IDEAL INVESTOR: A COMPOSITE

Is a medium-to-high-level executive.

Has a family with school-aged children.

Has home equity*.

(*Bonus points if they own their own home, free and clear!)

Maxes RRSP contributions annually.

Has limited time to do all the work.

Knows the value of having an expert around that can take care of all the details.

Has already developed his or her own version of a Personal Belize and will talk about it.

Dresses like a professional.

Enjoys dining out.

Interested in JV investing but does not want a hands-on role in managing the property.

EMMA: This exercise gave us a new way to think about the assets and skills we could share with our ideal JV partners, and which assets and skills we would require that they bring to the deal. This is great information to have when you go into your first formal meetings. If it's money you need, and they don't have it, the negotiations are done before they're started. This approach helps us focus on the kind of JV partners we want to work with, and we use that focus to identify and attract the right people.

Step #3: Decide whether or not to continue

Now that you've reviewed the questionnaire and given more thought to what your ideal JV partner will look like, it's time to take the next step. If the information you have collected shows significant gaps in the expectations between you and a prospective partner, let them know you aren't ready to take your relationship to the next level. Be honest. If their positions regarding ROI or timelines cannot be met by your deals, let them know that those are key issues. Be especially mindful of your Level 1 relationships. If they are not ready to invest or do not understand your system, move on to the next lead without compromising your ties. You have given these individuals valuable information about how your JV deals work. That information may encourage them to learn more about JV real estate investment and that may bring them back to you later.

The filtering process could also generate other leads if these people feel that they were fairly treated and then share what they learned with others.

EMMA: That's exactly what happened with us. When we told some individuals why we could not complete a JV deal with them, they listened to what we had to say and most agreed with our decision. Regardless of whether our expectations weren't in sync or they didn't have the money a deal would need, they respected our honesty—and business sense.

That led to pro-McTavish discussions with their own Level 1 contacts, and sometimes with Level 1 contacts we shared. No one was "mad" at us for not doing specific deals. On the contrary, they seemed to like that we were so fussy because that augmented our credibility as sophisticated real estate investors who sought win-win deals for our money partners.

REALITY CHECK!

Seed today, harvest tomorrow

A lack of available money will keep some would-be investors out of your deals. These same individuals may seek a JV partnership in the future. Leave those doors open.

THE TAKE-HOME LESSON: HOW TO PRESENT A DEAL TO A POTENTIAL JV PARTNER

When the prescreening process doesn't reveal common ground, you should contact the individual and discuss the situation. A face-to-face meeting may not be necessary—unless you think the issue stems from the prospect's lack of knowledge about what you do and how you do it. If you have a close relationship with the individual, you may want meet with them anyway so the lines of communication remain open. Again, you are following a system that cultivates relationships through appropriate follow-up.

When the prescreening process reveals common ground, set up a formal business meeting. This is where you can review the questionnaire together and ask questions about why they gave particular answers. Never assume a potential investor has the same real estate investing knowledge as you. Novice JV partners may not know why you are asking about RRSP investments and may need more information about how they might invest RRSP funds with you. That same lack of information may also come into play with rent-to-own deals or deals financed with home-equity loans. Make this meeting an opportunity to educate.

Once you've reviewed the questionnaire and clarified why certain information is valuable, present a professional investor package. The details of this package should depend on the prospect's level of expertise and might include the following items:

1. A review of the fundamentals
If you haven't yet done so, this may be a good place to present a copy of *Real Estate Investing in Canada 2.0* to the potential partner. Be prepared to talk about the Authentic Canadian Real Estate (ACRE) system and how investment fundamentals guide your investment decisions. Address your own aversion to risk and talk about how your investment strategies focus on long-term wealth creation. Again, your goal is education. Real estate investment is not risk free, but you manage that risk with real estate fundamentals. Be prepared to talk about how you do that.

2. Special reports
Include special real estate investment reports that clarify why real estate investing is a good way to generate long-term wealth. Real estate networks like REIN may make available special reports you can use to illustrate your business plan for a certain neighbourhood, town or city. Sophisticated investors may also allow members of

their professional networks to use reports they've generated. You could also use these as templates to create your own special report. Also provide prospective investors with relevant news articles about economic development in a particular community and how it's expected to impact housing. Sharing solid information with prospective partners is another way to demonstrate your market awareness and commitment to due diligence.

3. A deal or three

If you've already executed a JV real estate deal, share that information at this meeting. Outline how that deal works and draw attention to its win-win focus. You can also share details of a deal you're working on, or walk the prospect through the kind of deal you propose to complete with him or her. If you have a specific deal on the table, share those details.

While every JV deal is unique, the following three templates give you a starting point for discussion and can be used to guide the first round of talks on an actual deal. You can use the worksheet templates to show how JV deals work, or to help you collect the specific information you need to advance negotiations toward a Letter of Intent, followed by a formal Joint-Venture agreement.

If you get to this point in your business development plan and have not yet completed a transaction on your own yet, don't worry, there is still hope. Many investors, including the workshop leaders, have completed a successful JV deal without having completed a deal on their own.

To bring a money partner online without previous investing experience requires that you show your potential JV partner that you have mastered a system (i.e., the ACRE system) and will do whatever it takes, ethically and legally, to get the job done. My first JV partner was secured based 100 per cent on my confidence and my willingness to do whatever it took to make the venture a success. The bottom line is that even if you are starting at the ground floor in terms of investing experience, you can still have what it takes to complete your first transaction with a JV partner.

If you use the templates to collect information on a prospective deal, the information you negotiate and collect can serve as another prescreening tool.

WORKSHEET: CLASSIC 50/50 JOINT-VENTURE DEAL

Project Name and Address:

Investor #1 (you)	**Investor #2 (partner)**
• Real estate expertise	• Minimum $50K in cash or investment capital
• Real estate contacts (research team, real estate agent, property manager, lawyer, accountant, insurance agent)	• Covers down payment, closing costs and reserve fund (details to be confirmed)
• Local market knowledge	• Independent legal counsel
• Financing pre-approval	• Covers 50% of negative cash flow
• Covers 50% of negative cash flow	• Signs JV agreement
• On title and mortgage	• 50% ownership
• Signs JV agreement	

Exit strategy:
Upon sale of property, Investor #2 receives all investment capital first, and then the balance is split 50/50.

Minimum five-year hold.

Each investor has first right of refusal.

Notes:
Management costs paid out in cash flow.

WORKSHEET: THE RENOVATION

Project Name and Address:

Investor #1 (you)	Investor #2
• Real estate expertise	• Provides all labour and renovation expertise
• Real estate contacts (research team, real estate agent, property manager, lawyer, accountant, insurance agent)	• 50% of all costs (down payment, legal, reserve fund)
• Finds property	• 50% of all renovation materials
• Negotiates purchase	• Bulk discounts with retailers
• Arranges financing	• 50% of cash shortfalls
• 50% of all costs (down payment, legal, reserve fund)	• On title and mortgage
• 50% of all renovation materials	• Signs JV agreement
• 50% of cash shortfalls	
• On title and mortgage	
• Signed JV agreement	
• 50% ownership	

Exit strategy:
Upon sale of property, Investors #1 and #2 both receive all of their cash first. The balance is then split 50/50.

Hold period is determined by renovation (8- to 12-month window).

Notes:
Budget set in advance, funds for renovation set aside in advance.

WORKSHEET: PARTNER GUARANTEEING A MORTGAGE

Project Name and Address:

Investor #1 (you)	Investor #2
• Real estate expertise	• Guarantees mortgage
• Real estate contacts (research team, real estate agent, property manager, lawyer, accountant, insurance agent)	• Signs JV agreement
	• Independent legal counsel
	• 25% ownership
	• No cash flow
• Covers down payment, closing costs and reserve fund	• On title and mortgage
	• Arranges financing
• Finds property	
• Negotiates purchase	
• Manages property	
• Covers 100% of negative cash flow	
• Signs JV agreement	
• Registers caveat against property	
• 75% ownership	

Exit strategy:
Upon sale of property, Investor #2 receives 25 per cent of the total equity appreciation and is fully discharged from the mortgage.

Minimum five-year hold.

Notes:
The guarantor is never a "straw buyer," someone who is paid to sign documents that are not true. This is for legitimate JV buyers.

Workshop Action Step: From Filter to Follow-Through, Always Use a JV Worksheet

Successful real estate investors know there is no substitute for a pattern of investing behaviour that values systems, relationships and follow-through. While every JV deal is unique, that does not mean it is sometimes okay to skip the basics.

Every time you prescreen a lead, honestly assess what you bring to a JV deal and review what you need from a JV partner. Then take the time to complete a JV worksheet like those on pages 145 to 147.

The worksheet is a convenient way to work through the nitty-gritty details of a particular JV deal. It also provides a formal record of what you and the JV partner agreed to. Always keep a copy on file. The worksheet will be invaluable when you write a formal Letter of Intent. If a prospective partner questions the details of that letter, you can pull out a copy of the worksheet to show where the information came from. The worksheet and Letter of Intent lay the foundation for the JV agreement that comes next.

JV ACTION PLAN STEP #8

Advance the deal with a formal letter.

Once the questionnaire is complete, two kinds of letters can advance your deal. Neither are legally binding, but both set the stage for a future relationship. The first is a formal Expression of Interest Letter like the one in Appendix E. Prepared by the real estate expert and signed by the prospective partner, it directs the real estate expert to start looking for property deals that would meet the needs of both parties. It is signed by the prospect and outlines what the expert will do to put together a deal for the co-venturers.

The second letter is a Letter of Intent, and it carries more weight than an Expression of Interest Letter. While not legally binding on either party, it is signed by both parties. This letter typically provides a critical point of reference for a formal and legally binding Joint-Venture agreement between the parties.

Use the details of the following worksheet for the property at 456 Townhouse Road to figure out the details of a proposed JV deal, and then write a formal Letter of Intent based on those details. This letter would be sent after a potential money partner has completed a Potential for Relationship questionnaire and the two of you have met and completed a worksheet on a specific deal (or type of deal).

WORKSHEET: CLASSIC 50/50 JOINT VENTURE DEAL

Project Name and Address: 456 Townhouse Road

Investor #1 (you)	Investor #2
• Real estate experience • Real estate contacts (research team, real estate agent, property manager, lawyer, accountant, insurance agent) • Local real estate market knowledge • Financing pre-approval $300,000 • Covers 50% of negative cash flow • On title and mortgage • Signs JV agreement • 50% ownership	• Minimum $50,000 in cash or investment capital • Covers down payment, closing costs and reserve fund (details to be confirmed) • Covers 50% of negative cash flow • Signs JV agreement • Independent legal counsel • 50% ownership

Exit strategy:
Upon sale of property, Investor #2 receives all investment capital first, then the balance is split 50/50.

Minimum five-year hold.

Each investor has first right of refusal.

Notes:
Management costs are paid out of cash flow.

JV ACTION PLAN STEP #9

Personalize the strategies you use to show the win-win nature of your investment deals.

Here is another example of a template you could personalize to show a prospective money partner what you bring to the table as the real estate expert. Modify this template to fit your personal situation and the specific deal. Never lose sight of the fact that templates like this are tools you use to reinforce your commitment to the Solid Oak Marketing rules we learned in Workshop #5. You need to:

1. Stand out from the crowd.
2. Always tell people what's in it for them.

Investors who stick to these rules approach every potential money partner deal as a win-win proposition for both parties.

What Each Party Brings to the Deal

Investor:
To cash in on your investment you
- invest ONLY your money and a minimal time for due diligence
- qualify for a mortgage (if required)
- seek independent legal advice
- [insert here what you want the investor to do and bring to the table]

- _____

- _____

The Real Estate Expert:
To cash in on an investment, I must learn how to and then diligently complete the following list of tasks. I will only get paid based on the performance of the investment. If the investor does not make money, the real estate expert does not make money. To make this happen I must

1. Access and tap into a real estate power team. Building a team of these professionals may take years and many thousands of dollars in fees. My team includes the following professionals:
   - research analyst with access to up-to-date local market information
   - top mortgage broker
   - realtor
   - financial planner
   - real estate accountant
   - bookkeeper
   - real estate appraiser
   - insurance specialist
   - suppliers who offer preferred pricing
   - different lawyers, each experts in specific legal practices
   - maintenance and construction:
     - general handyman
     - mechanical and plumbing
     - electrical
     - general contractor
     - professional home inspectors
   - property management professionals:
     - I select the property manager, onsite manager and other professionals (such as tax advisors, inspectors, appraisers, bankers, engineers, roof experts, boiler mechanics) that may be required to inspect the property initially and then operate the property on a day-to-day basis
2. Complete the property search
   - searching for the right property can be exhausting and time consuming but it is critical to find the right property that fits the business model as closely as possible
   - screen and filter potential investment properties using realistic rents and/or expenses
   - conduct property due diligence
     - macro and microeconomics trends
     - completion of the Property Goldmine Score Card™
3. Write offers
   - write offer on selected property (this may involve multiple offers and multiple iterations since typically not all offers will be accepted)

- negotiate terms and conditions of offer (This is one of the most important tasks, and paying the right price for the property can be the make or break step for the investment. Understanding how to write offers not only protects investors but can save thousands of dollars using effective negotiating techniques.)
- finalize offer
- manage lawyers and accountants through buying process
- sign the documents
- ensure that all the proper steps and forms are taken to protect investors and deliver financial clarity

4. Secure financing
   - apply to the banks or through mortgage brokers to secure the right financing for the property
   - continuously monitor the mortgage portfolio to ensure best rates and terms to manage cash flow and maximize investors returns
   - sign required personal guarantees for required mortgage(s) (if required)

5. Structure the deal for flexibility and protection of all parties
   - set up the legal structure/corporation, and co-investor structure usually via a Joint Venture or limited partnership agreement

6. Handle property management and day-to-day management
   - act as the primary interface to property manager or, alternatively, manage properties in-house
   - secure tenants
   - manage issues or complaints
   - coordinate repairs or improvement services
   - manage rents and adjust rents frequently with market realities
   - market, rent, fix up, repair, paint, landscape and/or enhance said property to standards that expert sees fit to achieve appropriate rent and/or resale value

7. Keep the books in order and report on a timely basis to the investor
   - keep a record of such fixtures, repair material and/or landscaping material expenditures and/or all other expenses, such as property management fees, subcontractors, onsite managers, taxes, insurance, realtor, legal, advertising and/or related expenses to market, upgrade, rent and later sell said property

- provide simple and easy to understand statements on an agreed to timeline
- file annual or quarterly statements/documents that may be required by various jurisdictions

8. Be the leader of the marching band
   - certain team members play crucial roles at different times of an investment life cycle. Knowing when to apply a team member's unique talents to the issue at hand can solve problems faster and create peace of mind
9. Know how to flawlessly execute the detailed business plan and provide regular updates as conditions change
10. Maximize the investment's exit strategy and know how to reap the rewards of our work
    - utilize key relationships to sell the property at market value for minimum costs
    - negotiate the deal
    - stick handle the sale through lawyers and accountant
    - provide investor with proper split of the investment
    - provide the investor with a simple statement of account to be used for investor's taxes

[Insert any other duties you perform for your investors.]

WORKSHOP RECAP:

From filter to follow-through: Always use a JV worksheet.
Choose the right JV partner.
Advance the deal with a formal letter.

Presenter: Don Campbell

You covered a lot of ground in that last workshop, and we're going to use this tutorial to focus on two key issues: how to filter leads and how to approach a potential JV partner with information that could lead to the development of a formal Letter of Intent. I want to review the letter Susan prepared to follow up a lead with a dentist colleague of her daughter's orthodontist. We will also review a Letter of Intent written by Richard and Emma.

Susan: I've brought a draft of the letter I wrote based on a template I got from Russell and Don. I'd love your feedback.

Investor Name:
Address:
Phone and e-mail:

Date:

Level #2 Investor's name:
Address:

Re: Real Estate Investment Opportunity

Dear (Name):

I enjoyed talking with you by telephone the other day. I know that you also received a letter from me that noted my connection to our mutual colleague, Dr. X, along with a copy of the book *Real Estate Investing in Canada 2.0* by Don Campbell. As you know, I have been using investment real estate to create long-term wealth for several years, and Dr. X is also looking at coming on board as a joint-venture partner in my future deals.

I also appreciate your willingness to complete the Potential for a Relationship questionnaire, which I have included with this letter. This will help both of us zero in on an investment opportunity that meets both of our expectations.

As your request for more information was so specific, I am also forwarding more details about my investment portfolio. In addition to developing my portfolio, which now includes three properties, I have spent a number of years honing my skills as a sophisticated real estate investor. This included participation in several intensive real estate investment courses and active membership in a well-respected real estate investment network.

This month I plan to complete my fourth investment real estate transaction and I am looking to expand my portfolio by bringing people like you into my future deals. My primary goal is to put together and manage deals that will enable you to profit alongside me.

As you may already know, real estate is a proven way to invest money for long-term wealth creation. My own portfolio is founded on three investment pillars:

1. **I buy using a proven system.** The system I use is the Authentic Canadian Real Estate (ACRE) system as described in *Real Estate Investing in Canada 2.0.*
2. **I establish key relationships.** Over the past few years, I have built what I call my real estate investment dream team. It consists of the real estate agents, mortgage brokers, lawyers and property managers who work with me to create a successful real estate investment portfolio. Every member is an expert at what he or she does, and I have built relationships on a win-win principle that promotes loyalty and the quest for excellence.

3. I am committed to follow-through and taking action.
I built my portfolio beginning in 2007 and weathered the latest real estate market slump still making money. Moving forward, my ability to buy the right properties in the right locations is something I will expand with joint-venture partners, thus allowing others to profit from my deals.

The primary key to my success is my focus on **positive cash flow real estate** located in the Hamilton area. Further to that, I buy only when the price is right and the property fits my system as determined by my detailed due diligence checklists.

Once you complete the enclosed questionnaire, I would appreciate the opportunity to talk to you more about how working with me will allow you to benefit from my real estate knowledge and success. To help you understand more about my business, I have included an example of a recent deal I have completed. I also took the liberty of including a look at how these deals could have benefited a partner.

As you can see, the returns on investment, based on conservative estimates, are very strong over the next five years. I look forward to speaking with you in the coming days to arrange a meeting to discuss more details. Please contact me at: 123-134-5789.

Thanking you in advance,
Susan Templeton
Real Estate Investment Expert

Sample Deal

I bought this with equity from my primary residence. I was looking for a long-term buy-and-hold investment and used a line of credit to finance the down payment.

The numbers

Townhouse in Hamilton, Ontario

Purchase price	$ 169,000
Investment required	$ 36,000
Rent	$ 1,395/month
Est. positive cash flow	$ 150/month
Mortgage pay down	$ 234/month
($2,808.45/yr, 1–5% interest, 25-yr Amortization)	
Total profit + equity	$ 384/month
ROE (Return on Equity)	$ 12.8%

If the property values grow by 3% per year for the next 5 years, the property will be valued at $195,900. Mortgage owing will be $119,600. **Total equity $ 76,300**.

If this deal had been made with a 50/50 partner

Estimated equity	$ 76,300
Partner's down payment returned	$ 36,000
Net profit	**$ 40,300**

Profit breakdown (50/50 split)

Partner	$ 20,150
Myself	$ 20,150
ROI partner	56% (Total for 5 years)
	9.3% (Rate of Return Annual)

This looks good, Susan. I especially like the way you are "inviting" people into your deals. The example you gave did not include partners, but did a great job of showing how a partner could have benefitted. Showing potential money partners the rewards they could be earning is an awesome marketing tool. This is all tell, not sell!

Other principles of wealth attraction are also apparent in your letter. When I read this, I see that you are talking about an abundant universe; you know more deals are out there. Sharing the details of how you made these deals work on your own also shows imagination, decisiveness and expertise. Inviting people into these deals showcases your dedication to win-win ideals, and the fact that you did this in a recession demonstrates resilience.

Rather than critique what you've done, I want to focus on what more you can do with this letter moving forward. For example:

1. Share the good news.
I suggest you personalize the letter and send it to your daughter's orthodontist, too. Take the time to thank him for helping you connect with his colleague, and then share what you're telling the dentist. In essence, you're giving them both something to think about—and talk about.

If you get a positive response from one or both of these individuals, ask them for their help contacting other colleagues.

2. Keep it fresh.
This letter is very good. But I don't think it's the letter you want to send out six months from now. Once you have solid JV deals in your portfolio, use that information in the letters that accompany your questionnaires. I've seen investors make the mistake of sending out the same letter for too long. Unfortunately, some end up sending the same prospects the same letter, only months apart. That's not professional.

3. Target your Inner Circle contacts.
You've done a lot of work on this letter, and the deals you profile speak volumes about what you're doing with your real estate investment business. I know that you've been reluctant to bring partners into your deals, but I think you're starting to understand how this can be a win-win for you and your Level 1 contacts. Let's focus on the positives. When you're talking to Level 1 contacts this next week, tell them that you are going to bring partners into your deals. Be honest. Tell them, "I am good at this. I've got several years of success under my belt, and I am bringing on partners so that I can generate more long-term wealth for them and for me."

Then tell them you are looking for partners and ask if you can send them a copy of the letter.

SUSAN: That's great advice. I've actually had some close friends ask for more information about what I'm doing. I'll make a list and start calling people this week. Because these people know me,

I think I can skip the first letter and send out an updated copy of this one along with *Real Estate Investing in Canada 2.0* and the questionnaire.

Excellent. My one note of caution is that you also develop a system to track who you are talking to. You need to know who is getting what marketing materials, and you need to be able to follow up on those contacts. The prescreening process you learned in Workshop #6 takes time and due diligence. If you don't have time to prescreen several people at once, you will need to contact them and let them know that you are actively looking for deals that might work for them. That'll buy you some valuable time to focus on leads with the most immediate potential.

REALITY CHECK!

Keep it tight and personal

Personalize each letter you send, and keep the content as tight as possible. You may want to include additional documents, but keep the letter to two or three pages, maximum. If possible, vet your first letters through a sophisticated real estate investor. You want your letter to generate interest in a face-to-face meeting.

THE LETTER OF INTENT

Now I want to look at Richard and Emma's Letter of Intent. This is the letter you would send after you've vetted a potential partner and have held at least one face-to-face meeting to determine the kind of JV deal you would like to work on together.

RICHARD: The letter is based on the worksheet for a classic 50/50 deal Russell outlined in Workshop #6. We took the assignment a step further because we had already prescreened a potential JV partner and had completed a 50/50 deal worksheet based on what he was prepared to contribute. We've identified two properties that fit the parameters of that worksheet, and we're now ready to take that to our prospect. Once we've signed off on this Letter of Intent, we'll be ready to move on one of these properties.

Richard and Emma McTavish
Real Estate Investors
222 2nd Avenue South
Somewhere, AB
T1J 1L4
(403-322-2222)

Date
Potential JV partner's name
Address

Re: Joint-Venture Partnership between Richard and Emma McTavish ("JV Partner A") and Potential Investor ("JV Partner B")

Dear Potential Investor:

Emma and I are thrilled that you are interested in working with us as joint-venture partners on a real estate investment property deal. We appreciate the time you took to answer our questions and review our investment strategy. Experience tells us that this approach paves the way for a positive working relationship.

We have reviewed the worksheet we prepared at our recent meeting and have found a couple of deals that fit the parameters of a 50/50 Joint-Venture Agreement. Before we proceed with efforts to close that deal, we would like to outline our agreement in principle. More detailed paperwork will be drafted as specific details of the deal come to light.

Based on the worksheet completed with your input, we would like to pursue the following:

1. Property specifications:

- Property will be purchased within 6 months from today
- Price range between $180K and $230K
- Townhouse condominium
- 1,100 square feet or larger
- Three bedrooms and 2 1/2 baths
- Located in top performing economic region and neighbourhood

2. Estimated financial contribution:

- JV Partner B makes a commitment to contribute approximately $45,000–55,000
- Amount will be dependent on purchase price, closing costs and initial repairs needed on property; all of these costs are considered your capital investment
- JV Partner A makes a commitment to conduct and oversee all business relating to the acquisition, administration and management, and final closing on property

3. Property ownership will be as follows:

- JV Partner A: 50% share
- JV Partner B: 50% share

4. Targeted closing date on property:

- On or before [give date 6 months from now]
                                    Initials_____, _____

5. Mortgage funding:

- JV Partner A and JV Partner B will be qualifying and applying for the mortgage jointly unless mortgage is assumable without qualifying

6. Title on property:

- Title to be held in both parties' names (JV Partners A and B; 50% each party) in either personal names or corporate names
- Joint-Venture Agreement will be registered on title with lawyer; therefore, property cannot be sold without both parties' consent

7. Length of hold:

- Both parties agree that this is a long-term investment and agree to hold the property for a minimum of five years unless both parties agree to change this time period

8. Cash flow and equity appreciation

- Will be split 50/50 between JV Partners A and B
- Cash flow is defined as property revenues *less* all property expenses

9. Upon sale or refina nce:

- After five years, upon sale or refinance of the property, JV Partner B will receive capital investment first (as outlined in point #2), and then remaining funds will be split 50/50

We agree to the above-mentioned items and conditions of this Letter of Intent:

Joint-Venture Partners A:

| _____ | _____ |
| Print name | Signature |

| _____ | _____ |
| Print name | Signature |

Joint-Venture Partners B:

| _____ | _____ |
| Print name | Signature |

| _____ | _____ |
| Print name | Signature |

This Letter of Intent is very well written. I want to point out some specific things you need to watch as the JV deal proceeds.

1. Keep it professional.

I like the way you name your prospective money partner and include all of their contact information. That's exactly what a professional Letter of Intent should do. In many ways, this is an extension of your marketing program. Always assume that a potential partner will share your letter with someone you do not know. You want to make sure you are always presenting your business in the most professional manner possible.

2. Include deadlines.

This letter should put you one giant step closer to a JV deal. I like the way you stipulate a deadline of six months after the date of this letter. You are in business to make deals, not talk about making them. Besides, you can amend a timeline if you need to.

REALITY CHECK!

Modify where necessary

Sophisticated real estate investors know that the details of investment deals sometimes shift and that no one is to blame. A formal Letter of Intent is not a legally binding document. But it does spell out the rules of engagement, so treat it like it matters. Make sure changes are approved and initialed and keep up-to-date copies handy. This document contains a lot of information your lawyer needs to develop a formal JV Agreement.

---

3. Cite money details.

I also like the way you cite a price *range* for a property you anticipate buying with this partner. It is always good to know a partner's top number; the price at which he'll walk away from a deal. If you can, you probably want to keep a deal several thousand dollars under that limit. Again, it's all about your attempt to under-promise and over-deliver. A range also provides welcome flexibility. You are the real estate expert. Give yourself some room to prove it!

4. Outline property parameters.

It's also wise to outline the details of the property you plan to buy. This shows your partner that you know the kind of property you need to buy to make this deal work (e.g., four bedrooms, two baths) and you will follow that through. Would a 900-square-foot property at the right price and location still work? Maybe. But you'd need to tell your partner why.

5. Reinforce your position.

Each page should end with a place where you and your potential JV partner can initial what it says. And, the document should end with a place for formal signatures. Yours does. Brilliant! Would you substitute a changed page 1 to trick a partner? No way. But this strategy shows that you seek an honest business relationship.

Commit to the right partner

In sum, always remember that an Expression of Interest Letter (signed by your prospective money partner) and a Letter of Intent (signed by both parties) are still shy of a formal commitment to work with a particular partner on a particular piece of property. A joint-venture deal is not complete until the formal Joint-Venture Agreement is in place and the money in play.

Your primary goal through the process is to strike the best deal with the best partner. While the details of each deal will change as it proceeds toward closure, these pre-deal documents start the important process of clarifying all the details that will go into your Joint-Venture Agreement. Indeed, by providing specific parameters, these documents will provide the clarity you need to protect your own interests and the interests of your partners.

I know exactly what my ideal JV partner looks like, what he does and how much money he has to invest. That profile makes it easy for me to focus on the right partners.

—Joe Ragona

Background

Joe Ragona started investing in real estate in 2008, about a year after he joined REIN and three years after he embarked on a deliberate quest to learn what sophisticated real estate investors were doing to create long-term wealth.

Following an investment strategy that was based on his new understanding of the economic fundamentals of real estate investment, the veteran entrepreneur then used his own capital to buy his first properties. By the time his portfolio consisted of six single-family homes and two commercial condo units, Joe had only one JV partner—and a plan.

With personal investing experience now tucked solidly under his belt, Joe felt he was ready to move his investing strategies up a notch by bringing more money partners into his deals. By early 2011, he was actively seeking deals for five potential money partners. He expected those partners to help him buy at least 10 new single-family homes.

A former celebrity club DJ, radio host/remixer, music producer and VP of a multi-million-dollar manufacturing company he sold in 2005, Joe admits that he finds it easy to talk to people about real estate investment. But he is equally sure that his business acumen and public speaking skills aren't ultimately responsible for convincing people to invest in his deals. Paraphrasing mortgage broker and REIN mentor Peter Kinch, Joe says a combination of confidence, credibility and integrity are the real deal clinchers. "But confidence is just the first step. When I pitch a JV deal, I already have a profitable portfolio on the table, and I use that portfolio to build credibility with the people I'm talking to. It's not just me talking anymore; it's money and action that do the real talking. Education and knowledge aren't enough unless they're backed by action."

Integrity is also important to his growing success. "I am all about credibility and my reputation. I do know what I'm doing, and I will show investors that I know what I'm doing; but at the same time, when I *don't* know something, I clearly admit it and find the answer. I don't just have a Plan B for what might happen if a deal doesn't close, I've got a Plan C as well. If I think a property fits my portfolio, then I want it. For me, the worst thing that could happen would be that I didn't plan well enough to make sure that I could meet my obligations. My reputation is too important to me to let that happen."

Still, it's important to choose "the right" JV partner. And to do that, Joe relies on the systems and follow-through he's learned from successful real estate mentors. "I agree with Russell Westcott when he says we should know exactly what our ideal JV partners look like. Mine actually has a face, and his picture sits atop my computer so that when I put together marketing materials, I'm reminded that I'm speaking directly to him. I even have a name for him. I call him John, and he helps me keep my JV presentations on track."

Profiling for success

And the profiling doesn't stop there. Joe also has specific ideas about the tenants who rent his properties—and that information narrows the kind of properties he buys. Focusing on properties in the Barrie and Kitchener/Waterloo/Cambridge regions of Ontario, Joe's properties rent to young professional couples without children, or to young couples with two incomes who have no more than two children under the age of 10 and want to raise them in a safe, clean environment. That profile also allows him to target specific kinds of neighbourhoods and single-family home floor plans. "I have to look at what's *not* on paper. How is the kitchen laid out? Are there derelict cars on the street? The answers to questions like that will tell me whether a property is worth looking at."

While professional property managers take care of the day-to-day issues, Joe's investment system is backed up by his own hands-on participation in issues related to property management and tenancy. "I know all of the tenants, for instance, and I have a good personal relationship with these people." Those who question his front-line role are easily dismissed. As Joe sees it, his tenants are taking care of his top assets. Why wouldn't he want to know them?

To learn more about Joe's investing strategies, take a look at his answers to three specific questions.

Why Do You Need JV Money?

Joint ventures are extremely important to my business because I know where I want real estate investment to take me. I have a salary I'm looking for, and I know what it will take to get that. I was lucky enough to have the money to get my real estate investment business started, but expansion definitely depends on bringing in more JV partners.

Knowing that I want money partners shapes my approach to the business. I obviously can't just wait for people to come to me; I need to reach out, too. In addition to talking about my business with people I know and networking with real estate investors, I also write a popular blog and Internet newsletter. I started the blog and newsletter to help my JV partners understand the real estate investment business, learn about the economic fundamentals that inform my strategies and see how my portfolio works to create long-term wealth. These tools also help me reach out to people who are beyond my Inner Circle, but are within the Inner Circles of my Level 1 investors. It's another way to build credibility with people.

These tools sometimes elicit queries from people who are well outside my first- and second-level prospects. I usually don't spend a lot of time with these queries because I know that they will take a lot of my time and aren't likely to invest with me. To open the door to a relationship, I ask them to send the question to my blog. This way, I can answer the question and use that information to help my first- and second-tier prospects learn about real estate investment, while at the same time, subliminally creating trust with those I don't personally know yet.

Why Do You Have a Detailed Investor Profile?

I spent some time developing a very specific investor profile because I know that speeds up the process of finding the "right partner." That's in line with an approach that seeks people versus money. Because I know that the person I'm vetting has the money to come into my deal, I am better able to focus on the *relationship* side of the business.

Be honest with yourself. If you plan to be in business with this person for a long time, why wouldn't you focus on the person? The only time I've had a JV deal fall through is when the deal fell apart because the individual couldn't follow through and take the action he said he was willing to take. The problem had nothing to do with money, but because I was *chasing* the money, I neglected the obvious challenges to come.

What's Behind Your Early Success with Finding JV Partners?

Besides the fact that I have a proven track record with real estate investment, I am open to putting together creative deals. I'll do a 60/40 deal in favour of a JV partner because I know that after they get involved with me for three to five years, they'll want to stick with me. Because I know my investors so well, I also know how they might be able to help me in the future. If the person can help me bring new people into my business, then I'm going to be a little more creative in terms of finding ways to make a deal work. In the end, it's going to be a win-win for both of us.

I know that not everyone can do this, but I've also got the capital reserves to make sure that I don't have to go back to my partners for a cash call, if they are concerned about that. Sometimes a potential partner will look at the numbers I'm showing them and ask why I need their $150,000 if I've got that much in reserve. I tell them that my conservative approach makes sure that I can close a deal if a potential money partner pulls out. That reserve fund opens the door for me to talk to them about how much I value credibility—and my reputation. When they see that I'm taking care of all of the people who help me put a deal together, they see my integrity at work.

By the same token, I work hard to never undervalue my contribution as the real estate expert. I'll take a 60/40 deal in my favour if I think the deal works. I also believe that the negotiating process should be a two-way discussion. When I start that process by asking for 60 per cent of the deal, I've got lots of room to negotiate. That strategy gives me instant bargaining power!

What really works to my advantage is the ability to walk away from any negotiation because I am not chasing money. If I walk away from a negotiation from one person, I'll do the deal with another sooner or later.

The money is important, but it pales in comparison to the need to pick the right partner and then manage that partner's expectations over the lifespan of the deal.

—Monte Dobson

BACKGROUND

Monte Dobson and his wife, Jamie, own seven buy-and-hold real estate investments in Saskatchewan and Alberta, four of them with joint-venture partners. Their JV partners put up the money for the down payments, leaving the Dobsons to qualify for the mortgages and fully manage the properties. They handle everything from due diligence to accounting and cash flow analysis, as well as property management, including tenants, repairs and maintenance. They are also the money partners in several land development projects and apartment buildings in Calgary and Edmonton, giving them hands-on experience on both sides of the joint-venture investment deal. They also actively loan their RRSP funds as mortgages secured on real property.

Like a lot of investors, the Dobsons bought their first property before taking a serious look at what real estate investment could mean to their long-term financial security. Pleased with that property's performance, Monte signed up for one of REIN's weekend seminars, an experience that prompted a closer look at real estate investing. It also piqued the couple's interest in what other people's money could mean to their portfolio and long-term wealth creation.

By 2006, they owned one property in rural Saskatchewan and two in Grande Prairie. Now motivated "to purchase more properties to enhance our financial well-being, joint-venture partnerships became the logical choice to continue down this path," says Monte.

Setting themselves up as the real estate experts on new deals, Monte took the lead on finding the properties, while their JV partners put up the money for down payments. Working with partners, they purchased two properties in Grande Prairie, a house in Stony Plain, Alberta, and a house in Regina with joint-venture partners.

Determined to structure the deals as simply as possible, their initial term is a five-year buy-and-hold, at which time they evaluate the property and, where necessary, make adjustments to the original plan (which may include lengthened timelines or a new exit strategy). Using the classic 50/50 structure that splits net profit, their partners get paid first upon exit, "and we do not get paid until the property is sold, so we have an extremely vested interest in ensuring that the property performs well and is profitable," notes Monte.

That attention to detail is also important when deals are being put together, since the most difficult part of the JV deal is what Monte calls "investor relations and setting expectations." Projecting a confidence based on their own investing experiences, Monte shares what they do to prioritize investor relations and ensure they and their JV partners understand how the deal works.

BE HONEST AND OPEN

When we entered into many of our partnerships, real estate values were climbing, rents were high and everything was rosy! Well, the real estate market changed, and that has caused us to alter the original plans, especially the exit timelines. When we formalized our agreements, they were based on a five-year buy-and-hold term, and I now expect that many of these will be extended, simply as a way to extract the returns on the investment that were originally sought. This is tough to manage, since it involves changing expectations. It's also taught me to be very cognizant about setting reasonable expectations upfront. It also underlined the need to have a contingency plan in place and large cash reserves accessible when necessary.

Our goal is to under-promise and over-deliver. To do that, we follow Don Campbell's advice and always try to "look behind the curtain" and "look past the headlines." When times get tough and things aren't going as planned, the frequency of communication with JV partners must increase. It's sometimes very hard to be the "bearer of bad news." We aim to give our partners the best "big picture" information we can, and to do that, we draw heavily on the research of numerous organizations and economists (including REIN Canada). This helps us show them that real estate is still a good investment, even though the media headlines sometimes portray a different story. All indications are positive for economic growth in the western provinces, and that bodes well for demand in residential real estate over the next number of years, which puts upward pressure on real estate values and rents.

Pick Your Partners Wisely

More than anything, experience has taught us to select our partners wisely. A bad partner can create a lot of stress and grief in your life and cost a lot of money. It is imperative to select partners with goals, expectations, values and morals that are in line with your own. Otherwise, it is a recipe for disaster if things go wrong or don't go as planned. You have to realize that this is not only a money partnership; it's a human relationship and needs to be handled accordingly.

We've also learned to keep our deals simple. The higher the number of partners, the more that can go wrong. But simple doesn't mean you can skip the lawyer! Have sound legal agreements in place that will protect your interests in the event a partnership goes bad. As REIN teaches, "plan for the divorce ahead of time." It's unlikely you will ever need to go down that path, but if you do, you'll have sound direction.

When it comes to picking the right partner, our system focuses on the due diligence of the following steps:

1. We ask our partners to fill out a questionnaire that provides an "initial picture" of who they are and what they expect from owning real estate as an investment. This questionnaire provides a simple snapshot of their personal and investment goals, timelines and strategies.
2. We then meet with the partner and anyone else who might be involved with their decision (such as a spouse). Our goal is to make sure all parties are on the same page, so there aren't problems down the road.
3. We take background checks seriously. Because lots of people can talk a good talk, it is very important to "trust, but verify." Talk to references, do credit and criminal record checks, and take whatever means necessary to ensure there will be synergies going forward.
4. Don't be afraid to walk away from a deal. Trust your instincts and your "gut feel." The best deal in the world can go very bad if it's made with the wrong partner. These are people you will be dealing with typically for many years, so ensuring there is a "fit" from the onset is essential.

Commit to Doing Better

Sophisticated real estate investors will tell you that they make money when they buy a property. We know that's true, but the first property that we bought with a money partner in Grande Prairie has ended up being a "money pit." With lower-than-anticipated rents, downward pressure on rents and real estate values, and a problem tenant, this has not been a fun property to deal with from afar! One positive is that we have continued to pay down the mortgage on a monthly basis, so our equity is remaining intact. But the cash calls, lower cash flow and repairs and maintenance have forced us to make some tough decisions.

As part of managing our money partner's expectations, this property has also made us better prepared to take care of our business in the long term. Lessons learned include the following:

- Do not overpay for the asset, regardless of how "hot" a market is.
- Do not expect that rents and real estate will always go up.
- Have a clear contingency plan and multiple exit strategies in place.
- Do hold significant cash reserves; we now hold onto a value equal to a minimum of three months' worth of mortgage payments, taxes and insurance.
- Review each party's roles and responsibilities and make sure that both understand who manages what, who pays for cash calls, when those cash calls might be required and who determines when it's time to sell or hold a property.

Build a Team You Can Depend On

I've also learned to make sure to have a team in place I can rely on to deliver the things that aren't in my area of expertise (such as accounting, bookkeeping and property management). I have found myself trying to do too many of the tasks involved in a successful partnership, and at times, it can be overwhelming. Don't be afraid to "outsource" tasks, and value your time by focusing on your own areas of strength and skill set.

WORKSHOP: SECURE COMMITMENT—MOVE YOUR DEAL FROM TALK TO ACTION

It was character that got us out of bed, commitment that moved us into action, and discipline that enabled us to follow through.
—Zig Ziglar

WORKSHOP OVERVIEW

Presenter: Russell Westcott

The first workshop focused on the question: Why do you want JV money? Well, look how far you've come! Every one of you knows why you need that money, and you've taken some serious steps to line up "the right" JV investors for your deals. This is exciting. But it's also scary. Even though you may have found the right person for your JV deal, you now have to take some more steps to make sure you can move that deal from talk to action. Working with your JV worksheets, you have each written a formal Letter of Intent. Some of you with potential deals at stake are ready to translate that information into a formal Joint-Venture Agreement.

I am here to take a little bit of the "emotional wind" out of your sails and to tell you that reaching this point is no guarantee your JV deal will be completed. In fact, writing a JV agreement right now is probably premature—it's not impossible, just premature.

Why am I saying this? Because all you really have right now is talk. What you need is action—and you can't take action until you have secured your co-venturer's commitment.

SUSAN: Really? Because I think I'm ready to forge ahead and structure a deal. I've done the worksheet, amended it with my partner, and we've got an agreed-to Letter of Intent that's been signed by both parties. That letter was pretty specific with regard to a deal, and now I feel like you're telling me to back up the bus.

RICHARD: I know how you feel, Susan, but Russell's right. When I get to this stage of a potential JV deal, I am all about taking the next step and structuring a deal. But you don't want to put the cart before the horse. Even with a detailed Letter of Intent, a deal doesn't always go the way I've planned, and I like what Russell's saying. Emma and I have gotten this far before and been left holding the bag—mostly because we thought we had a commitment, and all we really had was a lot of talk. Our problem wasn't the wrong deal—it was the wrong partner.

REALITY CHECK!

Watch for delays!

Novice JV investors might confuse caution with delay. Be clear. Caution is all about due diligence, and it saves you money. Delays are typically about fear and greed—and they will cost you and your partners money.

THE BACKGROUND CHECK

That's the voice of experience talking. And I've been there, too. I've been ready to write a formal Joint-Venture Agreement and structure a deal only to learn that I was the only one really *committed* to the deal. We both *said* we wanted it to proceed, but only I was prepared to walk the talk to get the deal done and to manage it successfully.

To improve the odds that this will never happen to you, you now need to conduct a formal background check on your prospective partner. In fairness, this usually happens before you have a deal on the table—and right after you work through the details of a "hypothetical" JV worksheet and hammer out the particulars of the deal you want to partner on (classic 50/50, renovation or mortgage guarantor).

At first glance, this might look like a step backward. Can anyone tell me why the background check is important at this stage in the game?

TOM: I think I know. When Robert and I started talking about working together, we were really caught up in the excitement of our shared vision and we leaped right into our first investment property without a lot of professional advice. Since these workshops started, we revisited our actions to date. As part of that process, we asked a mutual friend to meet with us so that we could bounce some ideas off him and get his feedback. He is a veteran entrepreneur and was pretty blunt. He told us that he was happy for us and he believed we could be successful real estate investors. Then he challenged us to talk about all of the what-ifs that might happen in our lives that could affect our business relationship. He threw all kinds of things at us: death, divorce, prolonged illness, and questions about how we would resolve business disputes or handle cash calls. The list was long and nasty.

ROBERT: At first, I was annoyed. Then it hit me. The guy talking to us had weathered most of these storms, some more successfully than others. What he was really trying to tell us is that business partners need to talk about issues even when there aren't any.

You've both hit the nail on the head! Some investors describe the early days of an investor/partner relationship as the "honeymoon" phase. At this point, everyone is looking for reasons to talk about why a deal *will* work. Even though you two have chalked up some success, you've made a potentially dangerous greenhorn mistake. It sounds harsh, but what you really need to do when you partner-up with another investor is "plan for the divorce ahead of time." You two didn't do that and it's a critical piece of business that you need to take care of as soon as possible.

TOM: We've already met with a lawyer and have agreed to have the partnership agreement vetted by individual lawyers, too.

That's good. All of us in this room have to apply that same wisdom to our dealings with money partners. The Potential for Relationship questionnaire that you reviewed in Workshop #6 will help you figure out if you *could* work with a certain money partner. The background check takes that a step further. With your JV worksheet and your Letter of Intent or Expression of Interest Letter (and any amendments) in hand, you now need to call a meeting to address all of the what-ifs that could throw your partnership—and business—off track.

When that meeting takes places, present yourself as the real estate expert and be clear about what you are asking. Regardless of any other relationship you might have with potential JV partners, this meeting is "all business." At bare minimum, you need to work through the eight questions presented on the following background check. Each of these questions helps to satisfy your need to get specific answers to the following four critical questions:

1. How much do I want?
2. When do I need the money?
3. What is the estimated return on investment?
4. What is the security?

BACKGROUND CHECK

What if...

1. The money partner backs out before closing?
- Are there any funds provided upfront in a trust account? What happens to this money?
- Are there any penalties in place (such as the loss of up-front deposit, payment of costs incurred or removal from list of preferred properties list)?

2. We don't have closing costs or a reserve fund?
- How much do we need? Do we have a detailed budget?
- What is the minimum amount of money we need in the trust account?

3. We need a cash call? Who will come up with extra cash?
- Will it take the form of a 50/50 split, or some other ratio?

4. One of us wants out? Should we have...
- a buy-sell agreement?
- a right of first refusal?
- a right to call for a sale?

5. It's a family JV?
- Do we understand that dealing with family is different than dealing with an arm's-length party?

6. The real estate expert is managing the deal but . . .
- is becoming so busy that attention to detail is being sacrificed.
- does not have the working knowledge (or team) to properly manage the property.
- is letting oversight of accounting and property management slip.

7. One of us dies or goes bankrupt?
- Have we thought through such an event and does the JV agreement cover this?
- What legal provisions have we put in place to ensure problems will be minimized if this occurs?

8. The bank says only one of us can be on title?
- Can both parties qualify for mortgages?
- Do we have two or three different plans as to how we will structure the title and mortgage?

Every one of the questions on this background check will be dealt with in a solid JV agreement. Going through the questions ahead of time is one more way to make sure that all parties understand what the JV agreement says.

Richard and Emma, I believe you have a story to share about why a background check is so important?

EMMA: The answers to these questions can make the difference between closing a deal and not. On one of our earliest JV deals, Richard and I were working with a relative. This individual had followed our portfolio for years and knew that we had bought an investment property with Richard's boss. In the end, all of that "familiarity" with our portfolio led to some pretty serious misunderstandings . . .

RICHARD: I'll say. We'd lined up a straightforward 50/50 deal and even had a formal Letter of Intent. Because we were working with family, we made some assumptions about how much that individual understood about how JV investment deals work. It kind of felt like the formal background check was more overkill; that all of the detail was unnecessary. That was naive.

EMMA: Following a system that taught us to always have a Plan B, we had secured financing with our own portfolio and money. But because we "knew" we could count on the JV partner, it did not seem at all likely that this potential deal could go bad and leave us on the hook for the down payment.

RICHARD: And then we learned that our prospective JV partner's money was tied up and he needed several weeks before he could cut a cheque. There was also a serious misunderstanding about return on investment. Our deal cash flowed, but its strength was in market appreciation. To make a long and scary story short, we had two more formal meetings to iron out the ROI issues and the relative stood by the deal. We got her 50 per cent later than anticipated, but it didn't cost us the deal. Had we been working on more than one deal, it might have proved to be a way bigger problem than it was.

Nolan, you're looking perplexed. What's up?

NOLAN: I can see where Richard and Emma's assumptions about a prospective deal led to problems. But what the heck is Plan B?

Great question!

WHAT'S YOUR PLAN B?

The whole point of a Plan B is that successful real estate investors *plan* for success. They don't just talk about it—they plan to make deals work. When you are working with money partners, a deal's success may sometimes be contingent on having a backup plan; this is a plan that can make a deal happen even if a money partner can't deliver. To put it simply, Plan B ensures you will do what you've said you will do.

Do What You Say You Will Do

Let me explain what that business philosophy has to do with prospective JV deals. Sophisticated real estate investors who've built their portfolios on JV partnerships will tell you that the next deal rides on the success of the current deal. I take this so seriously that I always enter a JV deal with a backup plan that will allow me to close on a property even if my money partner backs out.

To me, it's an issue of the team. Because I value the efforts of the real estate agents, brokers, lawyers and property managers who work with me to put together deals that will benefit my co-owners and me, I never want those team members to feel like they've been left holding the bag for a deal that didn't close.

By never buying a property that I can't afford to buy on my own, I make sure that I can close every deal I negotiate. My strict attention to the details of due diligence means I have never had to put my Plan B option into motion. Still, I like knowing it's there, and I am confident that it's another way to encourage members of my team to keep working on my deals.

NOLAN: That makes sense to me now. It also underlines why I am going to have to be particularly diligent about my money partners. Until I build my portfolio, I will not have access to a Plan B that involves my own money. It looks like maybe my Plan B will have to begin with a discussion with my parents. They've said they want to help me invest in real estate; I should find out what that really means.

Good idea. I know novice investors who line up family or friends to help them secure a first deal. With solid due diligence on deals and JV partners, most of them never have to call on those individuals for help. Still, they marshal that backup financial support so that they won't have to walk away from a good deal and burn team bridges in the process.

Again, if you have any questions about the level of detail required in this formal deal presentation, review the sample worksheets, Expression of Interest Letter and Letter of Intent that Susan and the McTavishes wrote as part of the tutorial for Workshop #6. Never think that the details are just the icing on the cake. In JV real estate deals, they are the foundation of a deal's success or failure.

Co-venturer commitment

JV money is not *extra;* your deals depend on it. It all comes back to the basics. Investors whose worksheets and Letters of Intent contain significant details that are backed by a background check will find it easier to write the JV agreement. (Investors who work through a background check will also find the JV agreement easier to *understand.*)

Assuming you have vetted the potential money partner and want them on board, there are ways to tell if your deal is moving in the right direction. I teach that sophisticated investors have four ways to gauge co-venturer commitment leading up to the creation of a formal JV agreement. They are:

1. Their word
2. An initial upfront cash deposit of $1,000 with $5,000 due upon removal of conditions
3. An Expression of Interest Letter
4. A Letter of Intent

Many investors respect someone's "word" but will demand a cash deposit and formal Letter of Intent in order to launch a deal. The Letter of Intent is more valuable than an Expression of Interest Letter because it outlines more details, including timelines, and is signed by both parties. A cash deposit backs up both, providing some financial security to back up a verbal commitment.

WHEN A PROSPECT SAYS NO: DEALING WITH REJECTION

In this business, rejection is a fact of life. I want you to recognize that, but never let it become an excuse for failure. I see wannabe investors let rejection take them out of the real estate investment business all the time. Part of me says, "Oh well," because that leaves more room for committed investors. Another part of me shakes my head because I know that these people are letting rejection get in the way of future success.

The bottom line is that duplication is the crux of a successful real estate investment system. But it is not enough to focus on duplicating what works. You must also look at what hasn't worked and find out how you can improve and what can be done better.

Learn from your mistakes

My point here is simple. I want you to be willing to learn from a prospective JV deal that comes undone before it's completed, especially if you'd already reached the Letter of Intent stage and then encounter problems with the background check.

Regardless of whether the lost potential JV partner came from a Level 1, 2 or 3 contact, your approach to a lost deal should always be the same. As long as you have followed the systems I've outlined here, you should be able to take that rejection and study it in terms of what you can learn from relationships and follow-through.

For example, every time we get past the Letter of Intent and someone turns down a deal I've pitched because we can't agree on the what-if scenarios, I deliberately ask them to take some time to talk to me about what it would take to get them to say yes. My rationale demonstrates my commitment to systems, relationships and follow-through. Regardless of where the individual started in my Circle of Influence, I recognize that the time I spend developing a potential deal is an investment in a relationship with a potential investor. I may never complete a deal with that individual. But if I have taken all of the steps necessary to secure a deal with that person, then I will be determined to learn from the experience so that I can continue my search for the right JV partner.

This approach requires that I do two key things.

1. I must recognize that the rejection is not personal.

I never take a rejection personally. This is about business, not friendship. If there is any confusion over that, I have not done my job as a real estate expert. As a sophisticated real estate investor, my willingness to learn from someone who's turned a deal down is further evidence of my commitment to success. By honing in on specifics (like misunderstandings about fiscal timelines, ROIs, profit sharing or who is running the deal), I have fine-tuned my approach. That helps me identify and deal with stumbling blocks much earlier in the process.

2. I reframe the problem as a solution.

Because I know that the rejection is not personal, I am able to listen and learn from what people tell me. I call this "reframing." Does the information I gather sometimes look entirely irrelevant to the deal?

Absolutely. If I have a formal Letter of Intent and a prospective partner tells me they didn't realize they needed to secure a mortgage loan on a 50/50 deal, this tells me one of two things. First, it may tell me that I did not do a good job of explaining the deal and joint-venture partnerships to this prospective money partner. Second, it may tell me that I did not perform solid due diligence on the individual. We will talk about that more in Workshop #9: Closing the Deal—How to Avoid Partner Pitfalls. What's important right now is that you realize that you cannot partner with everyone who says they want to partner with you. And the sooner you learn that lesson, the better!

Here are some examples of how I take a problem and reframe it positively so that I can improve the way I do business. Remember: reframing can get a deal back on track—and prevent the next deal from going off the rails.

REFRAME THE PROSPECT'S PROBLEM

Prospect's problem: I need a higher return on investment.

Reframe:
- Provide the JV prospect with more information about how real estate investment generates long-term wealth.
- What exactly does he mean by "higher return on investment"? My next Expression of Interest Letter or Letter of Intent will make sure that information is presented more clearly.
- I believe in an abundant universe and that I will find the money I need to close my deals and build my real estate investment portfolio.

Prospect's problem: I feel like it's all happening too fast. I am afraid.

Reframe:
- The prospect trusts me, but not necessarily the deal. I'll send her some more information about other JV deals I am involved with, and I will make sure the next deal I pitch has fewer time restrictions. Fear leads to analysis paralysis, and when I'm closing deals, there's no time for paralysis!

- I will take additional steps to make sure prospective JV investors understand why these deals may sometimes "feel" like they are moving so quickly. My focus on the right property at the right price in the right neighbourhood may demand quick decisions. I'll make sure that potential JV partners understand why I need to act fast and give them more information about how I make purchase decisions.

Prospect's problem: I am not comfortable with the amount of money you need from me.

Reframe:
- I need to provide more detail about why I structure deals a certain way. I want my potential partners to understand that I take care of them first.
- My next presentation package is going to be clearer about how much money the deal needs upfront and how that investment is protected in the deal.
- Maybe this deal could include an additional partner.

Prospect's problem: I don't think real estate investing is for me right now.

Reframe:
- I will continue to tell, not sell. I am proud to be a real estate investor, and I will talk about my business with my friends.
- I am in business for the long term and will nurture potential JV partners accordingly.

Prospect's problem: I hear all this talk about relationships, systems and follow-through, but all I can think about is "my money, my money, my money."

Reframe:
- By plugging into a network of experienced real estate investors, I have made sure that my business is built on many years of successful investing. I will add some of that experience to my face-to-face meetings with potential partners.

> I want them to know how I've learned the things I know.
> I want them to understand why I say my business is built
> on the shoulders of giants. I am not inventing anything
> new; I am duplicating success.

Your deal, your reputation

In a perfect world, the joint-venture worksheet will cover each of
the fine points you need to address in the Letter of Intent, and the
background check will merely help you move more quickly through
the formal Joint-Venture Agreement process. Your goal is to have
people describe you as "all talk and action." You are "talk" because
your deals won't sell themselves. You are "action" because you get
the job done right—and everyone on your team benefits from that.

Workshop Action Step: Real Estate Investment Is About Action

Sophisticated real estate investors build portfolios of property, not
promises. Secure your deal by following a proven system that advances
from someone's word to a cash deposit, and then do an Expression of
Interest Letter and Letter of Intent.

Make background checks part of your due diligence. The first check
should assess the potential for a relationship. The second should evaluate a prospective partner's commitment prior to writing a formal
Joint-Venture Agreement. You and your partners must know exactly
what you've committed to doing together. Misunderstandings will cost
you, and the price of confusion is higher if you are close to or have
already signed a deal.

Can they or will they put their money where their mouths are?

JV ACTION PLAN STEP #10

Study a Joint-Venture Agreement.

This action plan step prepares you for a deeper discussion
of Joint-Venture Agreements in the following tutorial. All

---

workshop participants should visit the REIN website at www. jvsecrets.ca, find the Joint-Venture Agreement template and review it in detail. Prepared for illustrative purposes only, these are vastly oversimplified documents that summarize the provisions of a JV agreement. Simplified or not, it provides a good introduction to the level of detail a JV agreement requires. The tutorial will look at the document in more detail.

JV ACTION PLAN STEP #11

Keep generating those leads!

Novice investors can get so caught up in the details of a JV real estate investment deal that they forget to keep generating leads. Don't make that mistake. Unless you already have all the money you need to make your Personal Belize come true, you need to be constantly looking for new JV leads. Nurture those contacts once you have them. One successful JV investor tells me that he keeps a list of potential co-venturers who would qualify as JV partners on his deals. He keeps in touch with these individuals, and when he's ready to close on a property, he can find a partner after making just four or five phone calls.

Are the prospects who didn't close on a particular deal disappointed? Not at all. They know that real estate deals are closed under tight deadlines and trust the investor to call them again.

Tutorial: Study a Joint-Venture Agreement | 7

Workshop recap:

Real estate investors take action.
Study a Joint-Venture Agreement.
Keep generating those leads.

Presenter: Don Campbell

I know the last assignment was daunting, even though all you had to do was *review* a Joint-Venture Agreement. Rest assured, you won't be writing a Joint-Venture Agreement without the help of an experienced real estate investment lawyer. But never think it is okay to leave all of the heavy lifting to your professional advisors. Successful real estate investors do not merely sign quality JV agreements, they understand what these agreements mean.

This tutorial focuses on the JV checklist I use to review my JV agreements with my advisors. I often show the checklist to prospective partners, too. It's another way to show them that I am serious about my business. Each of us will solicit independent legal advice, and if they want to take the checklist to their own advisor, that's good for me, too. I want them to be confident that I know what I'm doing and that the deal looks after both of our interests. Making a copy of the checklist available can reassure them that I am a good steward of other people's money. I let them know I use checklists to make sure our interests are protected.

Susan: I looked ahead at the checklist, and I'm already feeling better. I followed Russell's advice, went to www.jvsecrets.ca, downloaded the JV agreement template and went through it in detail. The notes on the checklist definitely helped me clarify what I was looking at.

That's our intent. Templates and checklists aren't for the lazy. They are for the successful. Every good Joint-Venture Agreement should have the elements noted in the JV checklist, and a good lawyer can put a solid JV agreement together with very little input from you.

But that's not what I'd recommend. If you want to create win-win relationships with money partners who will want to do business with you again and again, you need to be able to look at a particular section of a JV agreement and talk about what it means.

WARNING: YOU NEED
A FORMAL AGREEMENT

Closing a deal using other people's money without a formal Joint-Venture Agreement in place is like driving a car without a seat belt. Many sophisticated real estate investors will tell you that they never refer to their JV agreements. But make no mistake: they know where to find them.

This is a critical stage in a JV partnership because even though you may have found a great deal and are close to finalizing an agreement with a partner, you don't have a legal and fiscal commitment until you have a JV agreement. Once that agreement is in place, it should guide that investment—and help you complete more.

RICHARD: That's a good point, Don. Emma and I find that satisfied partners are our best advertisers. As legal documents, JV agreements provide a way for all parties to know exactly what they've agreed to do, or not do. When everyone has agreed to a particular plan of action, it's easier to keep a deal on track and your partners happy. When we hear our partners say positive things about who's managing our deals, who's making decisions about hands-on items like maintenance or repairs, or how rental proceeds are distributed, we know their satisfaction is rooted in a good JV agreement.

My point exactly. Now let's look at that checklist.

JOINT-VENTURE CHECKLIST

1. Who are the parties?
2. What are their contact details?
3. What is the legal description of the property?

---

4. What is the municipal description of the property?
5. Which partner manages the property/is responsible for issues related to management?
   - The agreement must clearly state who is responsible for management. The real estate expert does not want to "leave the door open" lest the money partner think he or she should get involved with this end of the business.
6. What percentage of interest does each party hold?
7. Who holds title?
   - What if only one party is on title? How might this change the JV agreement?
8. For tax purposes, what and whose accounting methods will be used?
9. Is transfer to a related party covered in the agreement?
10. Is it clear that all transferees are to be bound by the agreement?
11. Do actions and expenditures of money flow through the real estate expert, property manager or one party on their own?
12. Who has the authority to make major decisions?
    - What are the parameters or restrictions of those major decisions?
13. Whose names will be on the bank account?
14. What parties or affiliates are doing business with the JV deal?
15. Who provides the initial funds and additional funds?
    - What are the default conditions and remedies?
16. How will the rental proceeds be distributed and when (monthly, quarterly or annually)?
17. Who is responsible for accounting, both day to day and year end?
18. How often will financial reports be issued (monthly, quarterly or annually)?
19. Who provides guarantees, if needed, and how does the guarantor get released?
20. Is there a "finder's fee" on top of other expenses?
21. How is the transfer or sale of JV interests handled?
    - Does it cover time limits, first right of refusal, buy/sell arrangements, compulsory sale, and sale of a partial interest?

22. What are the specifics regarding the termination of the agreement?
23. Are defaults, rights and remedies in place (indemnification, partition or partition and sale)?
24. How will dispute resolution be handled (arbitration only; mediation first, then arbitration; court action or other)?
25. What are the applicable provincial laws?
26. How are notices and delivery of documents handled?
27. Does the agreement stipulate "no agency" to ensure each signatory is acting on their own behalf?
28. Is the agreement set up as a "joint venture" versus a partnership (which could compromise individual ownership as allowed under a joint venture)?
29. Does the agreement stipulate that obligations are several (each co-venturer owns a separate share of the asset), not joint?
30. Is there a provision in the agreement to prevent unilateral action?
31. Are invalid clauses declared severable in the agreement?
    • This provision ensures that if one clause is later found invalid, the rest of the agreement would remain in place.
32. Are insolvency and termination covered in the agreement?
33. Does the agreement allow "signed-in counterparts," meaning the parties can sign separate copies (versus the original)?
34. What are the costs of legal proceedings?

A lot of the points on this checklist are very straightforward, but JV agreements can be overwhelming at first. I encourage you to visit the REIN website (www.jvsecrets.ca) to download a JV agreement template and then use this checklist and work through the template. This will help you figure out how particular deals might differ in terms of details.

There is also more than one way to present a lot of this information. If you find particular clauses difficult to understand, ask your advisor and other real estate investors if they can show you other ways to present the same information. But be forewarned: with complicated legal documents, simpler is not always better. What appears complicated to the novice investor is not complicated to the legal professionals who put quality JV agreements together. Their goal is to make sure that nothing is left to chance.

SIMPLE VERSUS DETAILED JV AGREEMENT CLAUSES

Here is one example to illustrate the difference between an over-simplified sample JV agreement and what should be expected from a real agreement.

Non-Arm's Length Sale (oversimplified)

We may sell our share to a direct family member or other non-arm's length party.

Non-arm's length sale (from a detailed JV agreement)

Notwithstanding right of first refusal, any Investor shall be entitled, upon giving notice to the venturers but without requiring approval, to sell, transfer, assign, or otherwise dispose of any or all of his Interest to:

(i)   a direct family member;
(ii) a wholly owned corporation, provided that the future sale, transfer, assignment or other disposition of the shares of such corporation be subject to the approval of the venturers;
(iii) any other person, corporation, trust or other entity deemed non-arm's length by the venturers.

GET PROFESSIONAL ADVICE

This tutorial underlines the need to have a professional lawyer on your team. I recommend that you find someone with considerable experience in real estate investment work. Ideally, this individual will be an investor him or herself. You want someone who really knows how to write a Joint-Venture Agreement that will prevent problems for you and your money partners.

Russell and I also insist that our co-venturers always get *independent* legal advice. When people tell me they trust me and will work with my lawyer, I tell them, "thanks, but no thanks." I would never use their lawyer on a deal that included my money, and they should never use my lawyer on a deal that includes their money!

That insistence on independent legal advice generates two advantages to my business. First, money partners who vet my JV Agreements through their own lawyer always come back to me and say their lawyer is impressed by the level of detail and how the agreement takes care of both parties' interests. That is information they will share with their friends and family, and since most of my contacts come from my own Inner Circle or the Inner Circle of my partners, this is free advertising for my future deals.

Second, where a partner's lawyer finds an issue to address, I reap the benefit of having let someone else pay for advice that makes my JV agreements stronger. This hasn't happened to me in years, but it did help me out many years back, and I still hear stories of novice JV investors who benefit from the advice of their money partner's lawyer.

RICHARD: I think it's also important to realize that there is no one-size-fits-all JV agreement. You really should ask your lawyer or your investor friends if they can share examples with you. Emma and I benefited a lot from the JV agreement templates we got from REIN. One of the things I struggled with in our first JV agreements was how schedules were presented. We were using a format that was like a list, and I found them complicated to read. Then a veteran JV investor showed me how he likes his JV agreement schedules to be presented as charts. I liked how they provided information at a glance, and we adopted this format for our business, too. In addition to the chart I'm showing on the following page, Schedule B Cash Contributions, we use a chart format for the schedule Cash and Other Contributions of JV Partner. We also use a chart called Further Monies, showing the partner's contribution and our contribution, along with dates and initials. Another chart lists the Purchase Price of Units.

SCHEDULE B CASH CONTRIBUTIONS

Cash Contributions of First Co:

Unit #	Down payment	Cash to close	Vendor-take-back mortgage	Legal fees	Staying power fund
5	0	$26,000	0	$995	$1,200
6	0	$29,000	0	$995	$1,200
7	0	$26,000	0	$995	$1,200
8	0	$29,000	0	$995	$1,200
Total	0	$110,000	0	$3,980	$4,800

A word about templates: Why can't I just fill in the blanks?

Templates are a fabulous way to familiarize yourself with complicated legal documents like a Joint-Venture Agreement. But they are no substitute for qualified legal advice. Anyone can fill in the blanks. You need someone who understands each clause, someone who can provide you with specific advice regarding the provisions.

If I had to sum up my advice regarding JV agreements in a single sentence, I'd say, "Don't pursue a deal without one." These are complicated documents. They are also an investment in the short- and long-term health of your business, and they provide a solid win-win business foundation for you and your JV partners. A professional race car driver would never start a race without being securely belted in and helmeted. A professional real estate investor would never strike a deal without a Joint-Venture Agreement, nor would they sign a JV agreement that wasn't prepared and vetted by their own lawyer.

Protect your assets

Asset protection is the number one reason you need legal advice to structure the ownership of a real estate investment deal that uses JV money. You will do the due diligence required to make sure you are buying the right property with the right partner's help. But to really protect you and your co-venturer, you must assume the deal could go awry and plan accordingly. Experienced investors call this "planning for the divorce ahead of time."

Let's be clear. Many investors never need to go back to their JV agreement when issues arise with an investment. If one partner's exit strategy changes or a personal or financial situation demands a different strategy with their investments (think: divorce, ill health, family or business issues), the co-venturers should be able to sit down and negotiate fair changes like the adults they are. That's good. But an *ethical expectation* that you will be able to count on a co-owner's co-operation is not the same as making fair negotiations a *legal requirement*. If you wouldn't drive a car without a seat belt, buy a carton of milk that's already been opened or sign a mortgage document that contains fraudulent information, why would you enter a JV real estate investment deal without a formal, written, legal agreement that's been vetted by a legal expert who works for you? Russell Westcott and I see this point as a no-brainer.

We also look at what might go wrong—and plan accordingly. That's why our JV agreements always include provisions for dispute settlement. If we are unable to settle a dispute with a co-owner, our JV agreements include provisions to call in an independent third-party adjudicator. Again, good planning prevents problems.

THE THREE FUNDAMENTALS OF A JV AGREEMENT

There are three fundamentals to the legal foundation of a JV Agreement. They are:

1. Practise full disclosure.

Lenders, lawyers, real estate agents and co-venturers must all be privy to the details of the deal. This includes everything from the upfront cash requirements to the long-term plans for the property, including your exit strategy.

It is especially important to make sure that everyone knows who is going to be on title. Let's say your money partner is going to put up all of the cash, but you want to be on title even though you are not contributing any money. That is information your lawyer and lender need to have. If you're not putting up any money because you don't have it, your lender may take issue with your name being on the title since it won't be on the banking documents.

Similarly, you may decide to assign the title to somebody else, or add your partner's name as the deal proceeds toward close. Again, the members of your investment team need to know who they are dealing with. Unexpected changes might jeopardize a deal and endanger your reputation as someone who's serious about real estate investing.

Moreover, it takes time to close a real estate deal, and changes to title and ownership take time to process. For example, Land Titles in Alberta takes more than a week to register a set of papers. Regardless of where you are closing the deal, every time you add or subtract a name to the title, you add or subtract a partner to the JV agreement. That means you must change the details of that agreement to reflect that new reality.

SOPHISTICATED JV INVESTOR INSIGHT

Avoid mortgage fraud

Sophisticated real estate investors never sign false documents. Mortgage fraud can cost you your deal, your reputation and your future business. Think about it: no one can afford to strike deals with a cheater.

---

2. Design the entire purchase around the JV agreement.

A JV deal is not the same as a real estate deal that does not involve other people's money. If you want your JV agreement to guide your investment and exit strategies, you cannot arbitrarily change the details of the purchase, or the plan. Take another look at the written offer and make sure it accurately reflects who's involved in the deal.

Reverse engineer the deal so you know what happens if something goes wrong or the situation changes.

3. Seek qualified and independent legal advice.

Every JV signatory must seek qualified independent legal advice. There are no exceptions to this rule. Lots of lawyers can help you buy a house.

Others might have specialized knowledge in areas related to tenant disputes or commercial property deals. You may need that kind of legal expertise on your investment team. But once you start getting into deals that involve investment real estate, including those with an RRSP mortgage or lease-to-own terms, you need a lawyer who can provide expert JV advice.

Sophisticated real estate investors take that principle even further. Their JV legal advisors will have more than 10 years of experience in the field. They also insist that their co-venturers seek independent legal advice. A well-constructed deal that's well understood by all parties will likely come back to the table with very few revisions or queries. That does not mean it was a waste of time. The fact that an independent legal advisor finds little fault with your deal is more evidence of your willingness to make the deal a win-win deal for you and your JV partner. You can't buy that kind of boost to your credibility.

Where changes need to be made, take heart. Minor revisions are likely to tighten up loose ends for all of the co-venturers. Besides, your partner just covered the cost of a second legal opinion!

SOPHISTICATED JV INVESTOR INSIGHT

Your lawyer's expertise

Lots of lawyers can help you buy a house. As soon as you get into investment real estate, RRSP mortgages, lease-to-own or vendor-take-back mortgages, the rules change. You can pay your lawyer to figure it all out—or pay her for great advice based on investment-world experience that protects your assets and your deals. The choice is yours!

Talking about real estate investment is not the same as doing real estate investment. JV partners are essential to our success and every deal we do brings us closer to the next deal.
                                        —Jules and Ange McKenzie

BACKGROUND

Jules and Ange McKenzie started buying real estate investment property in 2001. Following investment techniques taught by U.S.-based "gurus," they found themselves sidelined by poor direction and frustrated by continual requests for more money from mentors who increasingly appeared more bogus than beneficial. The couple remained convinced that real estate investment provided a path to long-term wealth and security. They were also increasingly aware that the tactics they were using to buy that real estate simply didn't work in Canada.

Committed to finding strategies that did work north of the 49th parallel, Jules and Ange joined REIN in 2003. That's where they learned what others were doing to attract joint-venture money to their deals, and the couple welcomed their first money partners in 2005. By early 2011, the couple held more than 50 properties and was actively pursuing new investments. "The fact that our business continues to grow is all about the sheer amount of capital we've been able to raise," says Jules.

Their success also speaks volumes about the couple's commitment to the fundamentals of real estate investing and their decision to follow a proven investment system. True to that system, most of their properties are located in Barrie and Orillia, Ontario, two communities with healthy economies and solid rental markets. They also focus on condo-type apartments where they can buy at least four units in a complex. Approximately half their properties are professionally managed, with the McKenzies handling the others. With experience, they've found that this combination of condo-type properties is easier to manage at a distance.

"We found our partners through the REIN network. They tend to be people who value our knowledge of the Barrie and Orillia markets, or people we've met through our real estate contacts," notes Jules. "Our history of success and the fact that we remain so enthusiastic about real estate investing also help bring new JV partners on board," adds Ange. "We believe in what we're doing—and that helps market our business."

But their commitment to following a proven investment system and their enthusiasm for what that system allows them to do tells only part of the McKenzies' success story. The bottom line is all about their willingness to take action. "We have a reputation for closing good deals and for keeping our properties performing well. Ten years into the business, that reputation for action is what really sells our deals."

For more on what the McKenzies do to keep taking action, Jules offers the following pointers.

FINDING MONEY

I know that most investors find their JV partners through their Inner Circle contacts. I think that's true for us, too, but we've defined our Inner Circle a little differently. A lot of new investors will find it difficult to bring other real estate investors into their deals. We didn't encounter that. I think it was different for us because we were already investing in real estate when we joined REIN. Also, I was very adept at "talking about real estate all the time." Because I knew what I was doing, I was able to sell real estate investment opportunities to people who saw the advantages of my deals, and knew they could invest without doing any of the work.

If you are looking for joint-venture money, document your success so that you can use your own experience to talk to prospective partners about what you can do with their money. Potential partners want to know what you're doing, and it's your job to show them. A successful experience is the best sales piece you will ever have. Good news travels fast—but bad news travels a whole lot faster.

QUALIFY YOUR INVESTORS

Just because you want to invest in real estate doesn't mean you can be part of our deals. I make sure that I know the people I bring the table, and I conduct my due diligence on who they are and what they expect. As part of that process, I make it very clear that we are the real estate experts and will be running the deals.

Our Letters of Intent are very detailed. This way, our prospective partners have a document that outlines each party's expectations, and we want this signed before we will put an offer on a property. The Letter of Intent includes an exit strategy, and this information all becomes the foundation of the formal Joint-Venture Agreement.

BE FIRM AND FLEXIBLE

I have had JV partners come to us because they want out of a deal early due to the fact that their life circumstances have changed. We will do everything we can to accommodate that kind of situation, but we won't completely toss out the original deal. Our legal agreements are in place to protect our JV partners and our own interests. Never lose sight of that.

Experience with situations like this did lead us to stop making investments that involved pooling rental properties. If you have a rental pool with several investors and one wants out, you need a forensic accountant to separate all of the ownership details! When we tried to help an investor who wanted out of this arrangement, it led to hard feelings with other partners. Today, we avoid that by operating units separately by joint-venture partner.

We are also willing to set up different kinds of deals. Not all of our JV partners are interested in being on title. Those who want to be on title need to qualify for the mortgage.

TAKE CARE OF THE FUNDAMENTALS

While I respect what happened in much of the world in 2008 and 2009, it really didn't affect our business at all. Since we had weathered some significant financial hardships in 2004 (just after we joined REIN and started learning how to invest with a system), we were accustomed to bringing a mountain of support documentation to the banks to qualify for mortgages. Back then, I also had to find properties that supported interest rates of 7 to 12 per cent.

During the recent downturn, we were able to acquire more properties and to finance our portfolio at the lowest interest rates we've ever had. As well, our positive cash flow improved significantly, which benefited us and our joint-venture partners. None of this is about luck. It's about investing with a proven system.

As part of your sophisticated approach to investing, you need to seek the best legal advice you can, and you need to be prepared to do what you say you plan to do!

WORKSHOP: HOW TO STRUCTURE JV DEALS

A verbal contract isn't worth the paper it's printed on.
—Sam Goldwyn

WORKSHOP OVERVIEW

Presenter: Russell Westcott

Do what you say you're going to do. That's the mantra of a sophisticated real estate investor who uses other people's money to make both of their dreams come true. Of course, in the real world of contemporary business, one's word is never enough. Throughout this workshop, I will address the reasons you should seek the advice of a qualified tax advisor when setting up your deals with co-venturers. Generally speaking, however, this session hones in on exactly what you need to know to structure the ownership of your JV deals.

OWNERSHIP STRUCTURE: KNOW BEFORE YOU BUY

The individual leading the JV discussion is the real estate expert, and he or she should decide on an ownership structure before pursuing an investment property with a co-venturer. This is critical because it can impact financing and the Joint-Venture Agreement. For example, lenders may not want a name on the title unless that person's name is also on the mortgage. As well, you cannot buy a property using one ownership structure and then change that structure without it costing you money. Moreover, a change in ownership structure could be disallowed by the JV agreement. That makes change risky—and foresight critical.

To avoid future problems and expenses, you need to know the ownership structure before you write the offer. When writing offers, you must be able to answer the following three questions:

1. Are all parties on the offer?
    (Does the offer list each partner or only one?)
2. Is a personal name or corporation on the offer?

3. Is a personal name and/or nominee on offer?

(Where a specific partner's participation is questionable, you can write "nominee" on the offer and then add a partner's name later with full disclosure to all parties involved, including the bank.)

To help you understand why those questions are so important, we'll review the five ownership structures specific to the Canadian real estate investment market. While some ownership structures are much more common than others, sophisticated investors should be familiar with all five types. The most important thing to remember is that the terms of the JV agreement will depend on the ownership structure you've chosen for the deal. To reiterate key points from the last tutorial, a real estate investment deal involving a money partner must be designed around the partnership. You must never overlook the fact that you are working with other people's money. To make JV deals work you will

- practise full disclosure,
- design the entire purchase around the joint venture, and
- seek qualified and independent legal advice.

All of that begins when you choose an ownership structure, because that determines who *owns* the property, who is responsible for its mortgage and who will reap the rewards of the investment.

---

5 CANADIAN-SPECIFIC OWNERSHIP STRUCTURES

1. Simple, personal and basic
2. Simple, corporate and basic
3. One-partner ownership
4. Corporate ownership (unanimous shareholders' agreement)
5. Corporate ownership as trustee for joint ventures

---

1. SIMPLE, PERSONAL AND BASIC

This is the easiest ownership structure to understand and implement, which is why it is also the most common way for novice and sophisticated investors to buy their investment properties.

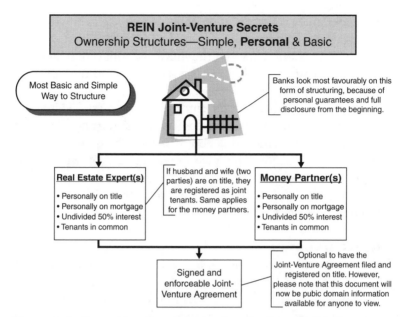

Figure 8.1: Ownership Structures—Simple, **Personal** & Basic

These deals can have more than one real estate expert and more than one money partner. Banks look favourably on this structure because they like the fact that the title carries personal names; lenders like to know who's borrowing their money and where they can find you.

Where all parties are on offer, you will need each party's signature. This is complicated if your partners are not in same geographic location as you, the property and your lawyer's office.

Clarity is the primary advantage of listing each party's name on the offer. But be careful because the need for multiple faxes or electronically scanned copies (carefully initialed and re-sent) can be troublesome. Faxes and scanned copies can be time consuming and the final document may also be difficult to read.

Too many on title?

Having personal names on the title offers you and your co-venturers the optimum protection in terms of who is responsible for the mortgage. Since you and your money partners' names are on the application to the lender, there is no confusion about whose names are listed on the mortgage documents.

But the number of names on the mortgage application and title can be problematic for real estate experts who are putting together deals with multiple money partners. As a rule, lenders do not like to see more than four individuals on a mortgage application. This is due to the fact that it costs more to foreclose on five or more people. From the bank's perspective, more than four names on the application is an issue of cost and litigation. This is why most legal advisors will say four is the maximum. As this can be an issue when two or more couples are investing together, you want to check out this detail with your lawyer and lender/mortgage broker.

Tenants in common

Under an ownership structure that is simple, personal and basic, all of those on the title are "tenants in common" under the law. This means that if a partner dies, their share goes to their estate versus to their partner. This differs from "joint tenancy," which is usually applicable to property held personally. For example, under joint tenancy, if you and your spouse own your home, one spouse's share of the property goes directly to the other upon death. In contrast, most investors are tenants in common, since they want their investment protected for their estate beneficiaries, not their business partners.

TOM: Does that mean Robert and I are going to have to use more complicated ownership structures seeing as one of us is married and the other is not?

RICHARD: "Simple, personal and basic" is still the way to go. To protect the interests of a married couple who is investing with a co-owner, the property can be purchased with all of their names on title, but in the Joint Venture agreement the ownership structure will note the percentage that is held jointly.

For example, Emma and I own property with several investors. Under a 50/50 arrangement, our ownership structure lists Emma and me together as 50 per cent of the joint tenancy. The other 50 per cent of the property is held with the investor as a tenant in common. If something happens to Emma or me, our 50 per cent stays with the other spouse. If something happens to our investor, his share goes to his estate.

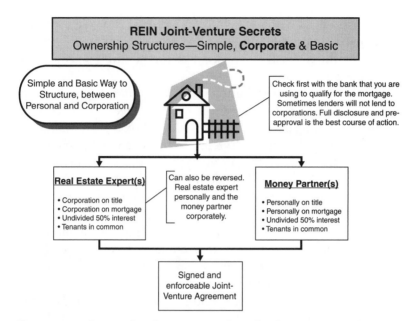

Figure 8.2: Ownership Structures—Simple, **Corporate** & Basic

2. SIMPLE, CORPORATE AND BASIC

Other offers may be written with a single personal or company name on the offer. But don't be confused by the use of the word "simple" on this ownership structure; some lenders will not lend to corporations. Even if you want your corporate name on the title, you will still need to sign a personal guarantee.

SUSAN: I am having this discussion about incorporation with my lawyer right now. I used to think that buying property in a corporate name was a good way to protect my assets from liabilities. My lawyer is saying that's not necessarily the case, and she wants me to talk to my accountant before I make a decision. What's up here?

To incorporate or not? That's the question every real estate investor faces at some point in his investment career. Unfortunately, there is no simple answer. But I can say your lawyer is right. The answer differs depending on your portfolio, your investment plans and your tax situation, and this is not a decision you can make without a lawyer and tax advisor. If liability is a central issue, you may be able to purchase liability insurance that protects your assets without mandating the expensive changes in your accounting records that incorporation requires.

The big-picture perspective holds that incorporation is not mandatory; nor is it necessarily a good idea for every investor, especially if you are just starting out. As I said earlier, even if you put a company's name on title, the lender is still going to want a personal guarantee.

On the plus side, tax advisors may tell you that incorporation offers greater liability protection and improved tax savings. That said, maintaining an incorporated business is also more expensive, since more complex accounting processes are required.

To determine whether incorporation makes sense for your business, ask your tax and legal advisors for their opinions. It can be a good way to shield investment income from employment income—but the additional expense is not always warranted. Besides, if you opt against setting up a corporation this year, nothing precludes you from changing that structure in the future.

What if the partner doesn't want to be on title?

A tougher issue arises when you want to use one of the "simple" ownership structures, and your partner does not want his or her name on the title of a property. (As titles are public documents, some investors, including some real estate experts, may not want to be on title as they don't want their assets to be traced that easily.) I've seen some deals where a money partner doesn't need to qualify for a mortgage because he has enough cash to make the deal work without going to a bank. Regardless of why an individual might not want to be named on the title, this partner would obviously seek a formal JV agreement with regard to responsibilities and rewards of the investment.

The general rule of thumb is that if your name is on the mortgage, your name is on the title when the deal closes. This is complicated if a property is owned 50/50, but only one person's name is on the mortgage. In that case, the person whose name is on the mortgage will only be able to mortgage his chunk of the property. As the bank will have lent against the "whole" property, they will want the co-owner's name on the title, too.

If the co-owner does not want to be on the title, but wants his interest to be registered, that might be possible. The solution to this can differ from province to province. For example, in Alberta, this could happen with a caveat. In Ontario, it would be a caution or a notice. As an alternative, the "non mortgage" partner could be registered as second mortgage holder on the property (pending whether the bank holding the first mortgage will allow a secondary mortgage to be registered). In all cases, the title would be considered "clouded," or have a registered "interest in land" on the property and the individual named on the title would not be able to sell the property without the co-owner's approval. (The co-owners' "interest in land" would have to be removed before the property can be transferred to another owner.)

Generally speaking, lenders will shy away from these deals. They want title to be less complicated. I typically recommend that investors work with partners who can qualify for a mortgage and therefore be on title, with no complications. While there may be times that you cannot work around that, those deals will be more complicated to manage.

A capital gains issue

Being the sole name on title could cost you money, too. Let's say you agree to be the sole name on the title of an investment property. According to the Canada Revenue Agency, that makes you the sole owner. If that property is sold, you are on track for 100 per cent of the capital gains. That's a major problem if you "do what you say you're going to do" and honour a JV agreement that says you will split the profits 50/50. Separating and keeping track of the beneficial ownership interest and the registered ownership is critical to create a proper paper trail.

SOPHISTICATED JV INVESTOR INSIGHT

Maintain a paper trail

Russell Westcott establishes a record of filing with the Canada Revenue Agency only 50 per cent of each property he owns in a 50/50 partnership with co-owners. Detailed Joint-Venture agreements, carefully signed and, where necessary, initialed, back up his claim to 50 per cent of the profits and losses. This helps him back up his claims should a partner fail to claim the other 50 per cent.

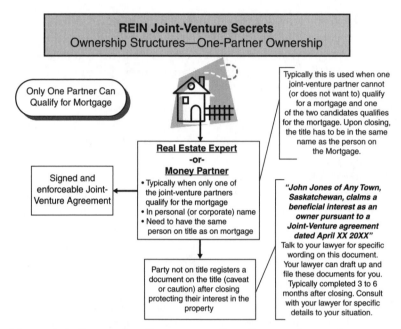

Figure 8.3: Ownership Structures—One-Partner Ownership

3. One-Partner Ownership

A one-partner ownership structure is applicable where only one partner can qualify for a mortgage. It is conceivable that the partner who did not qualify for the mortgage would be the real estate expert who found the deal and will manage it, even though he doesn't qualify for a mortgage. It could also be a lease-to-own situation where the real estate expert is helping his partner toward home ownership.

NOLAN: This looks like the situation I would be in if my parents qualify for the mortgage on an investment property that I will manage for them as the real estate expert. We are working out the details of how the investment will pay back their down payment, but I think it's fair to say we're all still a little gun shy. We don't want this deal to compromise our relationship, but it's got to protect their fiscal interest.

Here, the signed and enforceable Joint-Venture Agreement is critical, as is a caveat or caution registered on the title. The JV agreement and caveat or caution protect the investor on title and the money partner.

Laws can differ slightly from jurisdiction to jurisdiction. For example, to protect their interest in the property, the individuals not on title would register a caveat (Alberta) or caution (Ontario) on the title that is similar to the following:

"John Jones of Any Town, Saskatchewan, claims a beneficial interest as an owner pursuant to a Joint-Venture Agreement dated [month, day], 20XX."

That document is filed on title, and the property cannot be sold or transferred without its removal. Again, the document "clouds" the title and can complicate tax filing as the Canada Revenue Agency will see only one name on the title.

You can ask your lawyer to file the caveat or caution with a copy of the JV agreement, but that is not necessary. Filing it with a copy of the JV agreement makes it a public document. This may cause problems if you do not realize the JV agreement is now in the public domain.

What's most important here is that you recognize that while it is okay to have the money partner on title and not list the real estate expert, you must consult with a lawyer. And even when you're working with your parents, each party needs its own legal representation.

NOLAN: This is good. The Joint-Venture Agreement and caveat or caution would protect my parents' interest. I like knowing that we will be able to document that protection, and if the investment goes the way I want it to, I'll be able to oversee an investment that will repay their initial contribution and make them money.

What you're proposing is exactly the model a lot of new investors use to get into the JV market. In some ways, working with family is a really good way to start because these are not the people you want to disappoint!

4. CORPORATE OWNERSHIP OR UNANIMOUS SHAREHOLDERS' AGREEMENT

The corporate ownership structure, which works with new or existing corporations, can be quite complex, especially for novice JV investors. As discussed earlier, incorporation requires legal, accounting and tax

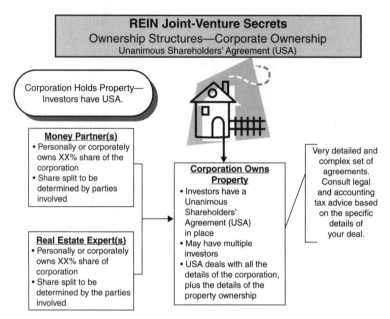

Figure 8.4: Ownership Structures—Corporate Ownership Unanimous Shareholders' Agreement (USA)

advice that is specific to the deal. Complications aside, a corporate ownership structure is used when there are multiple investors that hold a unanimous shareholders' agreement or USA.

In a real estate investment, the USA will deal with all of the particulars of the corporation, including the details of property ownership, and all business relative to officers, shares and voting requirements. Share splits will be determined by the parties involved, and the money partners and real estate experts, personally or corporately, will own a percentage of the shares of the corporation.

The one thing I want to emphasize here is that USAs cannot necessarily be amended to include a Joint-Venture Agreement. The USA, in effect, replaces the JV agreement.

5. CORPORATE OWNERSHIP AS TRUSTEE FOR JOINT VENTURES

Under this structure, a newly formed corporation holds the property as a trustee for the owners. Not all corporations can qualify for

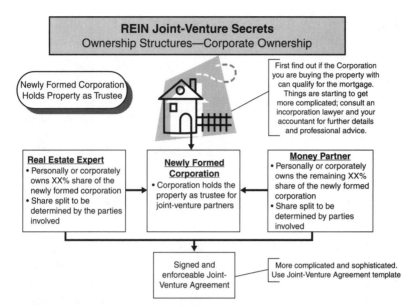

Figure 8.5: Ownership Structures—Corporate Ownership

a mortgage, so if this is the structure you wish to pursue, consult an incorporation lawyer and your accountant early in the process.

This structure can be especially useful with multiple shareholders. The real estate expert and co-venturer will hold, personally or corporately, a percentage of shares of the newly formed corporation, with the share split to be determined by the parties involved.

The newly formed corporation will then hold the property as a trustee for the JV partners. In other words, the corporation holds the title and the venturers are entitled to any benefits based on their shares. A signed and enforceable Joint-Venture Agreement is required.

THE TAKE-HOME LESSON: GET LEGAL AND TAX ADVICE

Decisions about how you structure ownership will impact your tax situation, and complicated ownership arrangements do not necessarily provide better tax or legal structures. Seek legal and tax advice and don't make decisions based on assumptions. Ownership structure must also be reflected in your formal JV Agreement.

Workshop Action Step: If You Have a Question, Ask it

The following tutorial is going to review the fundamental components of a JV agreement. In preparation for that review, I want each of you to come up with at least one question that still bugs you about investing with a co-venturer. I'll give those questions to Don and he'll address them in the tutorial.

This exercise is meant to remind you that there will be times when you just don't know what to do. That's okay. You should never pretend that you have an answer when you don't. But you should make it your business to find those answers for your partners and potential partners.

Learn to employ "nominee" language

Because there's not much an investor can do with a JV agreement without the help of qualified legal and accounting professionals, the second part of this workshop's action plan is really a bonus lesson in sophisticated real estate investing. To practise that lesson, read the following and then set up a meeting with your real estate agent and lawyer to talk about the use of nominee language. To put this into play, these members of your team need to be onside with what you plan to do.

To recap, this workshop taught you why it's important to know the kind of ownership structure you want in place before you buy a property and write a JV agreement. Ideally, that decision is made with a specific partner who is already committed to a particular deal. But what if that's not the case? What do you do if you come across a great JV deal *before* a partner is lined up?

First, exercise caution. This is where you need a Plan B in place because you should never sign an offer unless you can support it financially. Second, learn to exercise what I call the "nominee" action. Here's how that works.

Let's say a real estate agent has called me with a great deal on a single-family home in a buy-and-hold neighbourhood with appreciating value. I get calls like this all the time, not because I'm such a great guy, but because I've built such a great team. The real estate agents that I work with know what I'm looking for. In a case like this, I may put in an offer that names "Russell Westcott and/or nominee" as the buyers. You can only do this when you have a good working relationship with a mortgage broker, so beware. This may not be a tactic you can use on your first deals!

This works for me because my broker can make it work with lenders. And the approach is good because it leaves me in control of the contract and allows me to add another person at another time with full disclosure and approval by the seller and the lender. This may be particularly appropriate in a hot market or where there are time constraints. Keep in mind that an offer like this is never unconditional. I still want to see the property and conduct my due diligence. All I've done is get the process going.

If you want to use the terms "and/or nominee," you will need to make sure the bank lending the first mortgage is onside prior to using these terms on your contract. At the end of the day, you can always write the offer in your name and then get an amending document signed by both parties (buyer and seller), changing the names on the contract. Again, what really matters is that you make sure you get the bank's final approval prior to removing all conditions.

I also don't make an offer like this and then wait for a JV partner. I get to work lining up the right person as soon as I can. Once that partner's in line, I send a letter to my lawyer saying that while the offer reads "nominee," I've lined up the partner or partners and here are their names. That letter also outlines the split and it's also sent to my co-venturer and his lawyer. I expect the co-venturer to reply, likely through his lawyer, saying he agrees to everything the letter says, including the city or town where I will be signing papers.

This is not a formal Joint-Venture Agreement, but it definitely sets the stage for that document. So I am careful in my letter to my lawyer to state that I am the real estate expert on this deal, and I will be running the transaction. This underscores the fact that my lawyer is working for me, not the other buyers. It clears up future questions about who his client is, who he takes instruction from and how many people he needs to contact to proceed with action on the deal.

Let me make this as clear as possible: a letter like this will save you and your co-owner time and money. Because it establishes who will be signing the documents needed to close the deal, you prevent the frustrations that arise when you need two (or more) signatures or initials on every document. As such, the letter is a great management technique. Every time a notary puts his stamp on a piece of paper that includes a notarized change, it costs you money. It's simply not money you need to spend!

JV ACTION PLAN STEP #12

Set up a meeting with your lawyer and accountant.

If you're not convinced you need legal advice to put together a quality JV agreement, review the checklist Don Campbell presented at the last tutorial. Every good JV agreement should cover the elements on that list. Can you write an agreement that covers each element? Probably. Can you predict how your JV partner will *interpret* each element should some aspect of the deal need to change or be renegotiated? Probably not.

The bottom line is that smart real estate investors plan for success. Once you have lined up a JV partner, thoroughly vetted the partner with a quality background check and put together a real estate investment deal for the partnership, it's time to focus on an essential detail of a formal Joint-Venture Agreement: ownership structure.

That discussion must be held in conjunction with your tax advisor. A qualified tax accountant cannot remove your responsibility for paying your share of taxes. But he or she can ensure that you are not paying more than your share. Incorporation, purchase and sale decisions, and capital expenditures are all examples of business moves with tax implications. You can't un-ring a bell—and you can't undo a taxable decision.

As for a final note on incorporation, if your tax accountant's advice does not lead you to a specific conclusion regarding the need to incorporate, it's probably not a move you need to make now.

SOPHISTICATED JV INVESTOR INSIGHT

No grey-area deals!

Your reputation is your business. Stay away from deals that are not completely above board and honest. Signing false documents or promising things you might not be able to deliver are sure-fire ways to hurt your reputation—or kill your business. Full disclosure is a mantra you must have when investing in real estate.

WORKSHOP RECAP:

How to structure JV deals.
If you have a question, ask it.

Presenter: Don Campbell

The last two workshops have left you with some significant things to think about in terms of Joint-Venture Agreements and how to structure the ownership of real estate investment deals that involve money partners. What follows is a basic review.

THE THREE JV DEAL RULES OF ENGAGEMENT

1. A formal JV Agreement is fundamental to a solid JV deal. If your deal has a money partner, you need a JV Agreement.
2. Decisions about how to structure ownership of a JV deal must be made before the property is purchased. Ownership structure will dictate some of the terms in the JV Agreement.

JOINT-VENTURE AGREEMENT FLOW CHART

Make a decision regarding which of the five ownership structures you will adopt.

Use a Letter of Intent and information from the JV worksheet to write a JV agreement.

Customize the JV agreement.

Make sure your partner gets independent legal advice.

3. Lawyers and tax accountants are essential to the JV deal. Do not write a JV Agreement or purchase an investment property without their assistance.

Questions and Answers

Most of the workshop participants have now started or completed a JV deal. The fact that you still have questions is absolutely normal—and that's why I wanted to use this forum to address them. My goal is to help you understand that your job as the real estate expert is to be willing to act on the information you learn from your own experiences, as well as the experiences of other investors. You will never need to know every answer. You will need to know where you can find those answers and how you can use them to your advantage.

NOLAN: Real estate is expensive. I still worry that I don't have enough of my own money to get started. What can I do about that?

A. If you really don't want to swing a deal unless it has some of your own money in it, you'll simply have to find a way to get that money. You can work more hours or maybe talk to your lender about a line of credit.

But neither of those options is necessary. If you want to be the real estate expert on the deal, you may not need to have any money to put toward a deal. Again, learn the fundamentals of real estate investing and then find properties that will generate positive cash flow. Let your deals speak for themselves. If you want to *be* the real estate expert, *become* the real estate expert.

DAN AND CAROL: We are building a list of potential partners but still worry about what will happen if a partner backs out at the last minute.

A. Solid due diligence on your partner's commitment should make partner withdrawal a non-issue. Still, you need to have your Plan B in place because if the deal is close to completion, your real estate agent, broker and property manager may all have a stake in the outcome. Remember: you can always add a different partner to a deal that you have to close on your own. But if your deals don't close and your team members decide you're the problem, your deals may go to the bottom of their "to do" lists.

If a deal falls apart before it closes, take heart. Every experienced investor has been there. Instead of mourning what never was, figure out the lessons learned—and how to use them going forward. You won't close on every property. Get used to it.

TOM AND ROBERT: Incorporation versus non-incorporation seems like a really big deal, but we can't decide what to do. We've been floating the idea that we should hold off on any more joint-venture deals until this is decided.

A. That would not be the right thing to do. Real estate investors take action. That means they find, close and then manage investment real estate. Since your goal is to invest in real estate with money partners, do that. Decisions about incorporation are important, but they won't cost you deals. You can always incorporate later, and your tax accountant and real estate lawyer can give you the information you need to make that decision.

Again, this is not a decision you leave to water cooler experts. Your legal and tax advisors probably won't tell you what you *have* to do. (It's just not that easy!) But if you value their input, these are the people whose opinions you should seek.

SUSAN: I've completed the background check on a new co-venturer and now she's balking at the need to get independent legal counsel on the Joint-Venture Agreement. Help! What should I do?

A. First, I'm glad you find this disturbing. It is a really bad idea. Real estate lawyers are not in business to crash potential deals. They are in business to ensure their client's best interests are served. JV deals are complicated. As the real estate expert, you want to put forward a JV agreement that meets the needs of all parties to the deal. But that intent should never be an excuse for not getting a second opinion. Your money partner owes that to herself.

If this partner simply won't follow your lead, you may need to take other action. I know co-venturers who've paid for the independent counsel on the first deal they've closed with a co-venturer who they expect to work with again and again.

I've known others who add an addendum to the JV agreement that says the real estate expert (you!) advised independent legal counsel and the co-venturer refused. Honestly, your main goal is to establish that you know what you're doing and that you want your partner to heed your advice. No one wants to say "I told you so" if a dispute arises.

DAN AND CAROL: Our daughter has asked to come in on one of the properties we're looking at. Dan thinks a hand-shake deal is enough. Carol wants a formal JV agreement with independent legal counsel for both. Who's right?

A. Carol wins this one! If memory serves me right, this daughter is not an only child and she is going to be married next year. You simply have to work through all of the what-if scenarios and a JV agreement is the only way to really protect your interests—and hers.

Still not convinced? What if she's in a car accident and needs money? What if her new husband doesn't like the deal you've struck? What if they get divorced and he tries to claim the property as a marital asset? To be honest, every real estate property investment needs a formal and legally binding agreement, the terms of which all parties agree to. It doesn't matter if the deal involves co-ownership or a financial loan. If you are serious about making real estate investment a win-win for your co-venturers, you must be serious about planning for how the deal will unfold in certain situations. Let's get real. When it comes to love and money, all bets are off.

RICHARD AND EMMA: This is kind of embarrassing for us because we know that we have the most investing experience of the people in the workshop. These workshops really helped us fine-tune our commitment to systems, relationships and follow-through. But our Inner Circle contacts aren't exactly scooping up our deals the way we'd hoped. Are we doing something wrong?

A. If I've done my math right, you own five revenue-generating properties with four partners and you have held as many as nine properties with seven co-venturers. The four properties you sold were all disbursed in accordance with planned exit strategies. You are also working on a rent-to-own deal and are looking for properties with another partner. Considering that Richard is working full-time, I think your record speaks for itself. Find a way to remind yourselves that success is never about the number of properties you buy in a specific period of time. Success in real estate investment is about the relationships you build moving forward.

To nurture those relationships, you should always review and fine-tune your presentation of JV deals. Follow up rejections with questions about what would make the deal more attractive to a potential partner. Also remember that it takes time and patience to nurture relationships with prospective money partners. Russell Westcott has a friend who came on board as a JV partner after more than six years of listening to Russell talk about his investment business. Russell had never treated that individual as a prospect; they just enjoyed each other's company and sharing information about their professional and personal lives. Russell always made it clear that his preferred partners came from his Inner Circle, but his "tell, not sell" approach left doors open without his contacts feeling pressure.

I think it's fair to say that you have some regrets about the four properties you sold. You could have held onto those properties and pursued other partnerships. But hindsight is always 20/20 and regret is all about negative emotion, not positive action.

I suspect that what you really need is more time to follow up with the people you've been talking to. One of the best ways to do that would be to have a deal that's ready to go. That's right. Instead of waiting for potential partners to come to you, find the deal and take it to them. With all of the work you've been putting into your relationships, your record will do a lot of the talking!

RICHARD: That's great advice, Don. Listening to you talk has brought back a flood of memories about where I was at when you and I first met. I think I've been second guessing myself and I forgot how that breeds fear and analysis paralysis. Emma and I are going to see a property this coming week and we've got four potential partners in mind for that deal. Now that I think about it, what are we waiting for? Realistically, there's nothing to stop us from sharing that information with all four prospects. We can let each of them know that we've put the word out to our Inner Circle and that time is of the essence.

And that's what a plan looks like in action. Well done. The fact that you're second guessing yourself shows you're human, Richard. Real estate investors are allowed to have days when they don't think the world is moving fast enough for them. But take a deep breath and gain a little perspective. This is not a race to the finish line, it's a journey to long-term wealth creation. You and Emma have a win-win track record with your partners and that record puts you well ahead of the start line!

SOPHISTICATED JV INVESTOR INSIGHT

Create the win-win deal

Sophisticated real estate investors know that every JV partner is connected to a future JV partner or deal. Every JV partner with a win-win deal will come back to you to invest more, or refer you to others.

The right partner, the right property, the right business structure. You can't have one without the others.

—Gary McGowan

BACKGROUND

Gary McGowan likes his full-time job. But he loves his wife and three kids, and it's the family side of Gary's life that got him thinking about their long-term financial security. Looking for ideas, Gary turned to his dad, Richard. A man with more than three decades of real estate investing experience already under his belt, Richard didn't stop at advice. It turned out that Richard and Gary's mother, Pam, had also been talking about getting back into the real estate investment business. Intrigued by Gary's interest, the parents floated the idea of partnering with Gary and his wife, Michelle.

When their market analysis identified Lindsay, Ontario, as a good place to invest in buy-and-hold real estate, the couples took a closer look at that market. By the summer of 2008, they'd bought their first three properties in that community, two five-plexes and one four-plex. They'd also taken their first ACRE weekend through REIN, an educational experience that opened their eyes to the fact that other investors were building real estate wealth using other people's money.

"Before long, we were making a presentation to a long-time family friend who soon came on board with his son," recalls Gary. Three years later, the McGowans own 27 doors, all of them in the Greater Toronto Area, or within 100 kilometres of Toronto, and all of them with joint-venture partners. Eleven of the properties are in the rent-to-own investment category, with the rest held as long-term rentals.

"We now have five partners in the mix, one of whom is involved with about 15 properties and is the original partner. His are all 50/50 deals. He obviously understands our business model and likes what it does for him," explains Gary.

The McGowans like it, too. "When we started investing with my parents, we put together a five-year plan that looked at where we wanted to be. Three years into that plan, we're doing really well. I'm still working full time and that makes sense for now as Michelle and I have three young children," says Gary, who harbours no regrets about his and Michelle's decision to develop a real estate investment portfolio with his parents as co-venturers.

Gary's parents are also appreciative. Real estate investment lets Richard plan for his financial future while working (for one dollar a year) for a not-for-profit organization that does international aid work. Pam, an accountant, also does some work for the organization. More recently, the two couples hired Gary's sister, Kristy, to help run the office. "Ours is a pretty unique situation because we enjoy being together—and now that includes working together," says Gary.

Like other seasoned investors, Gary is adamant about what the people from their Inner Circle have meant to their business. "I'm not afraid to talk about what we're doing in real estate, and that has really helped us find joint-venture partners among the people we know. Because those people know us, they want to work with us. In the early days, that was a bit of a problem because I was kind of naive; looking back, it was like I wanted to take everyone along for the ride. It took me some time to learn how to be more strategic in terms of identifying who we wanted to work with."

What's developed is a three-pronged investment approach that views the partner, property and business structure as part of the same continuum for success. Here is a closer look at how Gary makes it work.

THE PARTNER

The fact that we've never partnered with the "wrong" person probably says a lot about how careful I am. In the beginning, I was really caught up in the emotion. If you wanted to invest with us, I wanted to invest with you. It took me awhile to figure out that I needed to be more strategic. Not everyone I knew and liked was going to invest with us, nor should they invest with us. Once I realized that, I was able to focus on the people who were real prospects. Honestly, it's neat to see how the people who fit your JV investor profile enter your life once you start looking for them. Three years into our business, our investors still come from within our Inner Circle, and I don't anticipate that will change.

THE PROPERTY

From the very beginning, we've focused on a business plan that valued real estate investment properties with positive cash flow. Using information we learned from REIN, plus my dad's experience, we stick with communities where the economic fundamentals show long-term strength for the rental market. Our rent-to-own properties are also located in communities where it makes sense for tenant-buyers to work toward the dream of home ownership.

One of the most interesting things that's happened over the years is that our track record with a certain kind of property now brings properties to us. Real estate agents and other investors will approach us with properties—and that's helping us grow our portfolio.

THE STRUCTURE

Most of our deals are 50/50. But since there are two couples in our 50 per cent, we are careful to make sure our Joint-Venture Agreements say exactly what we want them to say. My dad is my best friend; why would I want to compromise that?

In hindsight, I would say that our JV agreements have become one of our strongest assets. I really like going through our JV agreements and showing people that we have planned for what might happen down the road. And that approach pays off. When potential JV partners see how we secure their investment, and how much we value integrity, they like our deals even more. It's another way we show our investors that we know what we're doing.

As part of that approach, we also put a lot of emphasis on encouraging our investors to get independent legal advice. We've developed a solid JV agreement, but we think it's important for investors to have their own legal advisor look it over, too.

Do you need a partner, or money? Structure your deals so they make sense for your business.

—Ian Szabo

BACKGROUND

Real estate investing hasn't taken former chef Ian Szabo completely out of the kitchen. As an investor who renovates distressed residential properties so he can put them back onto the market for substantially more than he paid, Ian's no longer responsible for the kitchen—he's responsible for the whole house!

A few years ago, Ian's portfolio held close to 20 properties, most of them purchased for the long-term buy-and-hold market. Using what he knew about the fundamentals of sophisticated real estate investing, Ian realized he was pursuing someone else's dream. While he knew how to put JV deals together for the buy-and-hold segment of the investment market, it was a long way from what Ian *wanted* to do. Fast forward to 2011 and Ian's business doesn't just look remarkably different, he and his wife, Tanya, are a whole lot happier, too.

What changed? "Everything," says Ian. "I am still working with money partners, but I am not doing the classic 50/50 deals. Instead, my partners come in with money and I pay them interest until the reno-vated house sells. There's very little risk for them because they're on title and it works better for me because I take control of the whole renova-tion. No one can question what I'm spending money on, or infer that I'm not working hard enough or fast enough for them."

Ian's quick to say that his success in the "fix-and-flip" market is no fluke of fate. An experienced renovator with excellent contacts in the skilled trades, Ian parlays that expertise into successful deals pri-marily because he knows that he makes his money when he buys the property. "I really do buy the worst house in the best neighbourhood. Sometimes these houses are so bad they're sold for the value of the land. Other times, home owners can't get insurance for a mortgage, or I come across houses that are in such chaotic disrepair that real estate agents won't even go inside."

Ian's investment niche won't work for everyone. But his experi-ence has lessons for all. First and foremost, "this business is not easy.

I still hold some of my properties for five years, but working with 50/50 partners on those properties led to more complications than I was prepared to manage. The mental side of this business is tougher than people expect. I like working with investment real estate, but I like it more now that I've found a way to make it work for me."

Below, Ian offers sage advice for others who want to follow his investment strategy.

Be Honest about What You Bring to the Table

I was already in the renovation business when I started investing in real estate and then brought in JV partners. In the beginning, I think I sold myself short because I didn't understand what I brought to the table in terms of my experience and expertise as a contractor. I now realize it's my strength. It's because I know what I'm doing that people can be confident about investing their money with me.

Learn What You Don't Know

I've taken what REIN teaches about real estate investment and personalized it to fit what I want to do with real estate investment. Having my own niche is great. But I still need to understand how the market works because the fundamentals don't change.

If you're not willing to learn how the investment market works, and how the renovation-and-resell market works within the larger market, stay away. I buy a lot of my houses from people who did it the wrong way.

Do What Works

I am not doing the classic 50/50 deals. Instead, I'm looking for financial partners who want to treat their investment like a loan. Some of my investors want to come into a deal to learn how it works. Where it makes sense, these deals include teaching them what I do. Honestly, my money partners would probably be happier if a property doesn't sell because I owe them interest until the loan is paid. Since I'm in business to make money, that doesn't happen.

I also stick to neighbourhoods I know and can access easily. My properties all tend to be in the Durham, Ontario, region. It's five minutes from my house and, yes, that makes them easier to manage.

I find my properties by knocking on the doors of houses that appear to fit my system. I've even left sticky notes on front doors. Some of the people I buy from just don't know what to do with their properties, which are often vacant. Once we've established a rapport, which can take months, I look for ways to solve the problem. I never want to take advantage of a vendor, but there are definitely situations where people are looking for a way out, and if I can help them, I do.

WORK WITH PEOPLE YOU TRUST

You need to trust your money partners, and it makes sense to begin investing with people from your Inner Circle. For me, that's grown to include the contractors I work with. After they see what I'm doing, they want to get involved.

KEEP IT FORMAL

Every one of my property deals with a money partner includes a formal legal agreement. My deals are set up so that my money partners' names are on title. This reassures them that I can't refinance a deal or take money out.

GET A MENTOR

Align yourself with someone you can trust. It may be an investor who's already doing these deals. It's got to be someone with real-world experience. Steer clear of anyone who thinks a fixer-upper deal is as easy as what you see on television. Those shows condense weeks and months of hard physical work into an hour or less—and they don't ever show the heavy emotional toll of expected and unexpected expenses.

My track record with these kinds of property deals has led me to open a new business, Flip School. This is the direct result of the fact that I really enjoy teaching, and I want to fill a market void in terms of telling people what's really involved in these deals. I value mentors in my life and want to play that role for others, too.

WORKSHOP: CLOSING THE DEAL—HOW TO AVOID PARTNER PITFALLS

What do you want to achieve or avoid? The answers to this question are objectives. How will you go about achieving your desired results? The answer to this you can call strategy.

—William E. Rothschild

WORKSHOP OVERVIEW

Presenter: Russell Westcott

Successful real estate investment strategy is all about doing the right thing at the right time. But none of us lives or invests in a perfect world. No matter how much we *know* about the right way to go about doing our business, there will always be times when we, in fact, make a mistake. And when we are successful, we will come to realize that we could have improved on that success.

I'm here to set the record straight: mistakes are not the enemy. Mistakes only stop us in our tracks if we allow them to be an excuse for not taking action.

To help you avoid investment paralysis, I am going to work through the ugly details of 20 of the most common mistakes real estate investors make when putting together joint-venture deals. Let me be honest: I have committed every one of these errors. In fact, that's why I call them "landmines." I know what it's like to step on these bad guys—and I have learned what it takes to avoid them. In the first and final analysis, you must rest assured that errors happen and savvy investors put their lessons to good use. The great news about these particular mistakes is that they are entirely preventable. In fact, it's my mission to teach you what you need to know to avoid these hazards.

What's left after you've carefully avoided or made, and then learned from, every mistake possible? Success! Victory! Triumph! Call it what you want, a JV real estate investment strategy that avoids unnecessary pitfalls is a strategy where investments pay off and co-venturers come back for more!

Learn from the Mistakes of Others

A commitment to learning from the mistakes of others is the first and most important step you will take on this journey of landmine evasion. That begins with people like the ones in this room. Find out what your peers are reading, what seminars they are attending and whether they're willing to talk to you about what works and doesn't work for their own JV portfolios. To paraphrase Will Rogers, the late American cowboy-philosopher and social commentator, there are two ways to learn new information. The first is from reading and the second is "by association with smarter people."

Remember what I said about the importance of taking action? Make sure the smarter people you surround yourself with are action takers, not action talkers.

SUSAN: I'm hoping that's one of the avoidable landmines you are going to be talking about, because I've had my fill of "action talkers." I came into this series of workshops confident that other people were successfully investing with joint-venture partners, but lacking any confidence that I could do the same. That's turned around, but I've also learned that not everyone who *says* they support me actually serves as a positive influence. In fact, some of the prospective investors I've encountered seem determined to push my JV deals right off the road.

We are going to cover that issue. For now, it is important that all of you learn that you need to surround yourself with a support network that actually acts like a support network. Everyone can learn what Don Campbell and I have been teaching you. But not everyone who learns how to do it will actually *do* it. Wanting to invest in real estate with JV partners is like wanting to exercise to improve your physical fitness. You can't invest in real estate with JV partners without doing the work that it entails—nor can you hire someone else to do push-ups for you. If you're going to reap the rewards, you're going to have to do the work.

But look around this room. Richard and Emma are investing with co-venturers as a couple. Tom and Robert are approaching this venture as business partners with remarkably different personal goals. Susan wants to take an already successful real estate investment portfolio and grow it with JV partners. Nolan isn't in a position to invest in real estate unless he has money partners. Dan and Carol see real estate investment as a way to boost retirement income for themselves and their friends. My point is that you can commit to learning from others without committing to doing everything that others do. Your strategy can be completely different from the investors who mentor you, but you still need to follow a system, and if you want to be successful, the system you follow must be a proven system.

SOPHISTICATED JV INVESTOR INSIGHT

Take ownership

At the end of the day, your real estate investment decisions, good and bad, are your responsibility. When mistakes happen, own them and move forward. Don't blame others, but when appropriate, do give yourself credit for lessons learned. Drivers who stay at home until every light along their route is green will never leave the safe haven of their driveways. The road you take will have potholes and detours. You will avoid some, hit others and sometimes make the wrong turn. As long as you keep driving, you'll gain experience, make progress and enjoy the journey.

A Proven System

How can I stand here and encourage you to take action on JV investments when I know you are going to make mistakes? Again, it's not like I'm sending you on a life and death mission wearing a blindfold. To summarize my best advice on this matter, I am telling you to do the following three things.

1. Step carefully. Choose wisely.

There is no substitute for common sense tempered by education and due diligence. Do your own heavy lifting, but remember that real estate investing strategies are like a smorgasbord. Pick what works for you, pursue what makes sense for your plan, and learn to move slowly. This is not a race. Sophisticated real estate investing, with or without money partners, is about long-term wealth creation, not short-term riches.

2. Aim to be a settler, not a pioneer. Follow a proven course of action and always test your strategies.

Every JV deal you strike will be unique to a particular set of partners and circumstances, but real estate investing with money partners is not a new invention. Find someone who's doing what you want to do. Learn from them. Test strategies to figure out what works best for you. If you only have time to nurture Level 1 contacts, stick to that approach. Don't let yourself be talked into strategies that you don't have time to develop and perfect. If it works, go for it. If it doesn't, be prepared to make changes.

3. Get a good map. If you find a better route, go for it!

The strategies you adopt will be your own, but the mistakes you avoid can be based on lessons learned from others. Make continuous improvement, not perfection, a business goal.

EMMA: Aiming for perfection will just hold you back! When people like Richard's boss approached us about investing in our real estate deals, we didn't have the formal presentation package that we now give to prospective investors. Our first meetings were over coffee at a local café and we took everything from photographs of our investment properties to the business cards of the people on our real estate investment team. It's nothing like what we do today—but it worked because our investment decisions were following a proven system, and that's what our investors really wanted to hear about.

RICHARD: I look back on those early meetings as some of the best "pitch practice" opportunities we could have had. Because we had read the books, attended the seminars, were cultivating great mentors and had some experience in the bank, we did know what we were doing. What we lacked was experience talking about what we were doing. The information package we use today is the direct result of all the questions we fielded when we didn't have all the answers.

Richard and Emma are making a very important point. A "professional" investment package may help you sell your deals to money partners, but it is not essential to your first JV deals. In fact, I've seen novice investors spend so much time and money developing a professional investment package that they're worn out before their first deal is ever pitched. Again, keep your eye on the prize. What's more important in the early days of your JV business, writing reports or finding the deals others will want to buy into?

With an action-based foundation now laid, here are the 20 landmines I want you to study, think about and plan to avoid.

20 Common Landmines to Avoid

Here is the list of the most common mistakes that JV investors make while putting together JV agreements, along with a suggestion on how to avoid each one.

Landmine #1—Going it alone: You fail to build a real estate dream team

This landmine is all about the foundation you need to generate successful joint-venture deals in real estate. If you try to develop your business without a quality team behind you, you are doomed to fail.

Evasive action

Recognize that your role as the real estate expert on these deals means you must put together the team you'll lead. The team's success hinges on your ability to foster quality relationships with these individuals, every one of whom should have experience in real estate investing.

THE REAL ESTATE DREAM TEAM

Real estate agent

Lender and/or mortgage broker

Lawyer

Accountant

Bookkeeper

Property inspector

Construction and renovation tradespeople

Property manager

Prospective money partners

Landmine #2—Letting your team down:
You forget the win-win equation

Every member of your real estate dream team should be able to expect to be involved in a win-win relationship with you. What does that win-win relationship look like?

- Your real estate agent brings you sound deals because she knows what you're looking for. She trusts that you won't sabotage a deal and cost her a well-earned commission, so if a deal doesn't interest you, you let her know so she can shop it to another client.
- Your bookkeeper keeps your records up to date because he knows what you expect and that you won't burden him with last-minute requests for information unless it's absolutely necessary.
- Your renovation expert delivers solid quotes and quality work because he wants in on your next project.
- Your property manager takes care of regular maintenance, but makes sure you know where money is being spent.
- Your money partners like the return they're getting from their relationship with you and tell others about it.

Evasive action

These win-win relationships can be complicated, since some roles on your team may be filled by more than one expert and there may be times when you need to draft someone new to your bench.

The key is respect. Recognize that each of the individuals on your team will expect a win-win relationship with you. In the vast majority of cases, that win-win will have a financial component: these people are helping you make money and vice versa.

To have an endless supply of JV money for your deals, you need to keep the best on your team. Take care to offer something other investors do not and never forget that you want the members of your team to make money as a direct result of their relationship with you.

SOPHISTICATED JV INVESTOR INSIGHT

Develop a win-win mindset

Sophisticated JV investors know they can make money investing in real estate. They bring others into their deals so they can profit from deals that make money for their partners first.

Look at your team members and ask yourself: How can I help them? To bring them onside, answer the question: What's in it for them?

Under-promise and over-deliver by finding out how you can help them out!

Landmine #3—Staying too close to home: You choose the wrong partners

This problem is a lot more common than a lot of people realize. When you're new to JV investing, it's easy to talk about potential deals with other investors. But no hockey team needs more than one goalie on the ice during a game, and no real estate investment dream team needs a bench of real estate experts!

SUSAN: Very interesting. I was recently at a seminar with novice real estate investors, and several people in my working group were talking about getting together and forming a corporation to invest in real estate. They had all kinds of ideas about the kind of properties they were going to buy and the kind of people they wanted on their team, but they never talked *money.*

I've heard that kind of conversation a lot—and it misses the whole point of real estate investing. The critical action step all investors must take involves putting an offer in on a property, and you can't do that without money. The problem with assembling a team of real estate investment talkers is that the approach gets people all excited about taking action when they're not taking any action at all!

Evasive action

To avoid this landmine, take an inventory of what you have to offer and be mindful of what it tells you in terms of what you have and what you need. Are you the real estate expert? Do you also have experience with renovations? Is that experience hands-on or managerial? Do you know where to find investment properties with great potential for cash flow and appreciation? How are your legal or tax accounting skills?

If you're putting together your first real estate investment dream team, stock up on people whose skills are different from your own. What kind of investments do you want to pursue? Who can help you do that?

SOPHISTICATED JV INVESTOR INSIGHT

What are you waiting for?

Sophisticated investors take the time to figure out who they need on their real estate investment dream team. Taking a multi-faceted approach to their deals, they look at what they need and when they need it, and then identify the individuals who can help them do that. If you won't buy a single-family home without a property inspection, what are you waiting for? Line up that inspector before you make your first offer. Similarly, if you don't like what your mortgage broker offers, find someone else you can work with.

Landmine #4—A lack of confidence: You don't believe someone would want to invest with you

Remember the principles of JV wealth attraction? Sophisticated real estate investors attract money partners by practising the principles of attraction versus pursuit, abundance, expectancy, imagination, giving, decisiveness, expertise and resiliency.

Evasive action

Nolan, you've been struggling with this landmine. Will you tell us a little more about your experience with this?

NOLAN: I ran into this landmine head first! I'd been trying to focus on wealth attraction and was building a team of people I really wanted to work with. The one area I was struggling with was money partners; I just didn't seem to be able to attract any financial interest in my deals.

That changed when I took responsibility for the negative energy I was giving off. After the last workshop, I sat down with my parents and two brothers. It's not the first time we talked about real estate investment, but it was definitely the most productive. This time, I had a list of things I wanted to cover and every one of them linked back to the principles of wealth attraction. My parents and one brother told me they can't wait until I find them a deal to look at. My other brother said he's told a few close friends about my plans and a couple of them are interested, too.

That exemplifies the point I'm trying to make. Real estate investors need other people's money more than those other people need your deals. You can't just take that money, nor is it a gift. To attract it to your deals, you have to be prepared to tell people what's in it for them—and to show them how you will make that happen.

Landmine #5—Chasing the money: Desperation scares potential investors

A lack of confidence must be balanced by realism. Potential investors will not be won over to your deals if you seem desperate for the money, or too confident in what you can do with it. Some real estate investors do this full time. Others balance their property portfolios with full- or part-time jobs. Regardless, always conduct strict due diligence on the deal and your partner. Because bad news travels fast, avoid getting into situations where a deal will fall through if your money partner reneges and never let JV money go to anything other than an agreed-upon deal.

Evasive action

Put a solid Plan B in place. You do not want to lose a deal because a partner reneges. You do not want to close a deal that doesn't meet your basic goals (cash flow and appreciation) just because you're afraid you might lose a particular investor.

Learn the art of negotiation that practises the win-win approach. When necessary, walk away from a deal. If you can't come to an agreement, move on. You want to be flexible and still be able to do business on your terms. Remember your role as the real estate expert. When a prospective partner wants to elbow in on decisions that should be yours to make, think about what letting them do that will mean down the road. If you are the real estate expert, you want to own that role in your own deals.

Landmine #6—A lack of insight: You don't understand where your JV partners will come from

Review the REIN Circle of Influence. Joint-venture partners can come from all three levels in your Circle of Influence. But Level 1 candidates carry significantly less risk compared to prospects from Levels 2 and 3. Ignore this rule at your peril.

REIN Joint-Venture Circle of Influence

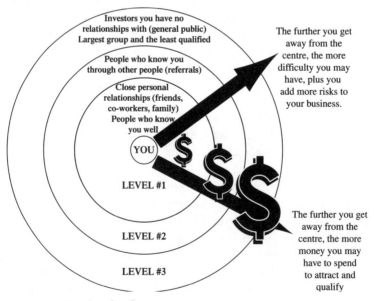

Figure 9.1: Circle of Influence

Evasive action

Make a list of your Levels 1, 2 and 3 contacts. Try to identify 15 to 25 people who are at Level 1 and design a plan that targets those Inner Circle candidates first. Once you have developed JV partnerships, look at how you can reach out to Level 2 contacts. Track all of the names and revisit the list regularly. Your Circle of Influence changes over time. Savvy JV investors track those changes and act accordingly.

Landmine #7—Sitting still: You can't attract more leads

Investors who step on the first six landmines are likely to step on this one, too. Generally speaking, investors who can't attract more leads are looking in the wrong places!

Evasive action

Your list of leads can never be too long! Aim to cultivate new leads. Take a critical look at your marketing materials. Do your business cards describe you as a "professional real estate investor"? Make that a priority. Get yourself 500 business cards that have your name, phone number and e-mail. Don't forget your website, if you have one. Hand these out to people you know.

Set goals for lead cultivation. How many people do you want to talk to about real estate investment on a weekly basis? Set your goal, make a plan to accomplish it, and then track your progress. Attend meetings, set up appointments, network and pursue direct communication. Letters and e-mails to get people thinking about your follow-up call or visit are critical. Following the principles of JV wealth attraction, assess what you're doing to get people to invest in your deals.

SOPHISTICATED JV INVESTOR INSIGHT

The best business card

Business cards can be tricky. But it's not rocket science, and professional real estate investors never leave home without them. Go through the cards you've collected from others. Copy the things you like and head down to a business store to place your order.

No time? Stop making excuses. Make an appointment with yourself and get the job done!

Landmine #8—Wasting time: You think everyone's a prospect

Potential JV leads are not prospects until they have been appropriately filtered to make sure they (a) have the money and (b) are people you want to be in business with. Be honest about the fact that you can't deal with every lead that comes your way. You can, however, devise a plan to filter that information automatically.

Evasive action

An unfiltered lead is a suspect, not a prospect. Prepare an information package that's easy for you to send to prospects. Include an Expression of Interest Letter and a special report about why, where and how you invest. If the lead comes from your Inner Circle and you want to showcase your credibility as an investor, include important background information like a copy of *Real Estate Investing in Canada 2.0* or *97 Tips for Canadian Real Estate Investors*.

SOPHISTICATED JV INVESTOR INSIGHT

Weed out the tire kickers!

Novice investors are sometimes overwhelmed when JV prospects ask for information. While the package you send is likely to evolve (and improve) with experience, knowing what you will send will save you a lot of time in the early days of building your portfolio.

Landmine #9—Prospects renege: You aren't filtering your JV candidates carefully enough

Every real estate investor, novice and veteran, has a horror story about dealing with enthusiastic JV candidates who turn out to be duds. Some of these people never planned to invest—even though they talked as if they did. Others won't have the money, so their intentions are moot.

Evasive action

While it's probably impossible to avoid this landmine completely, a quality filter will help you separate the winners from the losers.

This is not harsh. You are in business to make money for yourself and other people. When people waste your time, it costs you and your partners.

Never let a prospective JV candidate skip your filtering process. Have them complete a questionnaire like the one found in Appendix D. If timing is an issue and you can't conduct a face-to-face meeting, set up a phone appointment so you can go over the questionnaire informally.

Never confuse business with friendship. You can do business with friends, but that is not essential to the JV partnership. Set this relationship table carefully—and early. You want to work with people who want to work with you.

SOPHISTICATED JV INVESTOR INSIGHT

Show me the money!

Work with money partners who can deliver what you need. Self-employed money partners may have more difficulty qualifying for a mortgage, especially if the lender can't reconcile the difference between the income they *say* they can access versus the income they report to the Canada Revenue Agency. If someone claims $12,000 in annual income, they are going to have trouble qualifying for a loan on an investment property.

The same goes for a bad credit report. The bank won't allow someone with a poor credit rating to borrow money. This isn't news. It's business.

Landmine #10—Confusion reigns:
Identify the decision maker

We've all seen the good cop/bad cop routine on television dramas. This is where one officer appears to not care about the suspect being questioned, paving the way for the more compassionate officer to elicit a confession. The same roles play out in real estate transactions with money partners. Here, one partner appears to want to make the deal and then another partner walks in and tears up the deal (hoping for a better offer).

Evasive action

Make sure your filtering process nails down the facts about who has the authority to sign the papers that will get you the money to make a deal happen. Does a spouse need his or her partner's approval? Are there other shareholders you need to bring on board before a deal transpires?

Asking this question in your formal filtering questionnaire ensures a prospect can't claim ignorance down the road.

RICHARD: Well, they can *claim* ignorance, but it won't earn back your respect. Emma and I have run into this problem on more than one occasion, and our approach is pretty simple. Our formal questionnaire asks: *Is there someone in your life who will be participating in your decisions related to investments, and do you expect that person to be named as a beneficiary of the investment?*

Even when a prospect says he or she can make decisions on his or her own, this is a question we ask more than once. And we're upfront about why this is so important. We sometimes tell them about a deal we tried to put together where a spouse objected and the deal fell through. We make it clear that we didn't go back to those prospects with another deal, even though both spouses later let us know they'd be interested. It wasn't about revenge, it was about business. That situation occurred with a couple from our Inner Circle. We didn't want business to get in the way of that relationship—but we also couldn't let that relationship shape our business practices.

EMMA: It was all about trust. Richard and I work really hard to let our partners know they can trust us. We apply that same principle to our partners. If we can't trust you to follow through, we don't want to work with you. It saves us a lot of time.

Landmine #11—Picking the wrong deal:
You invest in the wrong property just to get
a partner on board

Nothing will derail your business plans faster than investing in the wrong property. Believe it or not, this can be easier to do when you have a money partner. Sometimes, the issue is the sheer desirability of the partner himself. Don't let your desire to work with a particular individual cloud your due diligence. There is no question that some partners can make a huge difference to an investor. These folks may have the money and contacts to help you bring deal after deal into your portfolio. Protect that relationship—but not at the expense of the wrong deal!

The other reason people make this mistake is related to greed. The fact that you are working with someone else's money should make you more diligent, not less. Personally, I do more due diligence with JV deals, and I always make sure that the deals I'm offering to co-venturers are deals that I would be willing to invest my own money in even if the partner didn't get involved. I don't want to let the emotional high of closing a deal cloud my judgment. Instead, I focus on the deals that make sense. Remember what I said about my Plan B? If I'm not prepared to swing a deal completely on my own, then it's not a "good enough" deal for me to risk someone else's money. I would never look for a partner to help me finance it.

Evasive action

The "perfect partner" is only perfect when the deal makes sense. Be honest with your prospects about why you want to work with them (e.g., they have the money), but tell them you won't work on a deal that's not a win-win deal for both of you.

Practise the same due diligence when it comes to choosing the deal. I told you how I "qualified" my own mother before we invested together. Because I truly value that relationship, I use it as a kind of measuring stick by asking myself, "Would I put my mother's life savings into this deal?" I encourage you to do the same. In the end, your reputation is your most valuable commodity; a couple of bad deals and you could be done. This is not an area where you make mistakes. It's where you under-promise and over-deliver.

Landmine #12—Not enough information: Your prospect doesn't understand the deal

When a potential money partner turns down a deal, I always ask them what I could have done to get them to say yes. Their responses have taught me the importance of making sure my deals are well understood. Sticking with the principle of attraction versus pursuit, I now know how important it is to "tell, not sell."

Evasive action

Every one of my prospective partners gets a one-page executive summary of the deal we're working on, or a deal I have recently completed. That summary for a completed deal covers the items in the following list.

EXECUTIVE SUMMARY

Profit and loss summary (quarterly and annually)

Cash-flow summary

Balance sheet summary:

>   Assets
>   Liabilities/mortgage
>   Equity
>   Initial investment
>   Joint investor share of gain

Highlights of the past quarter:

>   Profit and loss, and the cash-flow position (positive or negative)
>   Plans such as a property rent increase
>   Summary of any deduction in the mortgage

Economic update:

>   Regional/provincial
>
>>   Four specific items regarding the economic fundamentals of where the property is located
>
>   Local/municipal
>
>>   Key factors impacting the local real estate market

The goal of an executive summary is to provide financial detail without overwhelming your potential partner. This showcases your due diligence and your knowledge of the economic fundamentals.

The table in the appendix of the report you present to your money partner would then detail property cash flow, showing total income, total expenses, net income, total liabilities and total assets, ending with net cash flow. That table would be backed up by media reports that support your position regarding economic fundamentals.

RICHARD: An executive summary lays out the situation for a prospective partner. Here's an example of the property notes and economic updates Emma and I include in the reports we're sending out in 2011.

SAMPLE PROPERTY NOTES AND ECONOMIC UPDATES

Quarter #2 property notes

- Year-to-date [year] making a profit and in a positive cash-flow position.
- Rental income notice has been issued for September.
- New rent will increase $50/month for $1,250/year.
- This year (first 6 months) we have reduced the mortgage balance by more than $1,250.

Economic updates for Alberta [insert your area of expertise]

- Alberta is forecast to lead the country in economic growth.
- The forecasted growth is [X.XX]%.
- That growth will be fuelled by global demand for fuel, food, forestry and fertilizer (petroleum based)
- Forestry is also expected to increase to help rebuild Japan.

Economic updates for Edmonton

- Edmonton housing prices are flat with tremendous future upside potential.
- Even with increases, Edmonton remains one of the most affordable cities in which to own a home.
- The area northeast of Edmonton remains poised for speedy growth. Sometimes known as "upgrader alley," the area is expected to attract more than 80,000 construction workers to complete the upgrades. Most of these workers will be living in Edmonton.

The executive summary on page 240 shows what Richard and Emma know about the property they've invested in and the economic future of the geographic area in which it's located. I call these facts—and that's exactly what potential money partners will be looking for. This summary illustrates the value of relevant economic information. Another way to make sure you cover all of the bases is to use the following graphic and update it with current numbers from the area where you are buying investment property. This information is readily accessible from public sources, and networks like REIN can teach you where to look.

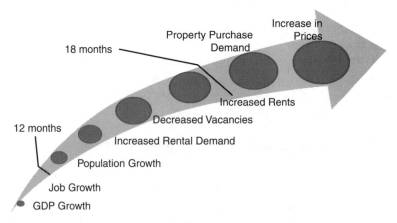

Figure 9.2: Long-Term Real Estate Formula

Landmine #13—The Pollyanna problem: You are overly optimistic and it scares prospective partners

When Don Campbell and I teach novice investors about real estate investing, we often talk about the need to "look behind the curtain." In other words, you never take anything or anyone at face value, but instead ask the tough questions so that you can be sure you've got the best answers. Your business partners will be doing the same and you should plan accordingly.

Evasive action

Be honest about what your partners need to know and then deliver the goods. When working with new investors, part of your role as the real estate expert involves education. You want to teach them how to "look behind the curtain" so that they can see that you know what you're talking about.

Real estate experts who focus on being realistic will deliver more than they promised. One of the easiest ways to deal with this issue is to provide estimates instead of hard numbers.

Landmine #14—Guaranteeing an outcome: You risk your reputation on assurances you can't deliver

There is no such thing as a guaranteed joint-venture real estate investment. I repeat: there is no such thing as a guaranteed joint-venture real estate investment.

JV investors who ignore this landmine are doomed to failure. Human nature is such that if you quote a range of return, people remember the higher number. So if you say the return will be between 8 per cent and 12 per cent, your partner will remember the 12. If you talk cash flow of $50 to $300 a month (which may be reasonable depending on maintenance and repairs), your partner will hear $300. Worse, they will likely do the math and calculate an annual return of $3,600.

Evasive action

Never guarantee numbers. Talk in percentages and be realistic about what can impact those figures. If a potential JV partner wants a guarantee, arrange to take their money as a loan and use it to secure a property. This may mean they'll make 10 per cent interest when they could have owned 50 per cent of the property. That is not your problem. They can't have a guarantee and half the property.

Tom: Robert and I have been running into a bit of this. I like this approach. It allows us to work with a particular investor without sacrificing our interest in the property, which we will manage.

Robert: And that's just the beginning. One prospect we're filtering is investment savvy, but not real estate investment savvy. This is a way to bring him on board, use his money for a win-win deal and teach him that he could have had a bigger piece of the investment pie if he'd come in as a money partner versus a lender. We can use that loan to build our relationship.

Perfect. And you're not sacrificing the win-win part of this equation. A deal isn't necessarily lost when a partner sets terms you can't live with. This is a creative approach to a problem. Some investors find it easier to deal solely with loaned money versus co-ownership. If that's what works for your system, that's okay.

Landmine #15—Stiffed: A JV partner walks out as the deal is ready to close

This is a major frustration and it's not a landmine you can necessarily avoid stepping on at least once in your JV career. Even with the four levels of commitment (a partner's word, cash in your lawyer's trust account, an Expression of Interest Letter and a Letter of Intent), some deals fall off the rails just as you're about to close.

Can you sue them? Maybe. But why would you want to revive a dead deal with a partner you can't trust to meet his end of a bargain? It's probably wiser to put that lesson in the bank and move on.

Evasive action

This is where your Plan B comes into play. Let's say your real estate agent doesn't actually look for a deal until he knows you've got your Letter of Intent along with a partner's word and some cash in trust. And now that agent is frustrated because it looks like the deal can't close. At this point, you may also have talked to other members of your real estate dream team, giving a heads-up warning to everyone from your lawyer to your home inspector and property manager.

Your Plan B should enable you to make the deal regardless of what happens with a particular partner. If you have been cultivating new leads, you may even be able to qualify a different partner and sell them 50 per cent of the property soon after the deal closes. This frees up your cash for the next deal—and your next Plan B backup plan.

For example, with a single-family home, to keep your Plan A option as open as possible, I suggest the cash deposit you request from your money partner be set at $1,000, with another $5,000 due upon removal of conditions on the deal. If your partner backs out before the conditions are met, you can still walk away from the deal and you won't have wasted a lot of your team's time. When potential partners realize they could lose $6,000 if a deal doesn't close with them on board, they are more likely to stay in the deal.

Landmine #16—The weak deal: Your JV agreement is not enforceable

Errors or omissions on your JV agreement can leave you vulnerable and at risk of failure.

Evasive action

This is an area where excuses never fly. You can fix an agreement after a deal closes, but why would you ever put yourself, your partner and your investments in that position? Seek legal counsel early and make sure your JV agreement is thoroughly vetted by your lawyer and an independent lawyer paid for by your money partner.

Use the JV checklist located in Workshop Tutorial #7 as a guide for the information you need to cover. But do not attempt this on your own.

DAN: Remember when I questioned why we needed a JV agreement with our daughter? Following Don Campbell's advice, Carol and I took the JV checklist to our daughter. We went over the details after we'd worked through the background check. She's a business woman and it turns out she was *expecting* a formal legal document as a prerequisite to us buying property together. I felt kind of silly.

Great story! Truly, the best way to avoid this landmine is to make sure you never let anything get in the way of seeking quality legal advice. That document is your single greatest asset to keeping a deal on track. This is where your due diligence heads off potential problems long before they ever materialize. This is where you plan the divorce ahead of time.

Landmine #17—Sacrificing legal diligence: You don't insist your JV partner get independent legal advice

Smart real estate investors don't like to waste money. But they don't cut corners that will cost them later.

Evasive action

Refuse to deal with a potential money partner who will not get independent legal advice on your JV agreement. You are the real estate expert, but your partners should want to understand how the deal works to protect their interests. They should be reading all the information you forward, and they should understand what they are signing.

If a partner simply refuses to get independent legal counsel, have them sign a document that states that they were advised to do this and opted out.

Landmine #18—Keeping secrets: You don't provide full disclosure to your lender and lawyer

This landmine is way too common. In addition to giving lenders and lawyers the wrong information, real estate investors are prone to leaving things out. This is not the way you want to conduct a professional real estate investment business—especially when you are using other people's money.

Evasive action

Information changes as real estate deals progress. That's no excuse for not making sure lenders and lawyers know exactly what you're dealing with. The documents you use to get lender pre-approval and then qualify for a mortgage with must be kept up to date. Anything less could constitute mortgage fraud.

Be cautious. Make sure your lender and lawyer know about changes, including the addition of new names to a mortgage application. These changes could alter the way you structure a deal (especially if a partner has trouble qualifying for a mortgage), and that may not be a decision a lender allows without input.

Always disclose changes as early as possible, since last-minute changes are likely to boost your legal fees and will most definitely annoy your lawyer.

Where a partner's participation is questionable, use "nominee" language to close the deal and then add the partner later (with full disclosure and approval by all parties involved).

Landmine #19—Poor communications: You don't provide quality communication to your JV partner

One of the main reasons JV deals encounter problems is that the real estate expert doesn't provide the communication the money partner wants. It's great to work with money partners who don't want a hands-on role in the deal; these people are attracted to joint ventures by the real estate expert's knowledge and the deals he or she proposes.

But you should expect your partners to ask questions—and they should expect answers. Remember, this is a relationship and that demands a commitment to two-way communication. There's a very good chance a new partner will ask a lot of questions precisely because they don't know the answers. They're seeking information, not trouble.

Evasive action

Real estate experts who want JV partners for their deals will always be cultivating new leads. But they also know that it is easier to work with existing partners and that these people are your best leads to new partners.

Make it your business to address issues upfront. Send your partners regular updates on the investment and on the economic fundamentals of the places you're investing in. Why risk an opportunity to let them know how well you know the business of real estate investment? Use regular communications as a way to remind them of why you are good at what you do.

Landmine #20—You sell yourself short

Real estate experts make this mistake when they fail to address all that they bring to an investment deal. This is how you end up owning less than your "fair share" of a property, or making other concessions you will regret.

The graphic on the next page comes from Strategic Real Estate Solutions (www.strategicrealestatesolutions.ca). It is a powerful reminder of why real estate experts are worth at least 50 per cent of a deal, and I sometimes show it to prospective co-venturers who may think that they can question my value as part of a negotiating strategy.

Evasive action

If you are not sure what you bring to a real estate investment deal or are unclear about all of the relationships you manage, deconstruct a deal. Write down every person you dealt with, from your real estate agent to your lawyer, home inspector and insurance agent and all of the assistants in between. Now calculate how often you phoned, e-mailed or met with them. Do you think this makes you worth 50 per cent of the deal?

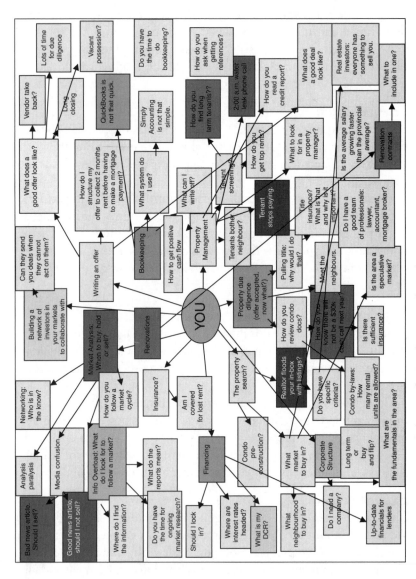

Figure 9.3: Responsibilities of a Sophisticated Real Estate Investor

The Take-Home Lesson: Take Responsibility for Your Deals

Sophisticated real estate investors set themselves up as real estate experts—and deliver on what that promises. The bad thing about investment landmines is that they can annihilate your deals and reputation. The good thing about landmines is that other investors have already stepped on them. Adopt a good system and you can learn from the mistakes of others.

Workshop Action Step: Walk in the Footsteps of Giants: Learn How to Avoid JV Landmines

Real estate investors make mistakes, but they do not need to make every mistake on their own. Commit to learning from the successes and errors of successful real estate investors already using joint-venture capital for their deals. Review the following rules of engagement and make positive action your focus!

Rules of engagement

1. Step carefully.
   - Every road has potential landmines.
   - The landmines can be revealed, but not removed.
2. Value experience over novelty.
   - Learn where the successful have gone before and follow their lead.
   - Study failure and emulate success.
   - Be creative when it works but innovate only when it equals win-win for you and your JV partners.
3. Get a good map.
   - Real estate investment is not a race, and success demands a long-term and "big picture" view of the world.
   - Rewards come to those who do the extra 10 per cent.
   - That extra 10 per cent includes following the clues left by investors with experience.
   - Detours aren't a problem unless they become an excuse for not taking action.

JV ACTION PLAN STEP #13

Avoid the landmines.

The 20 landmines just reviewed showcase the kinds of common—but preventable—mistakes investors make with JV deals. The following boils the list down to the top five steps to take to avoid landmines with JV deals. Review them and be ready to discuss in more detail.

THE TOP 5 STEPS JV INVESTORS CAN TAKE TO AVOID LANDMINES

1. Adopt a proven investment system.
2. Always create the win-win deal.
3. Choose the right JV candidates.
4. Pick the right deals.
5. Seek solid legal advice early and often.

JV ACTION PLAN STEP #14

Taking responsibility means taking action.

What is the number one mistake made by novice JV investors? Failure to act.

This occurs whenever an investor fails to take action when action is warranted. That mistake is compounded if a fear of failure is used as an excuse to prevent you from making or closing a deal.

So be honest. If the fear of failure is holding you back, look at what you need to do to turn that around. Step carefully, value experience over novelty and get a good map—but do move forward!

TUTORIAL: THE TOP 5 STEPS TO AVOIDING LANDMINES 9

WORKSHOP RECAP:

Learn to avoid JV landmines.
Taking responsibility means taking action.

Presenter: Don Campbell

This is one of my favourite topics. I don't like that it talks about pending disasters. I like that it talks about ways to avoid disaster, and that's what sophisticated real estate investment is all about. We take action based on proven investment systems. We get creative about making deals work—but only when that makes sense. Most of the time, we can find success simply by following the road most taken.

So forgive me if this seems a little repetitious, but I've seen the damage these landmines can do to an investor's portfolio and reputation.

THE TOP 5 STEPS JV INVESTORS CAN TAKE TO AVOID LANDMINES

1. Adopt a proven investment system.
2. Always create the win-win deal.
3. Choose the right JV candidates.
4. Pick the right deals.
5. Seek solid legal advice early and often.

---

1. ADOPT A PROVEN INVESTMENT SYSTEM

Sophisticated real estate investors aren't lucky; they're smart. Make it your business to learn from their successes and failures. The bottom line is that proven real estate investment systems are systems with a solid history of success. Investors follow these systems precisely because they know they work.

This is a complicated business with a lot of moving parts. The ACRE system gives you a way to deal with all of those parts. It helps you analyze what properties to buy, figure out where to put your money in terms of renovations and repairs, choose quality tenants and negotiate with lenders and vendors. This is all stuff you can learn to do on your own—but why would you reinvent a wheel that's already fully operational and moving in the right direction?

2. Always Create the Win-Win Deal

This is a big one, and I know it's a topic Russell and I have emphasized over and over again. We do that because it's a common mistake, and a mistake no one should be making. Successful real estate investors know they make money when they buy investment property. That's because they buy the right property at the right price, and make sure it fits their investment plan and exit strategy.

The "right deal" is even more important when money partners are involved. Never forget that your reputation as an investor will be strengthened by deals that make you and your partners money. But you will not be able to work with every partner who comes your way, and you should never pursue the wrong deal in a vain attempt to secure a partner, or vice versa.

If this ever confuses you, focus on what win-win means: wealth creation.

3. Choose the Right JV Candidates

This problem presents itself in many forms, since the wrong candidate may not have the money, mindset or integrity to bring to your JV deal. You avoid this obstruction with due diligence that thoroughly vets your partners.

Richard: Emma and I shared an example of this in the last workshop. We were working with a partner we thought we had vetted thoroughly, but we didn't have a clear answer on the question: *Is there someone in your life who will be participating in your decisions related to investments, and do you expect that person to be named as a beneficiary of the investment?*

We lost a deal because it turned out our partner needed his wife's approval to proceed with the mortgage application, and he didn't have it. It would be easy to blame him and his arrogance or duplicity. But the problem was us. We were required to do the due diligence, and we didn't.

Robert: Tom and I ran into a similar problem. In retrospect, we were chasing the money and let that focus compromise our due diligence on the deal. In this case it was a Level 2 contact through our other business dealings. Based on what we knew, this guy had everything. As we are looking to put together some buy-and-hold deals on properties that needed some renovations, we were especially pleased with the guy's renovation and construction experience.

TOM: We were worried that we might miss out on the guy and his money because he made it sound like he was looking at several JV deals. He also told us that he had $100,000 ready to invest, and he was pretty clear about the fact that it was his money to invest. But then we found out that the biggest "win-win" part of this JV deal wasn't going to work out. It turned out his construction experience included a history of over-promising and under-delivering.

ROBERT: The guy got caught up in the last real estate boom and faltered. He's got projects with long lists of construction and reno deficiencies. The cash flow part of our deals means we need to be able to put renovated properties on the market within specific time frames. It turns out we can't afford to take this guy's money!

What a great lesson. I often meet novice investors who tell me they can afford to carry properties that cost them money every month. Sophisticated real estate investors call these deals "alligators," because they'll eat you alive. I get that property appreciation is a major reason why real estate investment makes long-term sense. But get real. You are working with borrowed money that will have to be paid back. How much money can you afford to lose before you can't afford to keep investing?

A lack of commitment

Not choosing the right partner can also lead to issues with partner commitment. This is a brutal thing to experience no matter how long you've been investing. Due diligence will help you figure out if the partner you're considering has the money and desire to invest in your deals. It will clear up questions about whether this individual can deliver his part of the deal. *Filter. Filter. Filter.* And if you run into a problem that your filter did not help you identify, make sure you cover that issue the next time you qualify an investor.

Even the best filters may qualify an individual who then backs out of a deal. Stuff happens. Circumstances change. When possible, move to your Plan B so a deal can proceed. If the deal makes sense, you can always qualify a different partner later.

Communicate. Communicate. Communicate.

Solid communication will help you choose the right JV partner and close deals with the right JV partner. The JV agreement acts as a kind of legal guide, giving both parties access to a document that spells out your expectations. But closing the deal is just the first step. To make sure that JV partners will do business with you again, and that they will help you cultivate new leads, you need to nurture this relationship.

4. Pick the Right Deals

Never joint venture with someone in a deal in which you would not invest your own money upfront. This principle is as straightforward as it gets. As Russell likes to say, "Would I risk my own mother's life savings in this deal?" If the answer is no, then walk away.

Susan: Walk away *fast*. I'm still figuring out my first JV deal, and even though my filtering process is taking longer than expected, I'm getting a really good education about the due diligence required to adequately filter your JV partners. Last week, another real estate expert approached me with news about a deal she was putting together. I was secretly honoured to be considered—and that burst of ego almost cost me $50,000.

At first glance, the deal looked solid. She had a lead on a condo that was seriously underpriced, and she was talking about buying a bunch of similar properties. It looked like a fast way to build my portfolio really quickly. But then I drove by the place. It's in an up-and-coming neighbourhood, but almost half the units are up for sale and they are undervalued because they haven't been well maintained. Worse yet, the building beside it has a problem with squatters and a reputation with the police.

I know that some investors can take a deal like this and make it work. But I can't. I don't have the time or experience to turn a building around—and neither did my prospective partner. In the end, I felt like she was reaching for a rung on a ladder that was, at best, precariously positioned. She was so focused on price she was willing to ignore her proven investment system. I'm not.

The whole point of these filters is that they prevent problems. Real estate investment is all about long-term wealth creation, and there is always an element of financial risk involved with investing. That risk is mitigated by due diligence, and due diligence, including the filters you apply to potential JV partners, is all about avoiding problems that will cost you money. Susan's example illustrates what could happen if you fail to recognize that a bad deal is being sold as a good deal. But the problem with being "too optimistic" doesn't just apply to a bad deal someone else is selling you.

Even good deals have risk. It's your job to manage that risk, and to be realistic about what it means. As people tend to remember the highest numbers you cite, I recommend that you work with estimates instead of hard numbers. And honesty is always the best policy, but that's complicated because your co-venturers may not know very much about what's involved with managing a property. Let's look at what's involved in the total expenses line of a real estate investment.

TOTAL EXPENSES

Real estate expenses include the following:

Advertising

Appraisals

Banking

Closing costs

Condo fees

Insurance

Interest/mortgage payments

Legal costs

Maintenance costs/fees

Miscellaneous

Property management

Property taxes

Repairs

Taxes

Utilities

Vacancy loss

At this point in my investing career, my preferred partners are all very hands-off investors. They want the big picture, not the nitty-gritty. That won't be the case for investors who are just starting out. Your partners will want details. But building on what Emma just told us, those details may not make them feel better! Win-win deals will win them over in the long run. But if you're working with someone who's new to real estate investment, you can expect a lot of questions about the details.

It may seem like your partners don't trust you now that their money is already invested. What's really happening is that they are learning the business, and it's your job to help them understand you and the deal.

5. Seek Solid Legal Advice
Early and Often

Problems arise when JV deals are not based on a thorough and enforceable JV agreement that's both legal and binding. I don't even want to hear horror stories of real estate investors who tried to buy properties with partners without a legally binding Joint-Venture Agreement. To me, this discounts any pretension that you are a real estate investment *expert*.

I have that same frustration when I hear about deals where the partners did not provide full disclosure to the lender and lawyer involved. I know that deals change. Partners back out of deals, financial numbers change when closing conditions are altered (i.e., the cost of a new roof is deducted from the sale price after the vendor and buyer review a home inspection report).

What never changes is the truth. Regardless of what state a real estate market is in, fraud abounds. Don't do business with anyone who asks you to sign a legal document that includes false information. Everyone is *not* doing it. The crooks are—and they *will* get caught.

SOPHISTICATED JV INVESTOR INSIGHT

Risk and reward

There is no magic to real estate investing, but hard work is required. That hard work also mitigates the risks involved with a business that teems with long-term reward.

You can have a formal Joint-Venture Agreement in place when a deal closes, or suffer the consequences later. The choice is yours. If you call that a choice.

—Michael Ponte

Background

Michael Ponte lives in British Columbia, but his real estate holdings are all in the Edmonton area, where the economic fundamentals are a good fit with an investment plan that targets buy-and-hold properties in cities with strong rental markets.

Six years after he bought his first property in 2005, Michael is holding over 60 doors with close to 20 different partners. All of his doors are residential and multi-family properties. Most of his partners are repeat customers, a testament to a business plan that views every new partner as a long-term financial friend of the business. "I see my partners as 30-year investments. I want to exit deals that have matured, and then close new deals with the same money partners."

To do that, Michael invests a lot of time in managing his deals—and communicating with his co-venturers about their investments. "Once I've got a property in my system, I have an investor relationship to nurture. I call each of my partners once a month to let them know that I'm here and working for them. I tell them what's happening with the property and let them know that I am watching their money by keeping a close eye on the business. I also send out a monthly newsletter and I meet with my partners, in person, on a quarterly basis. That's where we conduct a detailed financial review of the property to track how the investment is performing," says Michael.

He admits that some other investors discount the need to spend so much time communicating with their partners. Michael disagrees. "My feeling is I'm competing with stock brokers and mutual fund advisors for investment dollars. I've looked at what they do to build relationships with their clients and I want to differentiate myself by providing a higher quality and more personal experience for my clients. I am serious about making money in real estate investment, and I build credibility with my partners when I show them what I'm doing to add value to our shared investments. This is how I build confidence for future deals."

That credibility and confidence aside, Michael also knows what it's like to make mistakes. In particular, he's learned what can go wrong when you don't have a formal Joint-Venture Agreement in place, or when you hire the wrong property managers. Here's what Michael has to say about the hard lessons he's learned at the helm of his company, Prosperity Real Estate Investments. Better yet, here's what he says about how other investors can avoid his mistakes!

Start with Who You Know

I like what Russell Westcott teaches about finding money partners, be they co-venturers or financial backers, by focusing on the people you know best. Like a lot of new investors, my wife, Dawn, and I ran out of money after we bought our first three properties. Because we wanted to keep investing, we started talking about what we were doing, and our first partners were my dad and my brother.

Develop Your Own JV Investor Profile

In addition to investing, I teach seminars on how to invest in real estate. It took me some time to realize that those seminars were expanding our Inner Circle. It turns out that a lot of the people who are in my seminars fit our JV investor profile. They have money to invest, and they like real estate, but they don't have the time or knowledge to put together and manage actual deals.

After they learn how my business works, some of them approach me to ask if they can co-venture with me. They may have come to my seminar thinking they needed to be the real estate expert, only to realize that maybe they could venture with someone else instead. In all cases, I'm honest about what I do and what I plan to do, and I tell them why I need their money. I also show them what I do to treat my JV partners' money as if it's all the money these people have.

Always Have a Legal Agreement

I'd probably done four or five JV deals before I ran into any trouble with a partner. In hindsight, the experience taught me that I needed to fine-tune my screening process to make sure I was working with the right people. The synergies you create with a partnership are a lot like a marriage, so it's important to work with people who share similar investing goals as you do.

In this case, I got caught up in the excitement of finding a partner, and I wasn't clear enough with my new partner on how the investment worked. He did tell me that he wanted to learn how to invest in real estate and that he wanted a role in managing this property. I underestimated what that meant.

We divided up the roles and went from there, but it turned out that only one of us knew—and was prepared to do—what the investment needed to work. In other words, giving up certain responsibilities for that property was a mistake because it compromised the investment.

Moving forward, I tell investors to make sure that they and their partners understand the deal the same way. This partner and I were able to move on from that experience, and we still invest together, but our relationship was rocky for awhile, and I know that the problem could have been avoided.

Unfortunately, I compounded the problem by not having a formal Joint-Venture Agreement that we could call upon to deal with any issues. I had a letter of commitment, but was wrong to think that was enough. In hindsight, that was really short-sighted because the letter didn't offer enough clarity.

I now insist on a formal JV agreement that establishes me as the real estate expert and the other party as the financial contributor. I explain how that protects both our interests. When deals go the way everyone wants them to go, you never have to reference a JV agreement. As long as it's in place, it will spell out exactly what happens if a partnership isn't working.

LEARN FROM YOUR MISTAKES

That situation was really troubling, and its resolution took a lot of energy I could have spent somewhere else. It also made me rethink the fact that I did not have formal partnership agreements for any of the properties I own with my dad and brother. Even though those deals worked out, not having a formal JV agreement was a mistake.

We now have that extra layer of protection, and I wouldn't do any new deal without it. It's good for each of us to know that there is a formal process we can follow if something changes and one partner needs or wants out of a deal sooner than expected.

Seek Legal Counsel

That experience also taught me an important lesson about making sure my deals and JV agreements are vetted through a lawyer and that my investors also seek independent legal counsel. If I had a prospect I really wanted to work with and he said the legal costs were the only thing standing in the way of a completed deal, I would offer to pay those costs. At this point in a deal, I would know that I really wanted to work with this person. As I want to work with this person again and again, I wouldn't let a few hundred dollars stand in the way of us building a long-term investment relationship.

Establish Impeccable Property Management

Property management is the other area where I've learned my biggest lessons. While property managers aren't partners in your business, they are critical members of your investment team and you can't underestimate their role.

Because my properties are not located in my home province, it's really important that I work with property managers I can trust. I've also learned that if I'm serious about managing my investments, I have to be serious about managing my managers!

Since I started investing in real estate in 2005, I have fired three property management companies. Those experiences served as good reminders that I always need to be looking for ways to strengthen my investment team with new members. You never know when you might need a new property manager, real estate agent or another member of your team.

Today, I work with two property management firms in Edmonton. That gives me some leverage as they know I don't have all of my eggs in one basket.

WORKSHOP: DUPLICATING SUCCESS | *10*

We are what we repeatedly do. Excellence, then, is not an act, but a habit.
—Aristotle

WORKSHOP OVERVIEW

Presenter: Russell Westcott

**Do I have all the money I need to buy all the property
I need to achieve my Personal Belize?**

I love asking that question because I know it's a question serious real estate investors ask themselves over and over again. As long as the answer is no, these investors will see the question as a call to action. That no is the reason they keep investing, and it's the reason they continually seek and nurture relationships with joint-venture partners.

This workshop is the last in a series of 10 workshops that walked you through a proven process that sophisticated real estate investors use to close deals with money partners. Some of those people will co-own investment property with you. Others will lend you money to buy revenue property. Here, we review what successful real estate investors do to make sure they can duplicate their success. It's all about the practical systems and follow-through or action they put in place as they build relationships that generate long-term wealth.

Before we jump into the topic of follow-up and duplication, I want to show you how these 10 workshops can be boiled down to a checklist of what I call the seven steps that unlock the vault of JV secrets. Let's review those steps. Pay particular attention to the way each step requires real estate investors to take responsibility for their business goals.

THE 7 STEPS THAT UNLOCK THE VAULT OF JV SECRETS

1. Understand why you want JV money.
- Ask yourself the question: Why do I want JV money?
- Tell yourself it's because you don't yet have all the money you need to buy all the property you need to achieve your Personal Belize!

2. Become a student of the principles of JV wealth attraction.

- Learn how to be a money magnet for your JV deals.
- Commit to the principles of JV wealth attraction: Attraction versus Pursuit, Abundance, Expectancy, Imagination, Giving, Decisiveness, Expertise and Resiliency.

3. Learn how and where to find JV investors.

- Map and explore your joint venture Circle of Influence.
- Focus on your Inner Circle/Level 1 contacts first.
- Find ways to help those Level 1 individuals put you in contact with Level 2 candidates.
- Be honest about the risks associated with Level 3 prospects.

4. Learn how to structure JV deals.

- Establish yourself as the real estate expert on your deals.
- Decide how you will structure ownership to create win-win deals for you and your investors.

5. Make sure your real estate team includes a good lawyer and tax accountant.

- Get legal help to write legally binding and enforceable Joint-Venture Agreements.
- Insist that your partners seek independent legal advice.
- Discuss deals with your tax accountant to optimize your tax situation.

6. Learn how to successfully close JV deals (and how to avoid common pitfalls).

- Filter potential partners and practise due diligence to avoid problems closing deals.

7. Practise success with systems that foster follow-up and duplication.

- Take responsibility for your due diligence. Errors will cost you.
- Keep developing new leads for potential money partners.

Practice Makes Perfect

The most important thing to remember about these seven steps is that they lead to success; they help you identify and work with JV partners to build a solid portfolio of real estate investment property. Following them also makes it easier for you to repeat success. Believe it or not, real estate investors who use other people's money in their deals will tell you that once you get some experience with money partners, it will be easier to find partners than properties. I know that catches a lot of you by surprise, but it will make more sense as you bring partners into your deals.

NOLAN: I'm already surprised by what's happening to me! First my parents and one brother expressed interest, and then two of my other brother's friends approached me. I am working with them on a deal for half a duplex, and we expect it to close in about a week. They are all about letting me be the real estate expert, and that's giving me an opportunity to practise everything I've been learning. I can see how these two guys can help me find other money partners, so I'm working really hard to avoid any problems. "Under-promise, over-deliver"—that's my working mantra!

Instead of moving ahead on a deal with my parents, they've agreed to be my Plan B financial partners in the event the deal with my brother's friends doesn't close. That has two benefits. First, it backs up my purchase if something goes wrong with my partners, and second, the sooner I close this deal without my parents' money, the sooner I can start looking for another deal with them as my partners.

RICHARD: Emma and I actually keep that list of seven steps posted on the bulletin board in our home office. It reminds us of what we have to do and how much we know. With a portfolio of five properties with four partners and more coming on stream, there are times when we have to be reminded about why we do what we do and why it's so important to stick with our systems.

Built-in Flexibility

Richard's point is important for two reasons. Following a proven system requires that we find ways to keep that system on track. If you want to create long-term wealth with real estate investment, you buy properties that help you do that. But the system doesn't stop there. It gives us a way to re-evaluate individual properties, relationships with money partners, etc. In this way, our commitment to a system provides a kind of built-in follow-up process that duplicates success. It doesn't sacrifice flexibility, but it does keep us moving in the right direction.

Let's say you've qualified a money partner, have a deal ready to go and your partner has taken your JV Agreement to an independent lawyer. This is fabulous as it looks like you're about to close on a deal with a money partner already signed up. But can you buy the property before you have a JV partner? If the property fits your system, the only answer is yes. When you buy real estate using joint ventures, you can line up the right money and then buy the right property, or line up the right property and then find the right partner.

What you can't do is ignore the fact that the second approach will add stress to your life—even if the property meets the needs of your system. This is especially true if you're working with an underdeveloped list of prospective co-venturers and you have to scramble to qualify a partner. Again, either strategy is workable, but there are implications.

SOPHISTICATED JV INVESTOR INSIGHT

Know your limitations

Stress contributes to sleepless nights—and mistakes you regret. While it's never too late to add partners to a real estate deal, it's far less stressful to qualify your partners for a deal before any property changes hands. Ditto for the Joint-Venture Agreement. You and your partners can work out the details after a deal is closed. It is much better to complete the mutual JV Agreement first.

GET YOUR DEAL STRAIGHT

One of the reasons novice investors run into problems with their follow-up communication is that they aren't clear on their investment strategy, so they get confused about how they are supposed to follow up and duplicate. In other words, they know they want to build long-term wealth through real estate investment but they don't narrow down the specifics of how they will do that.

I tell investors to focus on a strategy that fits the time frame that works for them and their partners.

WHAT'S YOUR INVESTMENT TIME FRAME?

1. Short term (<1 year): flips, bridge financing, loans, renovations
2. Medium term (1 to 3 years): buy and hold, lease-to-own
3. Long term (>5 years): long-term buy and hold

ROBERT: What Russell just said makes complete sense. It also explains why Tom and I have been feeling a great deal of stress—and like we didn't have a clue about real estate investment. I now see that we've been looking at *every* deal that was coming our way, and that's ridiculous because we only want to focus on long-term investments. That's the area where our real estate and renovation expertise is going to be a boon to our partners.

You're not the first investors to see how important it is to have a plan. And let me be clear. Some sophisticated investors spend their entire real estate careers focused on one category of investment. Others diversify, or switch between the categories. When you're starting out, it's way better to become an expert in one category. That approach will also help you identify and then match specific investors to your strategy. If I know that I want to buy-and-hold a property for more than five years, I don't need to do the due diligence to qualify an investor who wants his money out in three. Similarly, if a potential money partner is looking for a quick return on his investment, I shouldn't waste his time—or my time—trying to get him interested in a property that cash flows $200 to $300 a month.

EMMA: Richard and I learned that the hard way, too. One of the JV deals we still hold ran into some trouble about a year ago. Even though one of our JV agreements was pretty clear about how one of our long-term buy-and-hold deals worked, this guy was like a thorn in our sides about cash flow. In the early days, when the cheques for this single-family home with a suited basement were going out every month, he was relatively happy, but he was also sure the cheques were too low.

Then we had a few months with the basement suite vacant, followed by a repair bill for an unexpected plumbing issue with the mainfloor bathroom. Our relationship with this partner was almost unbearable. The JV agreement spelled out a long-term commitment to this property, but after three years, he was second-guessing everything we did.

RICHARD: In retrospect, the issue was education. Although we haven't exited the property yet, a combination of cash flow and appreciation shows the deal has made him more than $50,000 in six years. After we pulled out the JV agreement and looked at our options for his early exit, he took a closer look at the numbers. That helped him see what he would be giving up and that's when he really understood what long-term buy-and-hold meant. That was a good reminder about why we need to be really clear about what our *long-term* strategy means. In fact, we use that story when we're talking to potential money partners because it illustrates that we know what we're doing.

That's a great example of why it's so important to keep those lines of communication open, even when a partner appears to have a penchant for "selective hearing" on something as straightforward as the time frame linked to your investment strategy. As long as you have a solid JV agreement in place, you can keep doing what you're doing in terms of managing a property, regardless of what your money partner might be telling you to do. But it's a tough go when the guy who's causing you grief is from your Level 1 or 2 contacts.

DAN: This is really interesting in light of what Carol and I experienced with one of our daughters. Remember when I said I was reluctant to suggest a formal JV agreement. Well I wasn't just reluctant, I was afraid that this particular daughter would see this request as a lack of confidence in our relationship.

CAROL: Then our daughter surprised us both by asking Dan why he was avoiding the subject and why he seemed to be suggesting a formal legal agreement wasn't necessary. It turns out she was reading everything we'd sent her way about sophisticated real estate investing with JV partners and she couldn't believe we would ever invest without a solid JV agreement. She'd even discussed this with her lawyer and had decided to walk away from a deal if we weren't prepared to sign a formal Joint-Venture Agreement.

Your example showcases the value of helping potential investors understand your investment strategies and why you do the things you do. It's also a good reminder of the hazards associated with not sticking to a proven strategy. This potential deal involved a family member and I know that some investors believe you can break the rules when you're working with family. I am definitely not one of those people and would encourage you to follow my lead.

As I see it, the second you start to think that you need to modify your system to accommodate the needs of a particular partner, you are rowing directly toward trouble! I never want to have to go back to a JV agreement and figure out what to do if a deal goes off the tracks. But it's great to know that JVA is in place—regardless of whether my link to a co-venturer started with blood or business.

CAROL: Dan and I are starting to think a formal JVA may be even more important with family! At this point, it looks like only one of our kids is interested in buying real estate with us. That formal agreement makes it very clear that this relationship is "all business." I like the clear boundaries.

BUYING STRATEGIES

Your approach to real estate investing with money partners can be as simple or complicated as you want. Here is a look at what how one investor manages 14 properties with four money partners.

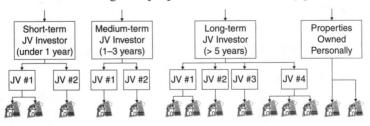

Figure 10.1: 14 Properties

PUT FOLLOW-UP IN ACTION

This is probably a good time to tell you that one of my weaknesses is following up with my co-venturers. I know that these people are the best source of money for my next deal. They either want in on another deal, or can refer me to someone who does. Still, it's an area where I've fallen short over the years. Because of that, I have developed a template that enables me to contact these individuals more often. My primary goal in developing this template is to optimize my ability to find out how I can better meet the needs of my money partners.

Pick a timeline

Before you develop your investor follow-up package, decide whether you will follow up with a co-venturer on a monthly, quarterly or annual basis. That timeline should be stipulated in your JV agreement. If it's not, write an addendum that you and your co-venturer both initial. This timeline can change over time but be sure to clear any changes with your partner.

> Well-established JV relationships get less of my time. Depending on the nature of the deal and my relationship with that individual, these contacts may be quarterly, semi-annually or annually. As long as the investment is performing to expectations, less is more when it comes to communicating with money partners with whom you have already developed a strong relationship.

YOUR FOLLOW-UP TEMPLATE

Cover letter

Executive summary

- Profit and loss summary
- Cash flow summary
- Balance sheet summary (optional)

Property cash flow statement

Good news articles (maximum of four)

Cover letter

Here is an example of the kind of follow-up cover letter I send to my JV partners. Note that it's headlined "Sophisticated Investor." You want to establish your role as the real estate expert. Don't just list your name, include a title: Sophisticated Investor, Real Estate Investor, Real Estate Expert.

Also pay close attention to how the letter focuses on the "good news" details of the property, and then concludes with a pitch for a new investment. The money partner receiving the letter has already had a phone call about the next deal, and this note confirms that the real estate expert wants to continue to do business with him.

> Sophisticated Investor
> Address
> Anytown, Canada

DATE

Joe Investor
Address
Anytown, Canada

Re: Q3 2010 Property Update Great news!

Dear Joe:

As per our agreement, please find enclosed the quarterly details of the property that we own in [insert town]. To date, this property has far exceeded our estimated projections. As you remember when we first entered into our joint-venture partnership, we factored in a 3 per cent per year growth model. To date, this property has increased by more than $40,000 ($200,000 Value minus $160,000 Purchase Price), and your share of the estimated increase is approximately $18,850.

Based on your initial investment of only $36,000, it looks like you have made a total return of about 51 per cent on your investment. I trust you are happy with the return to date. As you read through the attached documents, you will see that the forecasted growth is not to let up for the next five or more years.

As always, you have my direct phone number. If you need any further information or clarifications, please do not hesitate to call me directly.

Best regards,

[Your name]

Sophisticated Investor
Telephone:
E-mail:
Website:

P.S. As per our conversation earlier this week, I will be sending you over more information as to our next property purchase in [insert town], closing shortly. I look forward to working with you on this upcoming property purchase.

Executive summary

I like to include a colour photograph of the property with the financial details of the executive summary on the back side of that page. A picture is worth a thousand words and an up-to-date picture of a great-looking property is exactly the kind of thing a money partner may show off to business contacts, family and friends.

That cover letter, along with a great-looking photograph of the property, provide a good introduction to the dry facts of the executive summary, which should include a profit and loss summary like the one noted here.

SAMPLE EXECUTIVE SUMMARY

Profit and loss summary:
- Quarter $760
- YTD $2,280

Cash flow summary:
- Quarter $361
- YTD $1,047

Balance sheet summary:
- Assets $200,000
- Liabilities/mortgage $126,300
- Equity $73,700
- Initial investment $36,000
- J.V. share of gain (50%) $18,850

SOPHISTICATED JV INVESTOR INSIGHT

Keep it short

Keep your executive summary to one page. Include a profit and loss summary like the one above and property notes and economic updates as per those noted on pages 240 and 241 in Workshop #9. This may be the only page your co-investor reads in detail.

Property cash flow statement

The property cash flow statement that follows your executive summary does not have to be a copy of the detailed one the real estate expert needs to keep track of the profit and loss (P&L) details. Below is a sample of the information you must include on what I call a "top line" P&L statement. A more detailed statement can be found on www.jvsecrets.ca. Regardless of how you set up this statement, it must cover the fundamentals. Total income, for example, has to include real estate income, capital gains and rent. Total expenses must include all of the following real estate expenses.

Advertising

Appraisals

Banking

Closing costs

Condo fees

Insurance

Interest on the mortgage

Legal costs

Maintenance costs

Miscellaneous

Property management

Property taxes

Repairs

Taxes

Utilities

Vacancy loss

This statement must also include net income (total income minus total expenses), total liabilities (mortgage and mortgage principal reduction) and total assets (investment capital including cash deposits, property improvements and real estate investments). These are the numbers you need to provide a net cash flow summary for your partner.

NOLAN: At first, this piece of the follow-up package really scared me. It looked so complicated. But now I get it. If I'm serious about helping my money partners generate long-term wealth, I've got to be serious about my commitment to showing them how I am making that possible. The executive summary is great because it provides the highlights and a sense of the economic fundamentals behind my decisions. But the property cash flow statement is extremely useful and valuable because it shows details.

A lot of new money partners will look at the balance sheet summary on the executive summary and ask why it has the purchase price and doesn't reflect appreciation. That decision reflects your interest in dealing with what's happening right now. When it comes to the balance sheet, you are dealing with facts.

Your knowledge of the market may lead you to suggest an alternate exit strategy. But that's not the job of the executive summary!

Stress the fundamentals

Remember that you are the real estate expert, and many of your co-venturers will be looking to you for information about why their investment is a win-win for both of you. Present credible and supportable articles from sources such as the Canadian Mortgage and Housing Corporation (CMHC) and the banks or real estate investment research organizations to draw your co-investor's attention to some key economic fundamentals about the market you are investing in. In effect, these articles educate money partners about the real estate market and your superior knowledge of that market.

THE TAKE-HOME LESSON: MAKE IT YOUR BUSINESS TO KNOW THE MARKET

Successful real estate investors make it their business to know what's happening in the market in which they're investing. That's even more important when you're using other people's money! Keep a file of articles you can use in your follow-up packages. If a particular article is available online, consider sending it to your money partners via e-mail with a quick note that say you thought they'd be interested in what the article has to say.

I think you all understand why this follow-up package is so important to your business. This is a great way to keep in touch with your co-venturers, and it is the best way to get existing money partners interested in your next deal. In sum, always offer your next property deal to existing JV partners first. If they aren't interested, they might know somebody who is. Be clear about your strategy and your timelines. It is always easier to work with the right person on the right deal!

If you are unable to purchase another property with an existing partner, move on and find a new partner. It really is that easy.

Workshop Action Step: Follow-Up Communication Is Key

Sophisticated investors do not delegate the responsibility of regular follow-up communication with their co-investors. Once you develop a template for this follow-up, apply it to each and every purchase involving other people's money. Duplication is about repeating what works.

If an existing money partner wants in on your next deal, look at whether that deal applies the same purchase model and investing strategies, including whether it's a short-, medium- or long-term investment. If the deals are similar, you do not have to write a new JV agreement. Instead, add an addendum to your existing agreement.

Again, duplicate success. Do not skip the step that requires legal advice for you and independent legal advice for your money partner. You do not need to reinvent a JV agreement for each deal. You do need to duplicate your due diligence strategies.

JV ACTION PLAN STEP #15

Learn the top nine ways to duplicate your business success.

Quality duplication is all about systemizing your business to have an endless supply of JV partners. The tutorial for this workshop is going to focus on the systems you need to have in place to make sure you accurately track business data on a timely basis. Before that, review the following top nine

---

ways to duplicate your business success. After reviewing each point, answer the question and resolve to take action in each category.

1. Become an expert at something.

Whom would you invest your own money with? Answer that question for your money partners. Show them who you are.
- I am lease-to-own.
- I focus on RRSP mortgages.
- I buy townhouses that cash flow in [insert region].
- I buy single-family homes for professionals who want to live in walking distance of my city's transit system.
- I buy undervalued properties in northeast [town] to renovate and put back on the market in six months or less.
- My knowledge of neighbourhoods in southeast [city] helps me optimize cash flow from rental units I buy and hold for five or more years.
- I am all about cash flow and long-term appreciation!

Question: What is my real estate investment expertise and what am I doing to share that news with others?

2. Become a student of joint ventures.

We've all heard people boast about how they can "fake it until they make it." Sophisticated real estate investors learn the business, commit to a proven system and then take action. No one expects you to be an expert at everything. But when you don't know something, find out.

Search for ways to improve your system and replicate success. Avoid practising your new techniques with people who are in the same business. For example, pitch your next deal to a family member you can trust to be honest. Ask her: How am I doing? What can I do better? What did you hate about that presentation? Would you let me pitch this deal to your mother or best friend?

When you set your sights on continuous improvement, you focus on what works. Embody the motto: **be it until you become it!**

Question: What three things will I do this week to become a student of joint ventures?

3. Do not reinvent the wheel.

Other people are successfully doing what you want to do. Find out who they are and learn how they do it. Adopt their ideas and use their proven templates. You will need to personalize your systems, but you do not need to invent them. Never assume you have to start from nothing.

Question: Who can help me hone my real estate expertise in my chosen area?

(Call them tomorrow and set up a meeting.)

4. Be consistent.

There are a lot of ways to make money by investing in real estate. There are also a lot of ways to lose money by investing in real estate. Commit to excellence and make it easy to stay the course by practising the same strategies over and over again. This eases due diligence with properties, partners and all members of your real estate investment team.

Question: What am I doing to commit to consistent duplication of proven strategies?

(Identify two areas of concern and a plan of action: for example, qualifying JV partners, improving my presentation to prospective money partners, improving document management [see Tutorial #10 on page 280]).

5. Stick to one or two buying strategies.

Similar transactions allow you to hone proven skills. You can diversify your strategies, but that will mean more systems to duplicate. Until you have the time and resources to do that, less is more.

Question: Have I identified my buying strategies and what am I doing to promote those strategies in my interactions with potential investors from my Inner Circle?

6. Create less work for your JV partners.

Make it easy for people to do business with you. If you are the real estate expert, you drive the deals and that includes assembling the real estate investment team. Only work with people who want to work with you. If a partner or prospective partner always needs or expects "one more thing," be honest about how that affects you. You don't have to work with everyone—and not everyone has to work with you.

Question: What am I doing to help my partners understand and commit to my deals?

7. Only work with people who are committed as JV partners.

The world is full of investment opportunity. This is your deal and you are inviting a partner in on a win-win investment. Be upfront about what you are going to do and what you need them to do. Say, "You are putting up the money, and I am going to find and manage the purchase and operational details. I will lead the investment from start to finish, and my expertise makes this a 50/50 deal that's well worth your financial investment."

Spend your time on people who want to invest in real estate with you. Others will waste your time.

Question: What can I learn from JV deals (mine or a colleague's) that didn't close?

8. Take continuous action.

Always look for your next opportunity and don't let excuses throw your business plan off course. When you think of things you need to do to improve your business, write them down and commit to a time when you can deal with the issue. Never stop looking for money partners or new deals.

Question: What can I do to ensure that my business plan moves forward more quickly?

9. Build your team.

You are the real estate expert on joint-venture deals. Stick to what you're good at and what you're responsible for. Identify the gaps and eliminate them by stacking your team with qualified individuals.

Question: What am I doing to keep my real estate investment team relationships on track? Do I have a weak link?

SOPHISTICATED JV INVESTOR INSIGHT

Success leaves clues!

Unlock the vault of JV secrets and investment money will find you.

SOPHISTICATED JV INVESTOR INSIGHT

The perfect co-venturer

My favourite co-venturers expect the details, but don't want to have to manage a deal or investment. My ideal investor does five things:

1. Qualifies
2. Reads the documentation (also known as pro forma) and agrees to the investment
3. Gets independent legal advice
4. Writes a cheque
5. Smiles (every time he thinks of my name and real estate investment!)

TUTORIAL: TAMING THE PAPER TIGER AND USING ACCOUNTING STRATEGIES THAT WORK

10

WORKSHOP RECAP:

Follow-up communication generates new deals with existing partners. Duplicate your success.

Presenter: Don Campbell

The best thing about follow-up communication with existing JV partners is that these individuals are the primary source of future money partners. Letting them know how an investment is working out and showing them what we know about the economic fundamentals of real estate investing is the fastest route to *duplicating* our success and finding another money partner for the next deal.

As this workshop draws to an end, we are going to fast-forward past our first deal and assume that we now co-own a property with money partners who recognize us as the real estate experts. We found the property, worked out the details with our JV partners, signed a legally binding Joint-Venture Agreement and took possession of a three-bedroom, single-family home with existing tenants. Let me be clear: by following a proven system like the one outlined in *Real Estate Investing in Canada 2.0*, those tenants were thoroughly vetted before we agreed to let them stay, and we're thrilled to have them in our property. This is what our fellow sophisticated real estate experts will call a "quality" property, and these quality tenants are a great fit.

TOM: That proven system you're talking about was a huge help to Robert and me on our first JV deal. We followed that system from A to Z, and any time we encountered a problem, we went back and looked it up or found an experienced investor who could help us sort through the issue. We stuck to the due diligence outlined in the system and didn't take the first person who wanted to rent our place. Given the reality of the rental market, it was tough to turn prospective tenants away. It was also worth it!

ROBERT: Finding the right tenants was one issue, but so was placing our first offer, and we encountered a few hiccups with our first mortgage. Our first deal fell apart when the vendor didn't meet the conditions, but by then, we had a co-venturer and a whole series of systems in place and were ready to go on our next deal. Since then, we've even left copies of our Sophisticated Investment Binder with two mortgage brokers we want to work with, and one has already called us back for a formal meeting. We only have one property, but the broker told Tom he really likes what he's seeing. We're JV investment newcomers—but we are also real estate *experts,* and that shows in the commitment we've made to do what we know how to do.

It really is all about duplication. Several of you have also joined a real estate investment network or are developing one of your own that includes experienced and successful investors. Good work! There's no need to reinvent the wheel when you can follow in the footsteps of giants.

Anyone who invests in real estate, with or without money partners, soon realizes that due diligence is an ongoing commitment. Once the property is purchased and under your management, you are tasked with the responsibility to ensure it operates the way you intended. But even as that's going on, you need a plan to deal with what sophisticated investors call the "paper tiger."

TAMING THE PAPER TIGER

Let's get back to the scenario I painted earlier about being a real estate expert who owns his first property with a money partner. One of the things that often takes new investors by surprise is the sheer volume of paper this business generates. Even with electronic files playing an ever-greater role, real estate investors cannot go into this business without a plan to deal with the paper, which will overwhelm you if you don't use a proven system. On the plus side, a good organizational plan can be put into place very easily, and it will make required reporting (for the Canada Revenue Agency, lenders and partners) a breeze.

Filing system

The first thing you need is a filing cabinet that holds legal-paper-size files. That cabinet will also need to hold all of the information you need to access regularly, plus the information you will need to track and assess annual business activities.

You will need one accordion file per property, and inside each file, you will place four coloured file folders as per below.

Red file folder: Tenant information
Address

Rental information

Move-in inspection (with digital pictures filed on a CD)

Lease agreement

Tenant confirmation forms

All correspondence

All notices

Yellow file folder: Property miscellaneous
Address

Warranties on appliances

Copies of manuals

Dates of inspection

Dates, types and costs of repairs

Dates, types and costs of renovations

List of key contacts for property

Blue file folder: Legal documents
Address

Copy of offer to purchase

Your due diligence documents

Survey, Real Property Report

- The RPR is a legal document that shows the location of significant improvements to property boundaries

Title insurance

Appraisal

All closing documents

Purchasing statement of adjustments

Mortgage documentation
Source of down payments
Equipment purchased
Refinancing documents

Green file folder: Ongoing monthly receipts*
Address
All receipts for direct property expenses
(cash, charge or cheque)

*Write all details on receipts and take care to never miss an expense. You cannot deduct what you cannot trace, so failing to file well-documented receipts is akin to handing the government money to compensate for your laziness.

Annual business activities

Now that you have an accessible filing system in which to keep information, you need to set up a system to track annual business activities. The expense classifications you use provide a quick reference for year-end reports. The following example of a chart of accounts is based on the expense categories used by the Canada Revenue Agency.

RENTAL PROPERTY
MONTHLY STATEMENTS

Chart of Accounts

Your name: Real Estate Expert
For year ending: December, [20XX]
Partner's name and % of ownership: Joe Investor 50%
Rental property address: Street number, Anytown, Canada

1000 Rental income	**1300** Insurance
1010 Late fees collected	1310 Management fees
1020 Laundry and other income	1320 Strata fees
1030 Vacancy	**1400** Advertising and promotion
1100 Mortgage principal repayment	1410 Meals and entertainment
1120 Mortgage interest	**1500** Repairs
1130 Bank charges	1510 Maintenance
1140 Line of credit interest	1520 Updates
1150 Second mortgage repayment	1530 Utilities: rental property
1200 Mortgage interest penalties	**1600** Property taxes
1220 Legal fees	**1700** Office at home
1230 Appraisal fees	1710 Internet
1240 Accounting fees	1720 Computer and office supplies
1250 Bookkeeping fees	**1800** Travel
1260 Inspection reports	1810 Motor vehicle
1270 Other professional fees	1820 Seminars
	2000 Miscellaneous

Taking Action: Signed, Sealed and Saved

At the end of each month, the real estate expert (or her bookkeeper) must undertake three critical tasks:

1. Collect monthly receipts from the green file folder.
2. Enter information into a basic spreadsheet program (e.g., Quick-Books).
3. Write the date, address, amount and the expense code on the outside of a letter-size envelope, making sure the information is tracked *per property*, not for the whole portfolio.

SAMPLE RECEIPT SPREADSHEET

DATE: January 2011

Address:

Epcor	$145.00	1530
Bookkeeping	$85.00	1250
Rona	$73.29	1510
Walter's Windows	$278.00	1510
123 Condo Corporation	$167.67	1320
Total:	$748.96	

Once you've prepared your monthly statements (a monthly statement and a YTD summary as per samples in Appendices F and G), place each month's envelope back into the green file folder. At the end of the year, all of the receipts will go into one envelope for the accountant. When that envelope comes back from the accountant, put it in a box, label it with the year and file the box in a safe place.

SOPHISTICATED JV INVESTOR INSIGHT

Using a bookkeeper

A bookkeeper buys you time and saves you money. They keep the books while you are out finding and closing deals. They also make sure that business data is recorded in a timely manner and that reports are done accurately and on time.

As a general rule of thumb, investors with up to 10 properties can probably handle the bookkeeping on their own. But be honest about what bookkeeping time costs you. Sophisticated real estate investors who only have a few properties will justify the cost by sharing a good bookkeeper with another investor.

RICHARD: It's easy to think that bookkeeping is all about taxes, but that's only part of the story. Emma keeps our books, and having them done on time literally saves us money. In the early days, I think we would have lost track of the reserve fund we were keeping for each property (one or two months' rent) if it hadn't been for Emma's due diligence.

We had factored the reserve fund for each property we were buying at the time of purchase, and we knew it was to be put aside and not touched unless something needed to be fixed. But that plan would have been difficult to execute if Emma hadn't stayed on top of the numbers. Because our banking systems weren't as evolved at the time, it was imperative that Emma always knew where the money was—and what it was to be used for.

ACCOUNTING STRUCTURES AND BANK ACCOUNTS

That leads directly into my next topic: accounting structures and bank accounts. As you are the real estate expert on your JV deals, you maintain responsibility for managing the financial aspects of these deals. There is no room for complacency; after all, this isn't just money, it's money you are effectively managing for someone else.

I like to think about my financial picture as a score card. That data tells me where each of my properties is at in terms of cash flow, and I get to see the "big picture" as well.

SUSAN: Good financial records made my first JV deal. I've been investing on my own for several years and have three properties that cash flow $1,300 a month. (One is a rented suite in the home I live in with my daughter.) I decided to focus the JV side of my portfolio on similar properties (single-family homes with suites). One of the first properties I came across hasn't been well-managed; it's in a negative cash flow position of $58 a month. Using a business plan that focuses on long-term wealth, plus the expertise I've built regarding those first properties, I was able to convince a money partner to be a 50/50 partner on that underperforming property. We're just completing some basic repairs and upgrading and our first rent increase should generate a monthly cash flow of $160. That will be higher once our business plan kicks in as it includes some specific upgrades to the suite.

That property was vacant for a month, but it's looking great right now, and my co-venturer is hinting about doing a similar deal. If I hadn't had strong numbers on those other properties, he would have had 1,300 fewer reasons to trust me!

That's an excellent example of how quality financial records will boost your credibility. And let's be honest—the best way to build your own confidence as a real estate expert is to get some deals under your belt.

It's also worth noting that the reason Susan has such good financial records is that she runs a part-time bookkeeping business. A lot of investors who don't have that kind of built-in expertise will hire a bookkeeper to make sure they stay on top of the numbers.

EMMA: The bookkeeping side of the business is especially hard when you're just starting out. You definitely need to talk to your professional tax accountant and ask for advice about which accounting software package you might choose to keep your books. I like QuickBooks, but friends of ours use Excel spreadsheets.

The specific accounting program you use is less important than making sure the information is compatible with what your accountant uses. That's especially important if you're using electronic files. I always recommend that real estate investors talk to their accountants before they invest in a particular package. Some accountants will recommend a specific program, and their offices may even be able to offer some technical support if that program is new to you and your bookkeeper.

You will need to track the performance of each property and its relationship to each co-venturer. You also need a way to track the "master account." This is your account as the real estate expert on all of the properties in your portfolio. In the master account, each joint venture would represent a "class," with each unit separated out as a "sub class." Each category requires its own accounting numbers.

This sounds complicated, but it makes a great deal of sense once you look at the chart of accounts for each joint venture separately and then add them together so you can see your whole portfolio. For example, your JV partner on the first deal will want separate numbers on Unit A and Unit B. Similarly, the real estate expert needs numbers that reference each JV deal and each unit, as well as the "big picture" numbers related to his portfolio.

SOPHISTICATED JV INVESTOR INSIGHT

Understanding bookkeeping versus accounting

Bookkeeping and accounting are not the same thing. Bookkeepers track all of the in-and-out details of your business and may even pay bills and invoice suppliers for your business. They will also prepare the first round of data your professional accountant needs to provide you with quality tax advice and prepare your tax return.

The accountant's job is easier if your books are well prepared—and that will save you money.

Bank accounts

The issues relative to bank accounts are more straightforward, but this is a message a lot of novice JV investors ignore. The basic advice is simple. You need a business bank account for yourself, plus one account for each joint venture. Richard, I understand you've run into a problem that illustrates this point.

RICHARD: We sure did. Remember how we did our first JV deal with my boss? That deal closed before I'd opened a separate bank account and then I got busy managing the deal and used my personal bank account, including my debit card, to pay bills.

I compounded the problem by buying personal and property items on the same trip to the hardware store and not writing the details on each receipt. We sorted it out. But those mistakes cost me when I learned that I didn't have the records I needed for the Canada Revenue Agency. The problem was pretty simple: I couldn't use income from the property to pay for bills and expenses that I couldn't document. To make things worse, I also couldn't go back to my partner and expense items I couldn't explain.

And there you have it—a testimonial for good financial records! I thank all of you for sharing personal examples because they serve as great cautionary tales for your investing colleagues. It's also important to admit that we all make mistakes. The only shame in making mistakes is if we fail to learn from them.

Thanks again for attending this series of workshops and tutorials about investing in real estate with joint-venture partners! Russell Westcott and I look forward to hearing your success stories in the months and years to come!

You can't be an "expert" unless you know what you're doing and can do it again. Duplication matters.

—Todd Millar

BACKGROUND

Todd and Danielle Millar have been investing in real estate since 2001. Then in their late twenties, they bought their first revenue properties while they were living abroad and teaching English. Based in Japan, the two saw investment real estate as a good place to park—and grow—the money they'd worked so hard to make in Japan. "We knew we'd come back to Canada some day, and we didn't necessarily want to have to work for someone else. Real estate investment gave us a way to control part of our financial destiny," explains Todd.

Now living in Edmonton and expecting their second baby, the Millars figure their portfolio has, over time, held more than 64 doors in over 52 buildings. Their current portfolio includes more than 15 partners, including some couples and investment groups. All of their properties are now located in Edmonton, where Danielle oversees property management under a sister firm.

"Self-managing such a large portfolio is counterintuitive to what a lot of sophisticated real estate investors do," admits Todd. "But prior to this, we were overseeing our holdings from Japan. Once we moved back, it made sense to consolidate our resources and establish the property management standards that will be used to groom someone we can hire to manage these properties down the road." Self-managing their properties, which are currently all based in Edmonton, also helps the couple prepare exit strategies for their maturing portfolio.

Having weathered the global economic downturn triggered by the sub-prime mortgage fiasco in the United States, the Millars admit their current investment strategy is considerably more conservative than in past years. But a more conservative approach doesn't mean their portfolio will be standing still. In 2011, Todd and Danielle anticipate buying four multi-family properties with two or three JV partners. "More partners and more doors aren't necessarily a recipe for more freedom. We want to make sure we're buying the right properties with the right partners and hiring the right people to help us manage the business. When you feel pressure to do 'more,' you're more likely to make mistakes, too," notes Todd.

The shift toward a more conservative buying strategy also makes sense in light of their portfolio's size and the fact that they've decided to self-manage their holdings. "We still like JVs, but tough economic times mean you have to be more mindful of what you're doing. It's kind of like farming; if you're not there making sure the crops are seeded, managed and harvested correctly, you compromise your opportunities for success," says Todd.

The couple is quick to credit REIN membership for providing them with a solid foundation in the real estate investment business. They joined the organization in 2004, a few years after they bought their first investment properties in Winnipeg and Hamilton. Although Todd never attended a live meeting until after they moved back to Canada in 2010, he's grateful for information REIN regularly delivered via CDs.

Below, Todd offers his insights on why systems, follow-through and duplication are so important to their portfolio's success.

Systems Keep Your Business on Track

Systems give you a way of doing things. We follow those systems over and over because they provide structure to our real estate investment business. That doesn't mean we're not open to change. We fine-tune our systems all the time. But we don't second-guess them.

Take the recent recession as an example. It impacted our portfolio, but we didn't pull up stakes or bury our heads in the sand and wait for the market to shift. Instead, we went back to basics. We may have let some "details" slide when every property was cash-flowing and property values were always rising. Now that we're living in the same city as our properties are located, we've rolled up our sleeves to make sure our portfolio continues to perform the way it should. A recession sharpens everything from tenancy to maintenance and repairs. It's not enough to trim the fat; you have to know exactly what that means and where to cut.

Be the Market Expert

We started investing while living in Japan, and we could have invested anywhere in the world. Our first properties were in Hamilton and Winnipeg because we knew something about the economic fundamentals of those cities. Over time, we learned more about the value of being an "expert" on a particular market. That prompted us to focus all of our energy on Edmonton. Regardless of where our investors were from, our JV deals had a geographic foundation and our knowledge of the Edmonton market's fundamentals helped us attract money partners.

Be a Student of Joint Ventures

To be a student of JV investing, we focus on two things: the right deals and the right people.

The deals

We used our own money to finance our first deals, but I like JVs and have put together a lot of joint-venture deals. Once you start investing with other people's money, you've got to up your game. That's easier if you know what you're doing, so seek help early and often.

Remember, too, that a good Joint-Venture Agreement outlines what happens at every step along the way. Some potential JV partners may be scared off when you start talking about what the JV agreement says will happen in the event of future deaths, divorces or insolvencies. That can turn all of the sweet talk about a deal sour, very fast.

Depending on where the angst about these issues comes from, that may tell me that a JV deal is not for them. Unless those issues are dealt with, it also tells me that I probably shouldn't pursue a JV deal with this partner.

More than anything, I think both parties of a JV investment have to be committed to doing what the JV Agreement says you are going to do. That's always been very important to us, but it's not always easy and there have been times when we've changed the long-term plans for a property to help a partner who's dealing with a significant life issue. We do that because our relationship with these people goes beyond the paper a JV Agreement is written on.

I also tell new JV investors to be realistic. A detailed JV Agreement doesn't just spell out what happens if something bad happens to your money partner. It also spells out what happens if something changes in your life.

The people

We've always taken our responsibilities as the "real estate experts" very seriously. A lot of our co-venturers come to us through word-of-mouth referrals, so they already know what we do and how we work with our partners to generate long-term wealth. In the early days, we worked with some individuals who we wouldn't work with now. That's a factor of how our business has evolved with time and experience.

The problems we've encountered have typically revolved around different expectations. That's taught us to be very clear about how real estate investment works and how it works with JV partners. Moving forward, we're definitely more careful to choose partners who share our expectations. When your message is clear and consistent, it's easier to avoid problems.

I am pleased to say that our JV partners have never regretted their dealings with us and we are grateful for what their trust has allowed us to build. Right now we're working even harder to make sure that doesn't change. We're open to new JV partners—and we remain committed to serving our long-time investors as well.

ACTIONS SPEAK LOUDER THAN WORDS

Good news travels fast and bad news travels even faster. That's life. Danielle and I do what we say we're going to do. And we don't make our joint-venture partners pay for our mistakes. It bothers us when we hear about investors who've walked away from deals with joint-venture partners. This is our business and we want every one of our deals to help us secure the next one.

Workshop Wrap-Up:
Richard and Emma Look Ahead

Coming together is a beginning; keeping together is progress; working together is success.

—Henry Ford

Where To From Here?
Presenter: Russell Westcott

This book began with Richard and Emma's willingness to take an honest look at their real estate investment portfolio. They were serious about finding more money for investments with money partners, but had allowed a few bad habits to threaten their continued success by compromising their real-world commitment to systems, relationships and follow-through.

As this part of their journey started, the McTavishes owned five revenue-generating properties involving nine suites. The couple, who bought their first revenue property in late 2003, held nine properties by 2005. Two of those properties were sold in 2009. This was in line with the exit strategy devised with the JV partner who held both of these properties in a classic 50/50 split with the McTavishes.

The other two were purchased in 2005 and sold in 2010 as a direct response to market changes. One was not cash flowing, and the other was breaking even. Two co-venturers were involved, and neither was willing to extend the exit strategy. In both cases, JV investors got their money back plus appreciation well above contemporary interest rates. These properties were the McTavishes' only holdings in a community located an hour away from where they live. As property management presented ongoing challenges, Richard and Emma opted against buying out their partners and holding onto the properties.

RICHARD: I have some regrets about that, too, Russell. Even though we'd encountered some hassles with their management, these properties were purchased at the right price and would have continued to make us money once we got the property management issue under control and secured the right tenants. Looking back, I believe we should have found straight money partners who would have bought out our partners in return for a percentage of interest on the loan.

Emma: If we're being honest, I was the one who balked at the suggestion that we find a way to hold onto those properties. I don't have the same regrets as Richard. To me, selling those properties made sense for where our portfolio was at. It gave us a chance to focus on the properties that made obvious sense—and demanded less effort!

I appreciate both of you for your honesty! The bottom line is that you have registered some real success in real estate investing—and you've weathered your fair share of storms, too. More than anything, I like that neither of you is willing to let regret hold you back. Real estate investment is not about the past; it's about the future. Now that you've worked through these 10 workshops, where do you want the future to take you?

Richard: These workshops have helped us recommit to systems, relationships and follow-through. Listening to you, Don, and the others has also reminded us that we can be creative real estate investors. We are moving ahead with lease-to-own deals with two family members, and our long-time friend Auntie wants into our business, but not as a 50/50 partner.

She and her accountant are working on a plan to loan us money to buy real estate investment properties at a premium interest rate. We didn't expect that, but it's the deal she put on the table. The irony is that while she really likes real estate investment, one of her sons is very vocal about its risks. While she shouldn't have to justify where she invests her money, families are complicated, and she finds it easier to loan us money than get involved in our business.

That's a great story. It's also a great reminder of why investors who are looking for money partners need to *listen* to what the people in their Inner Circle are telling them. Sophisticated investors often call the 50/50 JV split a "classic" JV deal. But the fact that it's a common model shouldn't hold you back from other arrangements. In fact, the investor profiles we've included as bonus handouts after each tutorial are full of examples of what smart investors are doing to close deals that move them closer to their Personal Belize.

And speaking of those bonus handouts, I encourage you to read the one that follows this wrap-up. Jeff Gunther's story is a wonderful example of how experienced investors use their real-world understanding of systems, relationships and follow-through to develop their own approach to real estate investment. I think it's fair to say that real estate investing is a competitive business. Jeff's story is a really good reminder that it's okay to look at the "big picture" and ask yourself what it is that *you* really want from this business. In the final analysis, your ability to develop systems that work for your business model will enable you to adapt to market changes in ways that less-experienced investors cannot. As always, Don and I look forward to hearing the real estate success stories of those who've worked through this book!

Real estate investment is a risky business. But I know how to mitigate those risks and make my partners money. If I can talk a potential partner out of doing business with me, then that partner is not a good fit with my portfolio.

—Jeff Gunther

Background

Jeff Gunther bought his first real estate investment property at the age of 21. A business leader and former real estate agent who has trained realtors, brokers, managers and franchisees with one of Canada's largest real estate networks, his recent foray back into active investing has seen him purchase, renovate and rent a growing portfolio of properties that he and his partners anticipate holding for five to eight years. None of those properties, nor the ones he's working on today, involve Jeff's own cash or credit.

"My approach to real estate investment aims to build kingdom versus empire. I see 'empire building' as a very individualistic enterprise. 'Kingdom building,' on the other hand, is all about working together for a higher purpose, and that is essential to the joint-venture partnerships I put together. By focusing on kingdom, which implies community, shared values and relationships, I am able to put together deals that genuinely benefit my partners," says Jeff.

With that in mind, Jeff's business model puts relationships first. All his partners have some connection to Jeff's own Inner Circle of contacts. Because these are people who know him and trust how his business works, he rarely solicits new business. Instead, he waits for people to approach him and is then very honest about how his business works and how his partners benefit.

Jeff, whose MBA thesis looked at using demographics to forecast cyclical behaviour in real estate markets, says his decision to put his partners' needs first is the primary reason those individuals keep investing their money with him. "Our exit strategies typically focus on holding a property for five to eight years. That's a long time to be in business with someone who doesn't think their needs are being met. Experience tells me that if I have a good relationship with a partner on one investment, that partner will want to work on several."

Jeff knows investors can learn a lot from other investors. But he also believes that experience is the best teacher, and he encourages other real estate investors to use their experience to develop a personal approach to real estate investment. Here's a look at how he developed his particular niche—and what others can learn from that.

Perfect Your Own System

When I was selling real estate, I talked to a lot of very successful agents, and all of them were willing to tell me the secret of their success. They weren't naive. They did this because they had complete confidence in their knowledge that I couldn't do what they were doing. Sure, I could replicate some of the actions they were taking. But in the end, the best and brightest of these realtors knew that my success depended on finding my own system.

Real estate investing is the same. You can learn from others, but you have to make this business your own. That's what will make your business better. Something *you* do well might not work for me, but it's not about me.

Find Your Focus

There are a lot of ways to invest in real estate. You can buy-and-hold, flip, lease-to-own or develop properties, and you can do these things on your own or with partners. For me, the focus is on finding the right properties and partners to work with. If I am serious about inviting people into partnerships with me, I must be willing to develop an expertise that I can use to our mutual advantage.

Properties

My current property niche is in townhouses, and I've done so many of these deals that the due diligence is second nature. What I like about these properties is that they are a more affordable rental alternative to a single-family home, and that's attractive to the kind of tenants we want. From an investment perspective, my partners and I also like the fact that our condo fees cover much of the maintenance budget.

This means we don't have to worry about things like parking lots and windows.

As part of my due diligence, I also know the kind of tenant we're looking for, and that knowledge requires us to upgrade the property so that it draws quality tenants. Those upgrades are not extra, they are a deliberate part of our business plan. They are part of the system I've developed.

At this point in time, I'm also sticking to Edmonton. I moved here to invest in real estate and, for now, I like being close to my portfolio. Again, that's what works for me.

Partners

I work with partners who understand our model. I put together investments that make people money. If I can talk someone out of a deal, then that person is not a good fit with my portfolio. I want them to know that real estate investment is risky, but I also want them to know how we identify, mitigate and manage those risks. This information is vital to our relationship.

If you have a potential partner who can't swing a deal without bringing in a third partner, then I wouldn't work with that person. I simply do not want to make my life, or his life, that stressful or complicated. To me, it's important to work with partners who embrace the same values, and those values can include the parameters of the business model itself.

BE TRUE TO YOUR BUSINESS MODEL

Trust is a key consideration in every aspect of our deals. If I am serious about using real estate investments to build a kingdom, then the relationships I have with my partners are really about the kingdom we form by working together. By emphasizing integrity, I can make sure that the kingdom is based on the values my partners and I share.

One of the ways we build that kingdom is by making sure that our deals genuinely benefit all parties involved. As part of that, I work very hard to minimize capital requirements because I recognize that this is one of the ways we generate extraordinary returns. Because our model calculates a robust reserve fund into the equation, for example, my partners and I never have to put more money into a property.

That's not luck; it's good planning that is based on even better experience. Because we know what might go wrong with a property, we can plan ahead.

Use Experience to Earn Your Success

I believe that it's relatively easy to find cash and credit when you truly know how to find and describe a good real estate investment. But finding the cash and credit is just the start. Real estate investment success is in the details of the investment, not the pitch.

●

REAL ESTATE
INVESTMENT
NETWORK™

#1018, 105–150 Crowfoot Crescent NW, Calgary, Alberta T2G 3T2
phone (403) 208–2722 fax (403) 241–6685 www.reincanada.com

Property Goldmine Score Card

Property Address: _____

Town: _____ Prov: _____

Source: _____ Tel: _____

Property Specific Questions

❑ Can you **change the use** of the property?
❑ Can you buy it substantially **below retail market value?**
❑ Can you substantially **increase the current rents?**
❑ Can you do small **renovations** to substantially increase the value?

Area's Economic Influences

❑ Is there an overall increase in demand in the area?
❑ Are there currently sales over list price in the area?
❑ Is there a noted increase in labour and materials cost in the area?
❑ Is there a lot of speculative investment in the area?
❑ Is it an area in transition—moving upward in quality?
❑ Is there a major transportation improvement occurring nearby?
❑ Is it in an area that is going to benefit from the Ripple Effect?
❑ Is the property's area in "Real Estate Spring" or "Summer"?
❑ Has the political leadership created a "growth atmosphere"?
❑ Is the area's average income increasing faster than the provincial average?
❑ Is it an area that is attractive to baby boomers?
❑ Is the area growing faster than the provincial average?
❑ Are interest rates at historic lows and/or moving downward?

_____ = Total √s

Does this property fit your system? ❑ yes ❑ no
Does it take you closer to your goal? ❑ yes ❑ no

© 2004 www.reincanada.com

How to Use the Property Goldmine Score Card

As a sophisticated investor, you are looking for cities, towns or neighbourhoods that have as many of these factors in place as possible. For instance, if you find an area that has just one or two of these keys, then it's not a sure bet. However, as you reach seven or eight, you're starting to see a town with huge potential. Any score above that mark means you should personally go and check the area out, because that area may hold substantial opportunity. You should keep blank copies of the score card in your car at all times, because you never know when opportunity might strike. Keeping the card close at hand will ensure that you remember all of the critical questions to ask *before* you take action.

To find the answers to the questions on the score card, start with the web site of the economic development department of the city or town. Their job is to provide you with reasons to invest in their town, so they'll have most of the stats you need at their fingertips. If it is lacking in detail, pick up the phone or drop in and have a discussion with them; many have superb statistics. Go to the provincial government's web site, as well as the Statistics Canada site, to get the stats against which you're going to compare the town's numbers. To answer the rest of the questions, start digging. Talk to realtors, developers and other investors. Hang out at the town hall and talk to councillors and the mayor. Don't quit until you have the answers to all the questions; then, and only then, can you be assured that you've got your first level of due diligence complete.

If you want to be a successful investor, you need to do this due diligence for every property. Not doing it leads to mediocrity or worse. Those willing to do that extra 10 percent that others aren't willing to do are the people who become very successful. Those who skip the work or try to take shortcuts invariably create unremarkable results.

APPENDIX B

REIN™ PROPERTY ANALYZER

Property Data:

Address: _____ City/Area: _____ Date Viewed: _____

Asking Price: _____ Size (sq ft): _____ Age: _____

Major Repairs: _____ Est. Repair Cost $ _____

Owner: _____ Tel: _____ Fax: _____

Source: _____ Tel: _____ Fax: _____

Overall Condition: 1 2 3 4 5

Income & Inspection

Suite # or Desc	# of Bedrooms	Current Rent	Projected Rent	Increase Date	Inspection Comments

Total Monthly Rent $_____ $_____

Total Annual Rent $_____ $_____

Expenses:

	Current Annual	Current Monthly	Projected Monthly	Comments
Heat (gas, oil, electricity, hot water, other _____)				Paid by Tenant / Landlord
Electricity				Paid By Tenant / Landlord
Water/Sewer				Paid by Tenant / Landlord / Condo
Taxes				Included in Mortgage Payment?
Condo Fee				Last Increase Date:
Insurance				(for analysis only—actual cost factored in on page 2)
Property Management	%			Current Management Rating 1 2 3 4 5
Vacancy Allowance	%			Current Vacancy _____%
Rental Pool Mgmt.	%			
Repairs & Maintenance	%			Overall Condition 1 2 3 4 5
Resident Manager				Current On-site Impression 1 2 3 4 5
Other:				

TOTAL MONTHLY $_____ $_____

TOTAL MONTHLY INCOME less TOTAL MONTHLY EXPENSES (Before Debt Service) =

Current: $ _____   Projected: $ _____

TOTAL PROJECTED INCOME $ _____

(from bottom of page 1)

Mortgaging / Debt Service:

	Balance	Interest Rate	Expiry Date	Monthly Payment
1st Mortgage		%		P I T
2nd Mortgage		%		P I T
Vendor Take-Back		%		P I T
Other		%		P I T

TOTAL DEBT SERVICE $ _____

NET CASH FLOW $ _____

Purchase Details:

PROJECTED PURCHASE PRICE $ _____

1st Mortgage Funding   ($ _____)
2nd Mortgage Funding   ($ _____)
Vendor Take-Back   ($ _____)
Other Funding   ($ _____)

TOTAL DEBT FUNDING   ($ _____)
DOWN PAYMENT REQUIRED $ _____

Purchase Costs:

Professional Inspection $ _____
Value Appraisal $ _____
Real Property Report (Survey) $ _____
Mortgage Broker Fees $ _____
Legal Costs (incl. disbursements) $ _____
Staying Power (reserve) Fund $ _____
Immediate Repairs & Supplies $ _____
Immediate Renovations $ _____
Land Transfer Taxes $ _____
Title Insurance $ _____
Property Insurance $ _____
Other _____ $ _____

TOTAL PURCHASE COSTS $ _____
TOTAL CASH REQUIRED TO CLOSE (Down payment + Purchase Costs) $ _____

1. Does this property take me closer to my goal or further away?   ☐ Closer   ☐ Further
2. Does this property fit my system?   ☐ Yes   ☐ No
3. At what price would I have to buy the property for it to cash flow? $ _____
4. Will this property be impeccably property managed?   ☐ Yes   ☐ No
5. Who will manage the property?   _____

Appendix C: Prospective JV Partners—Follow-Up Letter

[Your name]
Real Estate Investor
[Address]
[Date]

Dear [name]:

Good day! Emma and I enjoyed our recent get-together, and we appreciated your interest in what we do as real estate investors.

You asked a number of questions about real estate investing, and we told you a bit about our commitment to what we call systems, relationships and follow-through. These are the crux of our portfolio and help us navigate the ups and downs of the real estate cycle.

Emma and I have been investing since 2006 and our growing portfolio includes several investments with joint-venture partners with whom we share real estate profits on a 50/50 basis. We are also active in one of Canada's largest and most successful real estate investment networks. In addition to benefiting from the mentorship of sophisticated real estate investors involved with the network, we now play that mentorship role with our own investors.

Our primary business objective is to source and manage real estate investments with win-win opportunities for our investors and ourselves.

I mentioned a couple of books on this topic that we really enjoyed, and I'm sending you a copy of one of our favourites, *Real Estate Investing in Canad 2.0.* We also recommend *97 Tips for Canadian Real Estate Investors* and *51 Success Stories from Canadian Real Estate Investors,* both written by Don R. Campbell, the president of the Real Estate Investment Network. If you would like to discuss real estate investing with us again in the future, we'd appreciate the opportunity.

Yours truly,
Richard McTavish

APPENDIX D: POTENTIAL-FOR-RELATIONSHIP QUESTIONNAIRE

Your Company Name
Address
Phone/Website information

Potential-for-Relationship Questionnaire

Name: _____

Address: _____

City/Town: _____

Province: _____

Postal Code: _____

E-mail Address: _____

Current Employment: _____

Do you own your own home?

_____

_____

_____

_____

How much equity is in your home?

_____

_____

_____

_____

What is the current value of your RRSPs?

_____

_____

_____

_____

Are you happy with your current return?

_____

_____

_____

_____

Please provide responses to the following questions as openly and as freely as you are able. This will provide the framework for determining how compatible you are with our investing programs and which of those programs best suits your situation.

1. If we were meeting five years from today and you were looking back over those five years, what must have happened, both personally and professionally, for you to feel contented with your progress?

_____

_____

_____

_____

2. What first-hand real estate experience do you have already? Have you participated in the market? What aspects of it? And what size deals have you been involved in?

_____

_____

_____

_____

3. How "hands-on" do you wish to be with the investment? What decisions do you want to be a part of?

_____

_____

_____

_____

a. Purchase decisions?

_____

_____

_____

_____

b. Financing decisions?

_____

_____

_____

_____

c. Property management decisions?

_____

_____

_____

_____

4. What is your primary focus in investing? Are you seeking to become a sophisticated investor yourself, or do you simply need a good
   return on your dollars and are happy to let someone else manage the
   problems?

_____

_____

_____

_____

5. What returns are you seeking?

_____

_____

_____

_____

6. How soon do you need to realize those returns?

_____

_____

_____

_____

7. What, if any, are your expectations for monthly cash flow?

_____

_____

_____

_____

8. What financial resources do you bring to the table? How much money can you invest in a single project, and what is your total investment capability? Are you prepared to sign personal guarantees? (This is a prerequisite as lenders do not operate without guarantees.)

_____

_____

_____

_____

9. Are the funds you are using cash or borrowed?

_____

_____

_____

_____

10. How available are your investment resources? Are they readily available or, if not, how much notice will you require to access funds?

_____

_____

_____

_____

11. Is there someone in your life who will be participating in your decisions related to investments, and do you expect that person to be named as a beneficiary of the investment?

_____

_____

_____

_____

Additional questions you may want to include:

- What is your personal risk tolerance?

  _____

  _____

  _____

  _____

- Are you prepared to take action? Or are you just wanting information?

  _____

  _____

  _____

  _____

- Do you know anyone else who may be interested in investing?

  _____

  _____

  _____

  _____

- Do you own any other investments, and if so, what does your portfolio consist of?

  _____

  _____

  _____

  _____

- What are your goals and how do they fit with real estate investing?

  _____

  _____

  _____

  _____

APPENDIX E: EXPRESSION OF INTEREST LETTER

Prospective Co-Venturer's Name
Address/Contact information

Date

Sophisticated Real Estate Investor
Expression of Interest

To: (Potential Investment Partner)

Further to our recent conversation, I am interested in forming a joint venture with you for investment real estate. I have funds available, not to exceed _____ dollars, for a suitable investment, and I will commit my money for a minimum initial period of not less than five (5) years.

I understand and acknowledge the following:

1. This expression of interest is not to be construed as a solicitation of funds on your part;
2. My expression of interest is just that; it is not binding on either you or me and is not intended to create a legal relationship of any sort;
3. I am not committing to paying any funds to you or any third party;
4. Although you are under no obligation to do so, please keep me advised if suitable investment properties come to your attention. I understand that as joint venturers, we each will have a personal financial interest in any such investment opportunities;
5. In the event that you are able to introduce me to an investment opportunity which is of interest to me,
   a. I will be solely responsible for evaluating the merits of any such opportunity as well as its appropriateness to my specific financial circumstances; and
   b. The decision whether or not to proceed with any such opportunity will be mine alone, and I will not hold you responsible for that decision in any manner;
6. I recognized that your time and efforts are valuable, and I agree to promptly notify you in the event my interest or intentions change;

7. I will not sign any fraudulent legal documents for the purpose of securing financing for real estate acquisitions. We wish to work with institutions and brokers operating a high standard of integrity.

Dated this _____ day of _____, 20___.

Witness: _____

Signature: _____

Name: _____

Address: _____

_____

Phone: _____

E-mail: _____

Appendix F: Rental Properties Monthly Statement

Your name—Real estate expert
For year ending:
Partner's name and % of ownership—Joe Investor 50%

Rental property address: 123–45 Avenue, Anytown, Canada

Expenses

Code	Description	Total
1000	Rent from Joe Smith, upper suite	$1,000.00
1000	Rent from Bob Jones, lower suite	800.00
1120	First line mortgage interest payment	640.00
1100	Mortgage principal reduction	118.00
1510	Rona: minor repairs	150.00
1130	CIBC: Bank charges	4.00
1140	Scotia Bank	97.46
1250	Bookkeeping fees	7.50
1300	Insurance	9.50
1310	ABC Management Co.	197.50
1320	123 Condo Corp	167.37
1600	Anytown Canada: property taxes	122.30
1410	Dinner with accountant	52.50
1820	REIN fees	25.00

Income

Code	Description	Total
1000	Rental income	$1,800.00
1010	Late fees collected	-
1020	Laundry and other income	-
1030	Vacancy	-
Total income:		$1,800.00

Operating income

Code	Description	Total
1120	Mortgage interest	$640.00
1130	Bank charges	4.00
1140	Line of credit interest	97.46
1150	Second mortgage repayment	-
1200	Mortgage interest penalties	-
1220	Legal fees	-
1230	Appraisal fees	-
1240	Accounting fees	-
1250	Bookkeeping fees	7.50
1260	Inspection reports	-
1270	Other professional fees	-
1300	Insurance	9.50
1310	Management fees	197.50
1320	Strata fees	167.37
1400	Advertising and promotion	-
1410	Meals and entertainment	52.50
1500	Repairs	-
1510	Maintenance	150.00
1520	Updates	-
1530	Utilities: rental property	-
1600	Property taxes	122.30
1700	Office at home	-
1710	Internet	-
1720	Computer and office supplies	-
1800	Travel	-
1810	Motor vehicle	-
1820	Seminars	25.00
2000	Miscellaneous	-
Total operating income:		$326.87
1100	Mortgage principal repayment	118.00
1520	Updates	-
Increase in equity		$118.00
Net cash flow		$208.87

Appendix G: Rental Properties Monthly Statement—YTD Summary

Your name—Real estate expert
For year ending:
Partner's name and % of ownership—Joe Investor 50%

Rental property address:
123–45 Avenue, Anytown, Canada

Code	Description	Total
Income		
1000	Rental income	$20,800
1010	Late fees collected	$0
1020	Laundry and other income	$800
1030	Vacancy	$0
Total income		$21,600.00
Operating income		
1120	Mortgage interest	$7,680.00
1130	Bank charges	48.00
1140	Line of credit interest	1,169.52
1150	Second mortgage repayment	-
1200	Mortgage interest penalties	-
1220	Legal fees	627.50
1230	Appraisal fees	-
1240	Accounting fees	-
1250	Bookkeeping fees	90.00
1260	Inspection reports	-
1270	Other professional fees	-
1300	Insurance	114.00
1310	Management fees	2,370.00
1320	Strata fees	2,008.44
1400	Advertising and promotion	-
1410	Meals and entertainment	630.00
1500	Repairs	247.00
1510	Maintenance	1,800.00
1530	Utilities: rental property	-
1600	Property taxes	1,467.60
1700	Office at home	-

1710	Internet	-
1720	Computer and office supplies	17.00
1800	Travel	-
1810	Motor vehicle	-
1820	Seminars	250.00
2000	Miscellaneous	-

Total operating expenses $18,519.06

Operating income $3,080.94

| 1100 | Mortgage principal repayment | $1,118.27 |
| 1520 | Updates | - |

Increase in equity **$ 1,118.27**
Net cash flow **$ 1,962.67**

Return on equity

Purchase price	$195,000.00
Improvements	$1,500.00
Actual cost	$196,500.00
Current value - net	$229,000.00
Profit	$32,500.00
JV partners profit (50%)	$16,250.00
Original investment	$50,000.00
Total return on investment	33%

Reserve fund

Reserve fund balance beginning	$1,750.00
Funds used	$500.00
Funds added	-
Reserve fund ending	$1,250.00

Mortgage amount

First mortgage beginning	$146,250.00
Mortgage principal repayments	$1,118.27
First mortgage ending	$145,131.73

Second mortgage beginning	-
Mortgage principal repayments	-
Second mortgage ending	

INDEX

●